Finnish Cities

presents a personal interpretation of Tampere, Turku and Helsinki, with an excursion from southern Finland to Rovaniemi and Lapland.

The fourth largest country in Europe, and the fourteenth in the world assessed in terms of Gross National Product, Finland is likely to become an ideal adventure destination for the discerning Anglo-American traveller during the next decade. With warm summers, winter sports, autumn forest tints, and invigorating spring hikes, Finland enjoys the full range of climates from the beaches of the south to the midnight sun of the Arctic north. In a stable country politically neutral, with a fascinating admixture of Swedish and Lappish cultural traditions, almost everybody speaks English and offers the friendliest welcome. Bus, train, and domestic air journeys are cheap, the standard of hygiene is exemplary, and the cultural life of the nation is as rich as its cuisine.

Turku's myriad islands, Tampere's magnificent new architecture in a shimmering lakeland setting, Helsinki's galleries, museums, and open-air markets; these and Lapland's exotic parks and virgin forests present an irresistible charm to anyone tired of Megapolis.

PHILIP WARD, FRGS, FRSA, ALA, has been travelling the world for thirty years, from Macao to Peru, from Indonesia to Morocco, from Hungary to the Philippines, from Pakistan to Chad. Among his best-loved books are *The Aeolian Islands*, *Albania*, *Bangkok*, *Come with me to Ireland*, *Ha'il: Oasis City of Saudi Arabia*, *Japanese Capitals*, *Touring Iran*, *Travels in Oman*, and *Tripoli*. Author of *The Oxford Companion to Spanish Literature* and *A Lifetime's Reading*, his latest book is a novel on the Spanish conquest of Mexico entitled *Forgotten Games*, hailed in *The Times* as 'brilliant in concept, written in prose as spare, lush and pointed as a cactus garden, as powerful and evocative as a rational nightmare, a logical daydream.' Philip Ward brings a poet's perception to a land still unfamiliar to the Anglo-American reader.

Finnish Cities

Travels in Helsinki, Turku, Tampere and Lapland

Philip Ward

THE OLEANDER PRESS LTD

The Oleander Press
17 Stansgate Avenue
Cambridge CB2 2QZ
England

The Oleander Press
210 Fifth Avenue
New York, N.Y. 10010
USA

In the USA and Canada the
paperback edition is published
by Hippocrene Books, 171 Madison Avenue
New York, N.Y. 10016 USA

British Library Cataloguing in Publication Data

Ward, Philip
    Finnish cities: travels in Helsinki,
Turku, Tampere and Lapland.—
(Oleander travel books; v. 13)
    1. Finland—description and travel—1987
I. Title
914.8.97′0434   DL1015.4

ISBN 0-906672-98-8
ISBN 0-906672-99-6 Pbk

Helsinki. Mannerheimintie runs north–south, with the National Museum in upper centre, north of the large Parliament Building, and the Rail Station lower right, east of the Central Post Office. (Courtesy of Helsinki City Tourist Office)   *Frontispiece*

Printed and bound in Great Britain

Contents

Acknowledgements

I am indebted to Felix Paasonen of Finnair, who kindly provided return flights London–Helsinki and Helsinki–Rovaniemi and Boris Taimitarha of the Finnish Tourist Board in London. Collaboration and hospitality were generously provided by Kaarlo Lidman of the Helsinki City Tourist Office, Irmeli Torssonen in Turku, Jouko Mustonen in Tampere, and Esa Peltonen and his successor, Arja Pietarinen-Björklund in Rovaniemi. Especial gratitude is due to my expert friends and guides who made me feel entirely at home: I was privileged to travel with Anja Saaristo in Tampere, Rauni Schleutker in Turku, and Sirkka Jääskeläinen in Helsinki. They have contributed to make this book what it is, except that its shortcomings must be debited to my account alone.

Only those already deep into Finnish life and lore can appreciate how much I have valued the assistance of Professor W. R. Mead, Chairman of the Anglo-Finnish Society, who has read the typescript but cannot be criticised for any errors that persist. In Helsinki and environs I acknowledge the help of Maija Tamminen, Anne Lappalainen, Simo Hankaniemi, Anita Ehrnrooth, Pia Mäkinen, Liisa Kasvio, Sinikka Vainio, Marja-Leena Rautalin, Eero Kaupinen, Aira Petrimäki, Marie-Louise and Gunnar Didrichsen, Nora Sommer, Birgitta af Forselles, Maria Rehbinder, and Marja Salonen. In Turku, thanks go to Eva Dziedzic and Rita Mattlar; in Naantali to Inkeri Mäntylä. In Tampere and surroundings, I thank Jaana Leppä at Iittala and Pirkko and Aivi Gallen-Kallela at Kalela, Virva Joensuu, Raimo Huhtamäki, Inger Franzen, and Maija Kanerva.

To all my friends and acquaintances, *Kiitoksia paljon*!

PHILIP WARD

Introduction

Finland and the Finns have a capacity to captivate and ensnare the visitor. It is probably a legacy from the days when they were internationally regarded as having a touch of the necromantic. Philip Ward, a much experienced traveller, has submitted willingly to their wiles. The result is a very personal and very different book about Finland which concentrates on the four cities and their environs which he chose to visit.

Finland lies upon the marchlands of the continent. The Finns have had to struggle to maintain their existence in the face of a high latitude climate and their identity on the frontiers of eastern Europe. As H.G. Porthan, a distinguished eighteenth-century rector of Åbo Akademi, put it – the Horsemen of the Apocalypse have ridden Finland hard. It is therefore not surprising that the republic lacks a great storehouse of treasures from the past. What is surprising is the richness and range of artistic contributions from more recent days.

No other book about Finland before this has given such an appreciative review of the content of the country's multitude of carefully maintained museums, galleries, churches and public buildings. And the applied arts reach their climax in twentieth-century architecture. The U.S.A. may know its Eliel Saarinen and Canada its Viljo Revell, but the inspiring work of others of comparable stature awaits the attention of transatlantic visitors. For Philip Ward, a professional librarian, perhaps the most exciting building in Finland is the new Tampere City Library. It is the product of Reima Pietilä, a social philosopher as well as an architect, whose professional objective has been to extend his country's 'temperate zone of well-being.' In all respects, contemporary Finland displays and enviable state of well-being: cultivating a healthy political consensus at home, creating positive relationships abroad, enjoying the fruits of a *per capita* GDP which exceeds that of West Germany and is close on the heels of neighbouring Sweden.

For the North American and British visitor who travels to a Finland now celebrating the seventieth year of its independence, Philip Ward's book will offer useful guidance as well as communicating the enthusiasm aroused in its author by the artistic achievements of this enterprising and tough, yet beguiling and imaginative Nordic land.

W.R. MEAD
Chairman, Anglo-Finnish Society

Illustrations

Photographs are by the Author unless otherwise credited. Colour photographs on the covers were kindly supplied by the City Tourist Offices of Helsinki (top left), Turku (top right), and Tampere. The Finnish Tourist Board kindly supplied the maps and plans

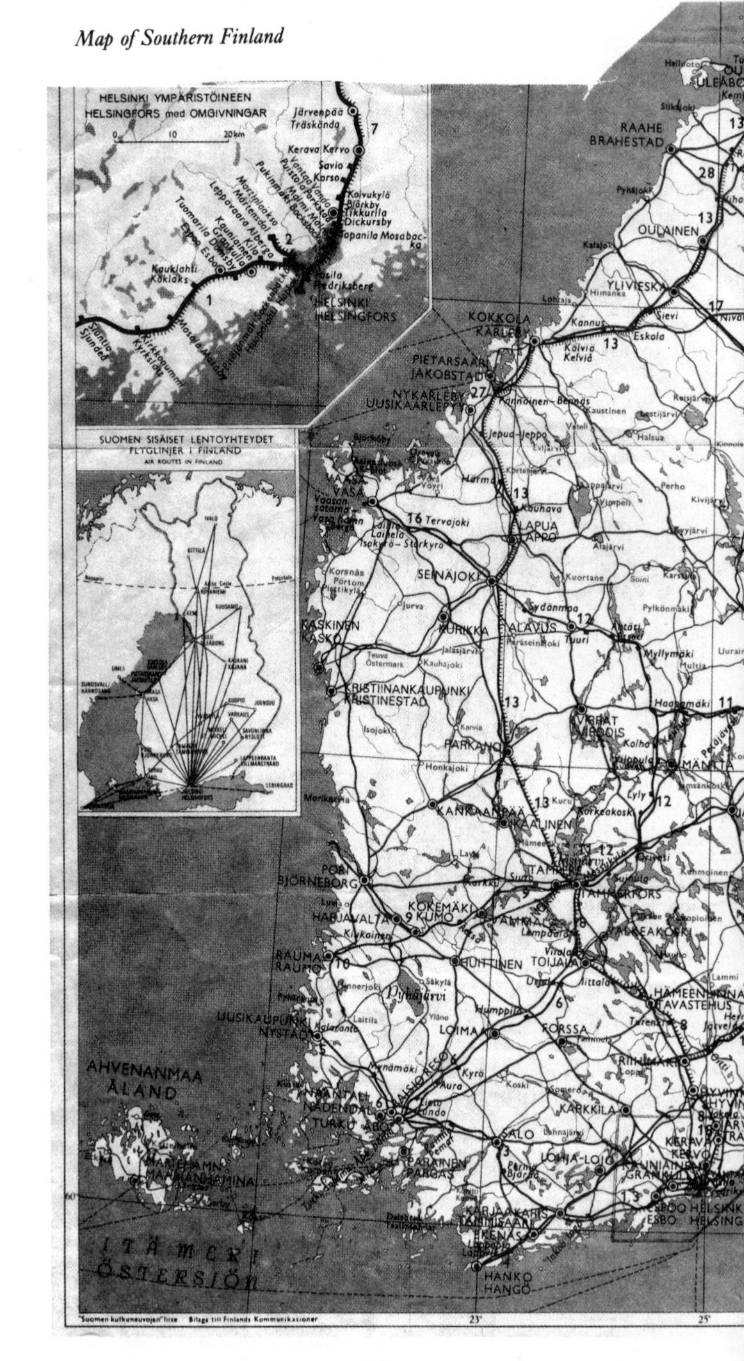

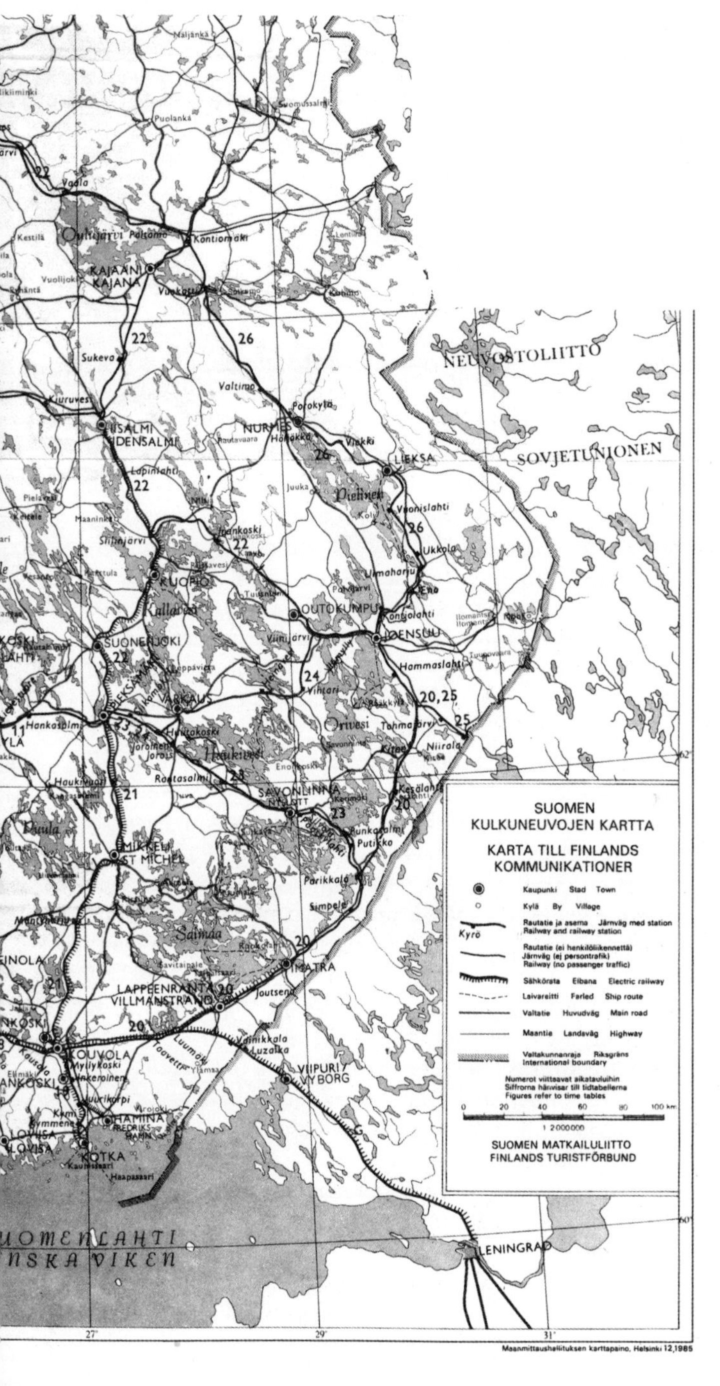

SUOMEN
KULKUNEUVOJEN KARTTA
KARTA TILL FINLANDS
KOMMUNIKATIONER
Kaupunki   Stad   Town
Kylä   By   Village
Rautatie ja asema   Järnväg med station
Railway and railway station
Rautatie (ei henkilöliikennettä)
Järnväg (ej persontrafik)
Railway (no passenger traffic)
Sähkörata   Elbana   Electric railway
Laivareitti   Farled   Ship route
Valtatie   Huvudväg   Main road
Maantie   Landsväg   Highway
Valtakunnanraja   Riksgräns
International boundary
Numerot viittaavat aikatauluihin
Siffrorna hänvisar till tidtabellerna
Figures refer to time tables
Kyrö
0   20   40   60   80   100 km
1 2 000 000
SUOMEN MATKAILULIITTO
FINLANDS TURISTFÖRBUND
NEUVOSTOLIITTO
SOVJETUNIONEN
KAJAANI
KAJANA
IISALMI
IDENSALMI
NURMES
LIEKSA
Pielinen
KUOPIO
OUTOKUMPU
JOENSUU
SUONENJOKI
VARKAUS
SAVONLINNA
NYSLOTT
MIKKELI
ST MICHEL
Saimaa
IMATRA
LAPPEENRANTA
VILLMANSTRAND
KOUVOLA
Myllykoski
VIIPURI
VYBORG
HAMINA
FREDRIKS
HAMN
KOTKA
SUOMENLAHTI
FINSKA VIKEN
LENINGRAD

By Way of Introduction

Finland is a western democracy, being a parliamentary republic in accordance with the Constitution of 17 July 1919, with a President elected every six years by an electoral college and enjoying powers somewhat akin to those of a French President. After centuries of subjugation to Sweden, and more recently Russia, Finland won Independence in 1917, and has firmly retained it ever since. Its population, below five million, occupies a sprawling land virtually uninhabited in its far arctic north above 70° latitude but gradually gaining demographic momentum until it reaches below 60° latitude at Hanko, level with Leningrad to the east and Uppsala in Sweden to the west. From Nuorgam in the north to Helsinki in the south the distance is 1,335 km. Of Finland's area, 338,000 sq. km., 56% remains forested, and 10% water, leaving a mere 8% for cultivable land. About 93% of the inhabitants have Finnish as their mother tongue, and about 7% Swedish but most are bilingual. In religion, 90% of the people are Lutheran, with a small Orthodox minority, mainly in the east.

Fundamentally capitalist, Finland has nevertheless created an enviably efficient welfare state, with only token payments for hospital treatment, medicines and doctor's fees. Taxes are high, and facilities equivalent. From pioneering beginnings in the wilderness, the Finns have created a civilization at once national and international: Klami's *Kalevala* suite, Wirkkala's glass, Pietilä's architecture, Sallinen's operas, new national parks, Haavikko's poetry, Kiaari Utrifo's feminist fiction, Simo Rista's photography. Why deprive yourself of exploring these wonders at first hand?

Certainly the weather forms no barrier, for the climate is temperate, and summers – lazy, warm and bright – lengthen into continuous light at Utsjoki in the far north from mid-May to late July, and into almost twenty hours of light in Helsinki during the summer months.

Helsinki is an obvious place to start, being the capital and by far the largest city (in 1984, 484,263 or 942,825 taking in the whole of the metropolitan area), with services and facilities to match.

Another gateway, this time from Sweden, is the south-eastern city of Turku (in Swedish Åbo), with a population numbering in 1984 some

162,282. While there, spend time in the archipelago of Turku, and at Naantali.

Finland's second city, roughly the size of Springfield, Illinois, or Northampton or Luton is Tampere, with a population of 168,150. Having long been Scandinavia's largest inland city, Tampere is becoming a civic showpiece, with glittering new architectural masterpieces that demand attention and comparison with the best anywhere, at any period. Visit the gentle woods of Pirkanmaa with its sweet berries; drive the country roads to Hämeenkyrö; enjoy lake cruises to Virrat and Visavuori.

These, then, are the Finnish cities discussed in the following pages, and frankly admired. All other Finnish cities have a population comfortably below 100,000, but that merely enhances their attraction, as we shall seen in Hämeenlinna for example or Rovaniemi, the capital of Lapland with only 32,369 inhabitants. In order of size, they are Oulu, Lahti, Pori, Kuopio, Jyväskylä, Kotka, Vaasa, Lappeenranta, Joensuu, Hämeenlinna, Hyvinkää, Kajaani, Imatra, Kokkola, and Rovaniemi.

Within Helsinki's greater metropolitan areas, Espoo, including Tapiola garden city, has 152,929 inhabitants, and Vantaa with Helsinki International Airport, 141,991. Don't miss Tarvaspää, Hvitträsk, or Ainola. I recommend a day's outing to Porvoo, to the east.

But Finns would be aghast at my insensitivity if I were to imply for one moment that Finland is a matter of three cities. Those very city-dwellers probably pride themselves on ancestry far inland, and almost certainly escape whenever possible to summer cottages, winter holidays, and weekends in the country. Many of them return year after year to the wilds of Lapland, an instinct you may understand only too well after travelling there yourself. So, after pounding the streets of Finnish cities, head for the solitude that the Finns understand, appreciate and often crave. You will not be disappointed.

The route-planning suggested is for a period of at least four weeks: one in each of the cities, and another in Lapland. I am far from proposing that Finland has nothing to offer beyond these ideas, however, and Savonlinna provides a splendid centre for touring the Great Saimaa, with evenings at the opera and music festivals in July-August. Those keener on lazing around would enjoy Åland in the far south-west, though the atmosphere is hardly typical of Finland.

The prices shown are of course merely indicative, and can be expected to rise. The opening hours have been checked as representative, but are subject to change in detail at any time.

Cynics may complain that my view of Finnish cities and Lapland is one of unrelieved enjoyment; that I chose only the most interesting places to visit, at the best possible time of the year. True. They will argue that I have brushed aside problems of alcoholism, drug abuse, and suicide, worries affecting all Nordic countries, no matter how socially responsible. True again. But these problems are likely to be worse in the countries from which visitors come, so that Finland will seem a very model of law-abiding tranquillity. You can discover the essence of Finland in a summer cottage with lakeside sauna, a boat trip through Turunmaa archipelago, in the glowing splendour of Tampere's new public library, in an ancient street of Naantali, or an open-air market in Helsinki.

I arrived in Finland with this challenge in my heart. I have travelled the world from Oaxaca to Wuhan, Muscat to Cape Cod. Show me something grand and yet intimate, stylish without affectation, calmly perfect. Thank you, Finland. You have passed the test: ten out of ten.

HELSINKI

A SHORT STAY in Helsinki of two or three days will involve walks in the centre, and possibly a ferry trip to Suomenlinna, with a bus to Seurasaari or Tarvaspää. But if you are travelling around quite a lot, you might benefit by buying a Helsinki Card (1, 2 or 3 days) including free travel; a day tourist ticket for unlimited travel on city transport but without the many other benefits a Helsinki Card possesses; or a ten-trip ticket saving 20% on a single ticket, currently 5.50 FM for adults and 2 FM for children, transfers allowable on both single and ten-trip tickets within one hour of the time stamped on the ticket. This is valid equally in trams and buses. The metro between Kamppi (near the bus station) and Itäkeskus stops near the rail station (Rautatientori), Hakaniemi, and the corner of Hämeentie and Helsinginkatu.

A Finnrailpass entitles you to unlimited travel on all passenger trains in the country over periods of 8, 15, and 22 days. But trains are cheap, like buses and internal air services, so it may not be worth your while. Expensive ways to see Helsinki are by taxi, and by hiring a car, either at the Airport or downtown Helsinki. Airport buses take you to Asema-aukio (between the rail station and the post office) about three times an hour via Hotel Intercontinental; to Ramada Presidentti Hotel about once an hour; and to the rail station (bus 615 at platform 62) about twice an hour. Allow at least 20 minutes for check-in at Vantaa for domestic flights, 30 minutes for European flights, 45 minutes for flights to the U.S.S.R., and 60 minutes for flights outside Europe. Ask about the Finnair Holiday ticket (valid for 15 days' internal flights), to see whether the price (currently US $250) would suit your needs: one factor is that many flights are fully booked because prices are low (and take a cold drink or flask and sandwiches, because there are no meal or snack services on most internal flights).

During my stay in Helsinki I lived in Töölö, a suburb sounding like the cooing of doves, just opposite Hesperia Park and Töölö Bay. The first building I ever explored in Finland was Finlandia Hall, in Hesperia Park, designed by Alvar and Elissa Aalto (1971) to occupy the terrace of Aalto's city centre plan. On a structure of reinforced concrete, the façades glow white with limestone and black with granite, stark planes being softened by surrounding greenery. The Hall itself has a large auditorium for 1750, a small auditorium for 350, and a restaurant to seat 300. Its lowest level is a car-park for each of the three separate entities; the entrance level offers pedestrian access from Hesperia Park to each; the auditoria level is the hub, including the restaurant, two halls and foyers; and the balcony floor provides administrative space. The congress wing has a drive-in level on Karamzinin-katu, an entrance level from Hesperia Park, a conference-room level, a congress-hall floor, and a technical level for simultaneous translation, film projection, and a radio and TV rooms. Opposite Finlandia Hall stands the National Museum of Finland (Suomen Kansallismuseo), open daily from 11 to 4 (and 6–9 on Tuesday evenings) every day but Sundays, when the opening hours are 11–6.

Founded in 1893, the Museum moved in 1902 into its present building designed by Armas Lindgren, Herman Gesellius and Eliel Saarinen in National Romantic style. Its central hall has monumental frescoes by Akseli Gallen-Kallela on themes drawn from *Kalevala*, the epic constructed out of folk poems by Elias Lönnrot (1802–82). The most disappointing department is the strikingly small Prehistoric section; the so-called Historic department comprises mediaeval sculpture, Renaissance, Baroque, Rococo, Empire, and Jugendstil sections; the best and most informative department is that devoted to Ethnography, with the splendid Finno-Ugric collections placing Finnish (and incidentally Lappish) life in its regional context, with such exotic bedfellows as Zyryans and Votyaks, Cheremis and Vepsians. One might have descended into science-fiction fantasy worlds devised by Lem or Heinlein, Wells or Bradbury. Depressingly, the most enjoyable aspect of Finland's National Museum during my stay was a loan exhibition of Chinese porcelain.

Finnish prehistory, expanding from the local Uusimaa prehistory seen in the City Museum across the road, starts in about 7500 B.C., nine thousand years after the last great sheet of ice began to melt. The first inhabitants, using tools mainly of quartz, were fishermen and hunter-gatherers living in pits or simple tents. You can see a fishing-net with bark floats and stone sinkers (found in the Karelian isthmus) which dates to about 7,300 B.C. The first named culture, called Suomusjärvi, lasted from 6,500 to 4,200 B.C., at which time stone tools, fishing and hunting implements were used. Comb Ceramic wares illustrate the next phase of evolution, when ornaments were made of slate, trade began, and the first preserved art objects were created. Asbestos from the Savo region of Finland was traded for pine from the Kama river, flint from Russia and southern Scandinavia, green slate from eastern Karelia, and amber from Prussia and Jutland. Paying due respect to the rule that nothing should be said of prehistoric religion that cannot be proven (and nothing can be proven), I merely note that figurines of game animals (like a fine wood elk-head) and human or divine beings were fashioned in amber, clay, wood and stone, and that rock paintings can be dated to the last Stone Age, and the early Bronze Age which began about 1,500 B.C. on the coast, under Scandinavian influence, characterised by long houses, round huts and cairn-building in high rocks. Simultaneously, the Stone Age persisted inland until virtually the beginning of the Iron Age, which began here as late as the first century B.C. Iron Age dwellings resembled those of the Bronze Age, but agriculture now began to spread, with the consequent stability of settlements. Contacts with the Roman Empire can be proved from such finds as a marvellous glass drinking-horn from Roman Cologne, and metal objects turned up at Soukainen, Laitila (West Finland, north of Turku). European influences increase during the Middle Iron Age (400–800 A.D.), also known in Finland as the Migration Period. Germanic animal ornamentation sets the same exotic mood at this time that Celtic art offered to Britain. A memorable example is the burial from Pappilanmäki, Eura, of the late seventh century, with grave goods belonging to a mounted soldier, notably a bronze-hilted sword plated with silver and decorated with animal- and plait-motifs. The Late Iron or Viking Age (800–1050 A.D.) provides evidence of local bronzeworking skills, and silver ornaments increase in quantity and quality, though large 'horseshoe' silver brooches were more commonly thought of as wealth than pure decoration.

Where did the Finns come from? Bluntly, who are the Finns? The evidence has been interpreted in two main ways. According to one reading, the ancestors of the present Finns (and we exclude the 3850 Lapps who still reside in Finland as an ethnic minority) were already settled by the Stone Age, a theory supported by the dating of some types of ceramics to the pre-Roman Iron Age (500 B.C. to 0). According to another, the ancestors of the present Finns immigrated from the southern shores of the Gulf of Finland (modern Estonia and region) early in the Christian Era, a view supported by enriched Iron Age culture during those centuries. Opponents of the latter theory argue that such enrichment might have derived from trade or travel, rather than from wholesale immigration.

During the Crusades Period from 1050 to 1150 Christianity spread, resulting in fewer burials with grave-goods, and in West Finland the most numerically significant finds have been textiles, from which the women's dress of the period can be reconstructed. Ornaments, commonly of silver, became generally smaller and lighter, with an increase in crucifixes among pendants. The silver treasure of Halikko consists of a round silver pendant, three silver chains with crucifixes, and 36 large silver beads.

'History' as opposed to prehistory in Finland dates from 1155 (or 1157?), when S. Erik, King of Sweden, is commonly believed to have led a Crusade to Finland with his British-born Bishop of Uppsala, Henry. The first Crusade is said to have brought southwest Finland under Sweden and

Christianity. The second Crusade of 1249 spread the Catholic faith to the province of Häme; the third Crusade of 1293 and the Treaty of Pähkinäsaari (1323) officially incorporated south-western Finland; recalcitrant Finns of the centre and north took even longer to become 'persuaded' of Catholic theology and Swedish paternalistic colonialism.

The National Museum shows few works of mediaeval art, compared with the Cloisters at the Metropolitan Museum in New York or the Victoria and Albert in London. For one thing, no large prosperous middle class existed to commission secular art, the churches were not wealthy enough to lure major artists from the Continent, and there existed no strong indigenous artistic tradition. None of the original wooden churches survives today, and no stone churches arose until the thirteenth century. Then, Gothic prevailed, reaching its apogee during the bishopric of Magnus II Tavast (1412-52). Many of the eighty-odd mediaeval grey stone churches preserve frescoes, original architectural features, sculptures in wood, and objects in iron. I was astonished to see a Romanesque Rhenish Virgin of 1200 from Korppoo, in the Turku archipelago, as much out of context in its way as a Giovanni Pisano. Flemish paintings imported by clerics or wealthy donors include a triptych of Christ's Passion from Vehmaa (near Askainen and the Manner-heim Museum) painted about 1470. Hanseatic artists are represented by Master Francke's 'Barbara' altarpiece (1415), produced in the Dominican convent in Hamburg and set in Kalanti church: look out for half the sheep turned into grasshoppers in the third painting and Bosch-like jeering figures in the fifth. The provincialism of Finnish ecclesiastical art is exemplified by the St Martin of Tours, a sculpture from Raisio church by the Master of Lieto, working in the early 14th century. The saint's mount resembles a child's rocking-horse. More than eight hundred mediaeval sculptures and reredoses survive in Finland, most of them *in situ*; here, the oldest are from the 13th century, such as the female saint from Nousiainen or the St. Laurence from Perniö, between Helsinki and Turku. Nousiainen, near Masku, was the hub of early Christianity in Finland and the original burial-place of Bishop Henry before his remains were transferred to Turku Cathedral in 1300. Henry, who became patron saint of Finland, was martyred, so the legend is told in the 'Ballad on the Death of Bishop Henry', by a peasant called Lalli on the ice of Lake Köyliö.

By the Edict of Västerås in 1527, Gustavus Vasa took the title of head of the Church of Sweden which incorporated the Church of Finland; he seized the assets of the Church, broke with Rome, forbade Mass, abolished ceremonial, and replaced Latin in Church services by the vernacular. The Lutheran faith was officially accepted in 1593, by which time Bishop Mikael Agricola of Turku, a disciple of Martin Luther, had produced the first books printed in Finnish, in the early 1540s. Though he made available the New

Testament in Finnish (1548), it was not until 1642 that the Bible was published complete in Finnish, by Eskil Petraeus: and it is essentially the language of Petraeus which is spoken and written by Finns today, with the necessary lexical addenda brought by three centuries of secular innovation.

Finland's transition from Catholicism to Protestantism was achieved without a great deal of bloodshed, and indeed the Convent of St Bridget in Naantali, near Turku, was not suppressed until some seven decades after the Edict of Västerås. The National Museum exemplifies this denominational change with a 'Lutheran Church Hall' containing pulpits from Parainen (1640s) in Late Renaissance style; and Sotkamo, decorated by Mikael Topelius (1734–1821). The Lutheran Church was financially poorer than its Romanist predessor, so that new wooden churches replaced the old stone buildings, but its ethos was more rigorously simple, even Puritanical in the avoidance of bright colours, and blazing iconography; lengthening sermons required built pews where worshippers might sit. The *Legenda Aurea* had been displaced by figures of apostles, prophets, church fathers and even Luther himself and his contemporaries. Officially, that is. In rural areas, Catholicism had held merely nominal suzerainty over men's (and particularly women's) minds. The old gods that rose again in Germany with the tide of Wagner's *Ring* survived barely touched in *Kalevala*, to which *Kalevipoeg* is the Estonian counterpart. William Canton knew what he meant when informing readers of his *History of the British and Foreign Bible Society* (1904) that central and northern Finland 'had drunk deeply of the cup of infidelity'. Today, and it must be admitted as far as one can predict the future, attendance in a church does not exempt the Finn from a mystic relationship with the great lakes and forests in which his fellow men seem utterly insignificant. You will see eyes glitter in mingling awe and delight and fear at the mention of *erämaa korpi*: backwoods, wilderness, where a man can be lost forever in the frost and snows of midwinter as surely as in any desert.

Such erratic thoughts put the 'Lutheran Church Hall' into perspective; I was now ready for the 'Last Supper', an altarpiece of 1725 by the first of Finland's distinguished women painters, Margareta Capsia (1690–1759).

Some splendid icons (and many more of lesser quality) have been deposited here from the Orthodox churches and village chapels of Karelia; after much of Karelia passed into Soviet hands in 1939, only two Orthodox monastic communites remain on Finnish soil: New Valamo and Lintula Nunnery in Heinävesi. And membership of the Orthodox faith now represents only 1.4% of the population. Note especially the icons celebrating Orthodox saints connected with Karelia: St Sergei and St German or Herman, founders of Valamo; Alexander of Svir; and Arseni of Konevitsa.

Mediaeval textiles are dominated by imports from Italy, Flanders and North Germany, but Finland is impressively represented by embroidery created by nuns of St Bridget's Convent in Naantali, such as an altar-front from Huittinen Church, showing the lives of the Virgin and Jesus, by Sister Birgitta, daughter of Anund, who entered Naantali in 1449.

The rest of the National Museum, presenting a tiny fraction of its holdings (a shortcoming endemic to all major museums), may be examined according to the visitor's whim, from the Renaissance, which in Finland begins as late as the 1550s when Duke John renovated his castle before and after his marriage in 1562 to the Polish princess Catherina Jagellonica, to the Jugendstil furniture and ceramics of the Iris factory working in Porvoo from 1897 to 1902.

By contrast the Ethnographic Department should not be skimped, for nowhere else can you see in one place the costumes and everyday life of every Finno-Ugrian folk. They are considered neither racially nor culturally, but only linguistically. The five linguistic groups are the Balto-Finnic, the Lapps, the Volga-Finnic, the Permian, and the Ugric. The most populous group is the last-named, with 12.7 million Hungarians, as well as small numbers of Ostyaks and Voguls who live in N.W. Siberia. The Zyryans and Votyaks of N.E. Russia comprise the Permian group. The Volga-Finnic group comprises 1.26 million Mordvins and 600,000 Cheremis, also within the Soviet Union.

The Lapps, who may be studied also in the Rovaniemi Museum, total 35,000 individuals, more than half of whom live in Norway. Of the 3,850 Lapps in Finland, only 2,900 speak Lappish, and my attempts to find literature by Finnish Lapps proved fruitless. The sole book in Lappish available at any bookshop I checked was a translation from the French of Saint-Exupéry's fable *The Little Prince*, which must perplex those seeking to promote Lappish culture as much as it dumbfounded me. Ecologically, Lapps fall into three groups: the Fell Lapps specialising in reindeer husbandry, the Forest Lapps specialising in hunting and fishing, and the majority: Sea Lapps, of Norway, specialising in fishing and small-scale farming.

Among the Fell Lapps, the reindeer plays much the same total rôle as the camel does among desert bedouin. They eat not only the lean meat and fat, but also most of the viscera, the blood, and the bone marrow. Wild reindeer have for the most part been replaced by scientifically tended herds.

But of course the largest part of the Ethnographic Department is devoted to the Finns: those of the west influenced predominantly by Scandinavia and the Baltic countries, and those of the east, most affected by Russia and eastern Europe. The *kantele*, Finland's national instrument, of the zither group, has enjoyed recent revival, having been the instrument used by Elias Lönnrot, to whom we owe *Kalevala* in its most familiar form. You can also see the kind of birchbark trumpet played by Finnish shepherds; ocarinas and whistles; horns and bugles.

The ceremonial drinking vessel from Rusko (1542) was carved from a spruce stump, with splendid Gothic decorations rising above it in a lyre shape.

Colourful folk costumes mainly of the 19th century are supplemented by a range of footwear, from old heelless moccasins, and the quilted cloth boots with flax soles and wooden shoes preferred in parts of the south-west Finland, to easily-fashioned and practical birchbark shoes. But of course the *ryijy* rugs *(rew-ee-yew* is a rough English equivalent pronunciation) stand out as a significantly Finnish contribution to art and craft. This type of knotted pile rug cannot trace its origin in the northern countries, so far does it go back. But we have excellent surviving examples of these patterned rugs from the 18th century, when they were used as best bed covers, mainly in southwest Finland. Many were hung on walls in absence of a native school of painting, and regional divergences of style and theme soon emerged. Two strands of influence in these magnificent pile weaves are the Baroque and subsequent Rococo styles which were called 'Gustavian' in Scandinavia after their period.

The darker side of peasant obscurantism is shown by amulets and charms, warding off evil to oneself and causing it to others. Ritual weapons for outbreaks of fighting between villages are displayed, dating to a time when young men of one community were 'dared' to confront the youths of another. Then there are implements concerned with sealing, fishing, trapping, cooking, baking, and a range of furniture including the Gustavian-cum-Biedermeier double rocking-chair.

Beside Finlandia Hall stands the charming Helsinki City Museum, housed in Villa Hakasalmi designed by E.B. Lohrmann (1844) for Attorney-General C.J. Walleen and occupied by the philanthropist Aurora Karamzin, his stepdaughter, from 1875 until her death in 1902. Opening hours are 12–4 from Sunday to Friday, with an extension to 8 p.m. on Thursday. Nobody can understand the growth of Helsinki without exploring this model museum.

After the Ice Age, most of the Helsinki region lay under water, the exceptions being the highest points of northern Helsinki and Vantaa; the oldest finds, dating back over 7,000 years, are stone, bone and quartz artefacts but, as these people had not yet learnt the use of clay, this is called the Pre-Ceramic period, identified at Korso, Myyrmäki, and Kaarela. Folk then lived by fishing, hunting, and sealing. Six thousand years ago ceramic skills were acquired, and this period is called Comb Ceramic from the decorative pattern found on pottery of the time, followed by the Rope Ceramic age about 4,000 years ago, when new immigrants arrived in south and west Finland from Central Europe, bringing with them an aptitude for farming and cattle-raising. Their axes, in the shape of boats, seem more confidently skilful in manufacture. Bronze arrived about 3,500 years ago:

two bronze axes of Scandinavian origin have been unearthed at Tapanila, but the most notable Bronze Age remains in the Helsinki zone are the burial mounds of Herttoniemi (*niemi* means 'peninsula'), Meilahti (*lahti* means 'bay'), and Lehtisaari (*saari* means 'island').

Iron Age finds in Helsinki are scanty, and indeed there is a theory that the population of Uusimaa ('New Land' or Greater Helsinki) declined to the point of extinction during the Iron Age. Another view is that the region's oldest fortress, Vartiokylä, may date from the late Iron Age.

Helsinki, excellently situated as it may seem to a modern visitor, did not begin its evolution from its present location, but at the mouth of the Vantaa river, in 1550, when the Swedish King Gustavus Vasa ordained that a new city should be established to rival the 'Reval' of the Hanseatic League, now Tallinn, Estonia, within the U.S.S.R. It was to emulate the League's success in trading with developing Russia, and Dutch enterpreneurs were invited to settle on the northern shore of Finland, mingling with merchants to be uprooted from such Finnish towns as Rauma and Porvoo, Ulvila and Tammisaari.

A castle was constructed, and a small export trade began in tar, lumber, furs, and butter. A modest shipyard was founded. But the few hundred inhabitants suffered from wars, political disturbances, and fires raging unchecked through vulnerable timber buildings: single-storey houses, church, school, hospital and town hall. The harbour facilities proved simply inadequate. So in 1640, Helsinki-Vantaa was abandoned and a fresh start made at Vironniemi, near the district we know today as Kruununhaka, on the open sea.

Kruununhaka, meaning 'Crown Meadow', is the second phase of the clockwise development followed by Katajanokka (adjoining the 'meadow'), Kaivopuisto ('Well Park', the spa), Töölö, and Hakaniemi. A multi-vision show lasting half an hour can be seen by appointment, and the City Museum's upper floor must be seen to appreciate urban interior decoration, such as the charming eighteenth-century examples, or the Frenckel room from the end of the nineteenth century.

If you stand in the monumental Senate Square today, you can imagine the little town as it gradually expanded from 1640 to 1654. A new church was named for Queen Christina of Sweden, who also ruled Finland. A town hall, district governor's office, school, and single-storey wooden houses even visualised in panorama would hardly have rivalled the Hanseatic League cities of the time! Since the economy had not yet flourished, businessmen engaging in shipbuilding, trade or construction had to combine their efforts with farming; fields and pastureland made up a great part of the early Helsinki, and it is relatively easy to explain the Finnish love of the countryside from their pastoral origins. Most of present-day inhabitants of

Helsinki not only have roots in the countryside; many actually have family properties or summer cottages outside the capital, and the excellent network of transportation throughout the country can best be understood through the Finn's traditional desire to escape from an urban setting to a rural setting as often as possible, even now.

Then, in 1654, fires swept through much of Helsinki: it seemed that the settlement was doomed. Again and again war, famine, and disease spread hardship and death. The Swedish rulers of Finland went to war with Denmark, Poland and Russia in 1700 and Finland was occupied by Russia from 1713 to 1721, after retreating Swedish troops had set fire to the town. Most of the residents who had survived the epidemic of 1710, the Swedish-Russian War, and the firing of their city in 1713, fled to Sweden, for the city had then (and retained until the end of the nineteenth century), a Swedish-speaking majority.

Some former residents returned to Helsinki after the Peace of Uusikaupunki ('Newtown'), a city south of Rauma, in 1721. After the War of the Great Wrath, Helsinki barely had time to rebuild its shattered homes before Russians and Swedes were at each other's throats again from 1741 to 1743, and again the Russians proved victorious. So the Swedish-Finnish union (not dissolved until 1809) determined to create a fortress in the harbour of Helsinki to defend the city from invasion by sea. Known in Swedish as Sveaborg, in Finnish as Viapori, the fortress is now called Suomenlinna ('Finnish Fortress), built on five connecting islands.

The security that its new defences offered the city may have been misguided, even quite illusory, since Viapori fell to the Russians in 1808 without firing a shot, but Helsinki grew in confidence. A new Finnish navy appeared from Suomenlinna's shipyards, and an influential group of Swedish officers led the city's intellectual and social life. In the middle of the eighteenth century Helsinki possessed only two or three stone buildings, and only two of its wooden houses were painted. The population of the district (six thousand) equally spread between Viapori and the mainland town, but the town's revived confidence began to express itself in growing trade and navigation, from bricks to ships, and cloth to spirits. The officers built manor houses on land acquired at this time: at Herttoniemi, for instance, at Stansvik, Kulosaari, and Tuomarinkylä. In the City Museum you can see a rococo desk made in Stockholm by the master-carpenter Tietze (1768–80), and a Gustavian silver jug by the Helsinki master-silversmith Sohlberg (1778).

1812 is not only the year of the celebrated overture: it marks the arrival of Helsinki as the nation's capital in place of Turku, not by any will of the Finns themselves, but by a political decision on the part of Tsar Alexander I. He designated Finland a Grand Duchy belonging to Russia, and appointed

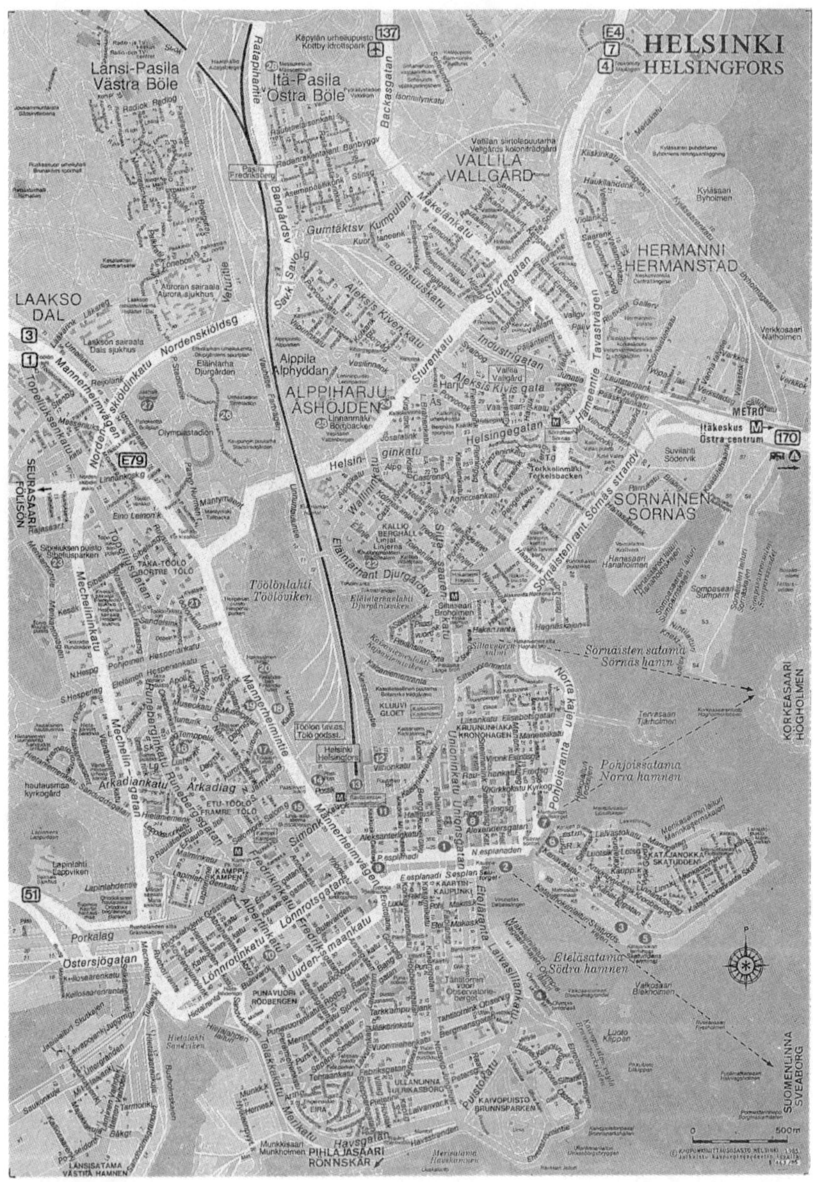

Helsinki. City Plan

himself Grand Duke, his action stemming from the fact that Turku lies geographically, linguistically, and culturally closer to Sweden, a tie which he wanted broken as soon as possible. The new Grand Duchy was awarded its own Diet, army and law courts. A new town plan was designed by Johan Albrecht Ehrenström, and the German-born architect Carl Ludwig Engel appointed by the Tsar was given the task of recreating the city's public buildings in a grand style reflecting Helsinki's new importance. A new university arose to replace Turku's university, destroyed by fire in 1827, eight years after the Senate had been transferred likewise. Taking as his model the neo-classical architecture of St Petersburg (present-day Leningrad), Engel produced a range of supremely elegant buildings: the Government Place or Senate Building of 1822, the University of 1832, the University Library of 1844, and the Cathedral of 1850–2. The narrow alleys of old Helsinki gave way to wide avenues on the grid system, incorporating ample squares and splendid parks. Engel's Helsinki is recognisable today with few exceptions, such as the Uspensky Orthodox Cathedral completed in 1868, as you approach by sea.

The only major change in central Helsinki was caused by the arrival of rail transportation with the opening of the line to Hämeenlinna in 1862, though

1	City Tourist Office	15	Bus Terminal
2	Market Square (Kauppatori)	16	Rock Church
3	Passenger Harbour (Viking Line)	17	Parliament House
4	Olympic Harbour (Silja Line; boats to Gdansk and Tallinn)	18	City Museum
		19	National Museum
5	Katajanokka Harbour (Finnjet)	20	Finlandia Hall
6	Uspensky Orthodox Cathedral	21	Air Terminal
7	Pohjoisranta (for Korkeasaari)	22	City Theatre
8	Senate Square (Senaatintori)	23	Sibelius Monument
9	Swedish Theatre	24	House of Culture
10	Finnish National Opera	25	Linnanmäki Amusement Park
11	Ateneum Art Museum	26	Olympic Stadium
12	Finnish National Theatre	27	Ice Hall
13	Rail Station	28	Helsinki Exhibition and Congress Centre
14	Central Post Office		

the buildings we see today were designed by Eliel Saarinen in pink granite in the so-called National Romantic style and date from 1919, with caryatids by Emil Wikström. Of course the railways fomented commerce and industry, as they had done elsewhere, and as well as the road and the sea nexus for Finland, Helsinki quickly became its railhead, and later its air capital. A glance at the map to see where a centrally-located capital might have been situated would evoke such names as Kajaani, Iisalmi, Kuopio or possibly Jyväskylä, but that is to overlook the sparse population density of Lapland and indeed the whole northern two-thirds of the country. Given the current population density, Tampere would seem by far the most logical centre for convenient growth as a second capital and, true to logic, this seems to be what is happening.

Low wooden structures continued to dominate Helsinki until, in 1875, a new building code permitted multi-storey building. Conflicting social interests, with a rising middle class and an increasingly large and powerful working class, led to the mixing of styles. Neo-Gothic buildings include the House of Nobility (Chiewitz, 1863) on Aleksanterinkatu, the Church of St. John (Melander, 1893) in Johanneksenpuisto, and the Roman Catholic Church of St. Henry (1860). Neo-Renaissance constructions of great note include the Bank of Finland (Suomen Pankki, Bohnstedt, 1882),the former Technical University (Sjöström, 1878), and the State Archives (Nyström, 1886). My own favourite neo-Renaissance buildings in Helsinki are those by Theodor Höijer on Pohjoisesplanadi ('Northern Esplanade'), but you will find a rich selection just by wandering the streets near the Senate Square.

Gas arrived in 1860, municipal waterworks in 1883, the telephone in 1891, and electric trams replaced horse-drawn trams in 1901, the city's electrical power plant operating from 1919. Growth of utilities meant accelerated industrialization, involving the migration of labour from the country to overcrowded tenements in Helsinki, mainly – after 1870 – in Kallio and Sörnäinen north of Pitkänsilta. The City Museum shows (in Room 15) a typical worker's rented room with a stove for heating, and cheerless it looks, in comparison with present conditions. By the 1880s, workers had formed housing associations to relieve intolerable conditions of congestion, poor sanitation, and spreading disease. Around 1900, when Helsinki's population had reached 100,000, a new city plan improved the potential urban sprawl of Kallio, Sörnäinen, Katajanokka, Töölö. Jugendstil spread from Germany, and the National Romantic style evolved, with such landmarks as the National Theatre (Tarjanne, 1902), the National Museum of Gesellius, Lindgren and Saarinen (1906), and the Kallio Church (Sonck, 1912). The monumentalism of the period after 1910 can best be exemplified by Saarinen's Railway Station, the classicism of the 1920s by the brick buildings of Töölö, the neofunctionalism of the 1930s by the Olympic

Stadium (started 1934–8) and the 1950s by the revitalising force of new garden cities such as Tapiola.

Recent architecture stands up especially well to comparison with the last six decades, whether one looks at the sparkling new shopping centres, the Municipal Theatre (Penttilä, 1967) or Finlandia Hall (Aalto, 1971). Aalto's name has been synonymous with that of Finnish architecture, and perhaps his name has unjustly overshadowed those of equally important architects. Nevertheless, it is only right and just to view his work in *situ* if you can: the Electricity building on Kampintori; the Akateeminen Kirjakauppa (Academic Bookshop) where Keskuskatu meets Pohjoisesplanadi; the House of Culture on Sturenkatu; and the Social Insurance building on Nordenskjöldinkatu.

Architecture has always presented a major challenge and stimulus to the Finnish imagination. The land is *extremely* flat, the only verticals being Bauhaus-straight conifers, telegraph poles and simple box-like wooden houses. Even if you have never looked critically at a building in your life, the Finnish passion for great design and superb buildings will stir your passions, inevitably. So many empty miles lie between one town and next (Alavus to Virrat, Oulu to Kemi), that each new building comes as a surprise, and a country so under-populated has far fewer buildings than trees, fewer towns than lakes. Each house becomes an event: any theatre is a piece of *architectural* theatre; every town hall is a bone of *architectural* as well as political contention.

So I chose to walk from the Helsinki City Museum south along Mannerheimintie to Erottaja, then into Eteläesplanadi, turning south again into Kasarmikatu. At number 24 stands the Suomen Rakennustaiteen Museo (Museum of Finnish Architecture, 10–4 except Mondays). Two exhibition halls regularly offer an overview of developments in Finnish architecture, and make compulsory visiting for anyone concerned with high art, good taste, and a beautiful, efficient enviroment. The museum moved in 1982 from an old wooden villa in Kaivopuisto; it is now housed not in a purpose-built area, but in an 1899 construction designed by Magnus Schjerfbeck for Finnish scientific societies in neo-Renaissance style, over-whelmed in effect by its great stairway, restored after the original plans.

The little peninsula of Katajanokka, with memories of the industrial and maritime past, is dominated by two buildings which, to landward, cancel out each other's effect: Alvar Aalto's functional white office block (1962) for Enso-Gutzeit, and the Uspensky Cathedral designed by A.M. Gornostayev on the model of the 16th-century stone church at Kolomenskoye, near Moscow, and completed in 1868. From the sea, however, the Aalto edifice is obscured: only the onion-domed Cathedral of the Assumption rises like its theme above the lowlying city. We might be approaching the invisible city of

Kitezh evoked by the magical music of Rimsky-Korsakov. The thirteen domes, in number reminding us of Jesus and the twelve apostles, have a shape which westerners call 'onions' but which the Orthodox Church considers emblematic of the flame of the Holy Spirit, descending on the disciples during the day of Pentecost.

The Holy Trinity Church and Sveaborg's Church of S. Alexander Nevsky proved inadequate to accommodate the increasing number of Orthodox believers during the period of Russian sovereignty over Finland, so the Cathedral was created to take the overflow, and offer counterpart on Helsinki's skyline to the Lutheran Cathedral. Within, the Uspensky refers like every other Orthodox Church to the relationship between heaven and earth, the dome supported by four massive monolithic Karelian granite columns representing the starry sky and the paradise of believers. The earthly paradise, as expounded by S. John of Damascus, can be found east in Eden, so the altar is placed in the east, and one prays towards it, using the rows of icons as symbols of heavenly prototypes. Little attempt at realism is intended, for icons are ideal in execution and purpose, the illusion being fostered by two dimensions, as opposed to the intrusive naturalism of sculpture.

The iconostasis, by Shiltsov, comprises three rows of icons, the highest being an icon of Christ above a copy of Leonardo's *Last Supper* in Milan, flanked by the four Evangelists. The final row portrays S. Nicholas of Myra, the Birth of the Virgin Mary, Constantine the Great, Archangel Gabriel, Mary the Mother of Jesus, Jesus, Archangel Michael, S. Vladimir the Great, during whose period Russia converted to Christianity, the Dormition of the Virgin Mary, and S. Alexander Nevsky. Some 60,000 Orthodox believers still reside in Finland, and many come to worship here, using for their practice of prayer such icons as The Virgin 'Comfort me in my Sadness', the Virgin on her Deathbed, with the Apostles and Church Fathers, and a Crucifixion. You may be unnerved by the eccentric use of red brick, but if you attend church services you will be deeply moved by the melodious tones of Church Slavonic, even if the Patriarch is He of Constantinople. The Cathedral is open from 10–4 on Mondays to Fridays but, even if shut, it is still worth visiting for the view from the terrace to the harbour, to S. Nicholas' Protestant Cathedral, and on the opposite side to the old industrial district, the power station, and the isle of tar: Tervasaari.

One is conscious that Uspensky is topographically and spiritually isolated from the rest of Helsinki: the beating heart of the city is Senaatintori, where parades are still held. But this is no massive, imposing Red Square: intimacy manages to break in despite its neo-classical ambience because of its small scale. Tsar Alexander II (1855–81) is celebrated in a statue (1894) by Walter Runeberg in the centre of the square, with vacuous symbols of Labour,

Light, Peace and Law. In 1827 the wooden Ulrika Eleonora Church was demolished, but the cobblestones at the west side of Senate Square are marked black to outline its walls, and in 1838 the old stone Town Hall went the same way, the new Senate Square quadrupling the area of its humble predecessor.

S. Nicholas' Cathedral (1830–52) must be one of the most serene, harmonious edifices of its period anywhere in Europe. Engel's dome was supplemented by four smaller towers and four smaller domes designed by Ernst Bernhard Lohrman, for it was believed that without extra support the dome would collapse. Inside the church, to a Greek-cross plan, I sat near the statue of Melanchthon, watched by companion figures of Luther and Bishop Mikael Agricola, the fourth corner in the square being occupied by the pulpit. The organist's tone reverberated throughout the whole building, its clean lines and brilliant white reflecting the glory that the worshippers attribute to their God. The invigorating atmosphere of brightness pervades also the crypt, opened in 1973 for art exhibitions and chamber operas.

At the top of the Cathedral steps, look to the right and you see the University (1832), extended in the style of the original by J.S. Sirén (1937). Next to it, and flanking the west side the Cathedral, is Engel's beautiful University Library (1844), elegant without and ceremonious in its quiet

Helsinki. University Library, from the steps of the Lutheran Cathedral

decorum within, a *trompe l'oeil* ceiling making as much as possible of the existing height. The twenty-six thousand students registered at Helsinki University are scattered throughout the city, adroitly avoiding overcrowding at any given site. Continuing clockwise around Senate Square is the former Russian School (Engel, 1823), subsequently a military hospital (from 1832), and since 1919 a university clinic. Behind the Cathedral stand the Orthodox Church of the Holy Trinity (Engel, 1827) and the Bank of Finland (Bohnstedt, 1882), with a statue of the patriot J.V. Snellman by Emil Wikström (1923). It was Snellman who completed the process of replacing the Russian rouble with the new Finnish mark and he, too, who achieved equality for the Finnish language at a time when Swedish was the offical language of culture and commerce. The neo-classical domination of Helsinki's architecture splits the country uneasily into urban, monumental, formal, decorous, even imperial and aristocratic; on the opposite side the rural, intimate, informal, impetuous, and democratic to the point of proletarian, the latter tendency tightening its grip on the literary scene from the folk rhythms of *Kalevala* to the woodnotes wild of Kivi and Sillanpää among the classic writers and Pentti Saaritsa and Tommy Tabermann among present-day voices. Armenians look totally out of their depth in Yerevan's immense Lenin Square; no less odd are the pretty blondes and handsome youths in fashionable clothes strolling in high Nordic summer down these cool porticoed streets, against classical columns that would seem more at ease in Augustan Rome.

Opposite the Bank of Finland you will see the old House of the Estates (Nyström, 1891), where the Diet of the Grand Duchy of Finland met. Emil Wikström's bronze frieze over the portal represents the moment in Porvoo when Tsar Alexander guaranteed to preserve the laws and religion of Finland intact. The House of the Estates is now occupied by a number of learned societies.

Continuing clockwise we come to the former Senate (Engel, 1822) or Government House, where the Senate of the Grand Duchy met. It now houses the nation's Foreign Ministry.

By contrast, the other corner of Aleksanterinkatu is taken up by an unobtrusive merchant's house, made in 1757 for Johan Sederholm and now the oldest surviving house in the city. Now the temptation is to go back into Kauppatori, Market Square, to see seasonal fruits and vegetables, the harvest of fish, and flowers, fresh bread and pastries, coffee-stalls and cold-drinks vendors. How beautiful are the girls, and how good-looking the men, fresh-faced and smiling with pleasure at the welcome sun! JESUS TULEE! ('Jesus is Coming!') proclaims a handbill offered to me by a young lady on behalf of a pentecostal group. I glanced around, but the only bearded man I could see looked distinctly more Nordic than Levantine, with a

Helsinki. Kauppatori. Open-air market in summer

twinkle in his eye, a mariner's step, and a bottle of beer clutched firmly in his right hand.

The beautifully-maintained little covered market comes into its own in winter, when ice covers the harbour.

From the South Harbour passenger ferries take fourteen hours to sail to Stockholm, 4 hours to Tallinn, and twenty-two to the West German port of Travemünde.

Before venturing into one of the major department stores, visit the Finnish Design Center, Kasarmikatu 19, south of Eteläesplanadi, open 10–5 on weekdays, 10–3 on Saturdays and 12–4 on Sundays. The exhibition constantly changes, but jewellery may be displayed by Aarikka, Carela, Finnmosaik, Eeva Hakkarainen, Kalevala Koru, Maija Käräva-Pitz, Lapponia Jewelry, Miessi, Rauni Mustonen, Ulla Poropudas, Jari Saari, Mauri Sarparanta, Outi Silfvenius, and Harri Syrjänen. Clothes could be from Bi-Ba, Flamant, Annikki Karvinen, LD Kari Lepisto (leather), Riitta Liski, Lena Rewell, Mirja Sarva (silk scarves), Villiruusu, Lissa Voima, Vuokko, and Willana. Articles of wood and other handicrafts may be shown by Aarikka, Juhava (candles), Juho Jussila (toys), Kotikäsityö, Laurituotteet, Modelyacht Company (ship models from 2800–3600 FM), Multi Mani (a collective selling in Senaatti-Center, Aleksanterinkatu), Nyanssi (mobiles),

Taisto Palonen (tin), and Piikkopuoti. Textiles other than clothes are often exhibited by Barker of Turku (napkins and tablecloths), Anette Bergman-Honkaniemi (tablecloths), Design Kaarina Nikkanen (handprinted interior textiles), Sirkku Kosunen (handprinted bedclothes for children), Maria Käld (handwoven coats), Tuulikki Mattila (interior textiles), Mikkelin Kotiteollisuuskoulu (tapestry), Palkkari (handprinted fabrics and tapestries), Piipariina (blankets) and Mirja Vehkaoja (handprinted bedclothes). Glass is dominated by Iittala (but in Helsinki use the sales office at Eteläesplanadi 14) and ceramics by Pentik or preferably their showroom at Pohjoisesplanadi 25a). My own favourites among offbeat items were the reasonably-priced postcards and posters of Finnish landscapes by Studio Pitkänen, and the flower vases by Seenat of Palojoki.

When buying presents or luxury goods in Finland, look for the sign 'Tax-free for Tourists', enabling you to receive a cheque for tax-reimbursement equivalent to about 10% of the purchase price, as long as you comply with three conditions: you must have your passport with you so the shop-assistant can check your country of residence; you must fill in your personal details on the back of the cheque; and you must show the goods, unopened, at the point of departure. These points are the airports of Rovaniemi, Vaasa, Tampere, Helsinki, Turku and Maarianhamina; the car-ferries of Tornio and Vaalimaa; the rail station at Vainikkala; and the seaports of Vaasa, Helsinki, Turku, Naantali, and Maarianhamina, on ships of the Finnjet Line, Silja Line, Vaasaferries, and Viking Line; and at the crossings to Norway, Sweden, and the U.S.S.R. Reimbursement will be in Finnmarks, and the minimum purchase in any one store must be 150 FM.

Finland's largest shopping centre is the Forum, with a hundred shops and restaurants, and parking for six hundred cars. Situated between Mannerheimintie and Yrjökatu, Forum is beside the bus station, and the rail station and Metro are only 200 metres away. The trams to take are 3B, 3T, 4, 7 or 10. Opening times are 9 to 8 on weekdays, and 9 to 4 on Saturdays. Forum Hall is devoted to food, with a wide range of fast-food outlets, such as Beefy King and McDonald's. Forumpiha Square concentrates on jewellery, gifts and fashion, in addition to banks, Finland Travel Bureau, and Forum Health Centre. Simonpiha Square possesses a range of boutiques, beauty shops, and handicrafts outlets such as Aarikka and Pentik. On Kukontori Square you will find furnishings, leisure shops, cafés and the Amos Anderson Art Museum.

Amos Anderson (1878–1961) owned and edited the country's largest Swedish-language paper, *Hufvudstadbladet*. Föreningen Konstsamfundet was established in 1940 as a foundation to administer his bequests of art objects and money. The museum occupies part of his home at Yrjönkatu 27: the ground floor and three upper floors, where major temporary exhibitions have enlivened the permanent display since the museum opened to the public in 1965, with an extension in 1985. Opening hours are 10-4 on Mondays to Fridays and 2–4 on Sundays, between May and mid–October, then 11–5 on Mondays to Fridays and 12–5 Saturdays and Sundays till year-end. The museum is particularly strong in Finnish art of this century, and the major show in spring 1986 was devoted to 'The Scandinavian 1880s', but the chapel demonstrates Anderson's enthusiasm for religious art, and past exhibitions have been devoted to Islamic musical instruments, Simo Rista's photographs from Mesopotamia, Mexican popular arts and crafts, African sculpture, Giacometti, Nolde and Turkish graphics.

While wandering from South Harbour (for boat trips round Helsinki or the waterbus to Suomenlinna), towards Senaatintori and the Lutheran Cathedral, you will find Senaatti Center, with access at Sofiankatu 6, Unioninkatu 27, and Aleksanterinkatu 26–8. Forty shops are open on weekdays 9.30–6, 9.30–2 on Saturdays, and also on summer Sundays 12–4. Ubiquitous cafés vie with Kotisaari bakery, knitwear from Kapteenska, Sypressi, Akanvirta and Framilla, jewellery, a sauna shop, postcards, art and antiques, fashion, shoes, and furs, numerous fine designers and the antiquarian bookshop TL-Divarit. New books can be bought at the Academic Bookshop. The Academic Bookshop is one of more than five hundred bookstores in Finland (more than one for every ten thousand inhabitants), and one of more than three hundred large bookstores maintaining 'sample' stocks from almost all Finnish publishers. Unlike the more selective system in Britain, in Finland the booksellers receive virtually every new title on publication. If they sell it, they must buy a replacement copy. If they do not, after two or three years they may send the samples back without paying for them, enabling them to keep a wider inventory than they could afford if they had to pay in advance. Books are nevertheless very costly, because they incorporate in their prices a 16% VAT charge from which British publishers are exempt. Fewer than 50% of books are sold through booksellers, according to 1983 estimates kindly supplied to me by Marja-Leena Rautalin of *Books from Finland*; direct sales by publishers account for 21% of the market; door-to-door sales of general and specialised encyclopaedias for 16%; book clubs for 12% and retailers other than bookshops for the balance.

Bookshops, as elsewhere, increasingly need to diversify into stationery, magazines, and other retail lines, because the level of profitability on books is relatively low. Finns are great readers, partly due to their love of quiet and solitude, partly due to the shortage of alternative indoor entertainment in isolated communities, partly because of the long winters, and partly because of their innate love of and respect for books, instilled by the Church, the universities, and society at large, where writers traditionally warrant great respect. Katarina Eskola's doctoral thesis on Finnish reading habits, 'Suomalaiset kirjanlukijoina' (1979), indicates that television has not reduced the amount of time Finns spend on reading. Each member of the population borrows an average of 15 books a year from the local public library, but library books constitute 'less than one third of the total number of books read in any year by the average Finn', who consequently reads about 50 books a year.

Finnish handicrafts are still based on the 'Arts and Crafts' renaissance led by William Morris and John Ruskin, which gave rise to Art Nouveau, or Jugendstil, each country incorporating national motifs in a cosmopolitan style based on the integration of handicrafts with fine art, the architect involving himself with all phases of the building and decoration processes down to the smallest detail, as we shall see at Hvitträsk, for example. Karelianism in Gallen-Kallela, symbolism in Simberg, and National Romanticism in a wave of architectural fervour incited artists away from their fellow-Finns: ceramics, glass, rugs, ornaments and forms both functional and aesthetically pleasing. Rationalism, as expounded by Gustav Strengell and Sigurd Frosterus, laid the groundwork for the functionalism of the 1930s. The society Ornamo was founded in 1911 to 'develop domestic crafts and design, to promote co-operation between artists and to improve the professional skill of its members', nearly all of whom studied at the Institute of Crafts and Design. When the building industry of newly-independent Finland finally recovered from the effects of World War I, the battle between cost-conscious planning authorities and strong designers wavered between the boom of the mid-1920s and crash a few years later. Egalitarianism in the 1930s called for mass production of homes and utility wares based on increasing mechanization and burgeoning technology. Ingenuity increased during the War years with the scarcity of raw materials and manpower. Standardization following the War was gradually replaced by rising aesthetic standards and individualism, but the migration of country-dwellers to the cities placed enormous strains on housing and utilities. Industrial art now benefitted from increased numbers of qualified artists with an innate grasp of form and sensitivity to material. Finnish design triumphed at the 1951 Milan Triennale. Plastics and fibre-glass entered the arena in the 1960s, when Finnish creators travelled more and became increasingly conscious of design's international dimension. Standards of living rose sharply, stride for stride with the quality of consumer goods, their range and quantity. Pop art, advertising, and the throw-away design of television and posters formed part of a new youth-oriented culture exemplified by the expansion of Marimekko's clothes for whole families, based on the young woman's wardrobe of printed textiles.

Ecological issues, feminism, and attention to the needs of disadvantaged groups such as the poor or the disabled, marked the 1970s, a phase which ridiculed the '60s optimistic emphasis on unlimited growth.

The 1980s have seen a return to pure imagination and reviving self-confidence, with a passionate devotion to past design which has seen craft objects of earlier decades sold at auction for astronomical sums, when their counterparts (also mass-produced) are sold for relatively little in every department store. Industry and business now rely on inventive, tasteful design to sell their products in a highly competitive market-place.

Artek was founded in 1935, primarily to produce and sell furniture designed by Alvar and Aino Aalto. Twenty-eight km by rail from Turku on the line from Helsinki stands the world-famous sanatorium at Paimio (1933) designed by Aalto as his Gesamtkunstwerk, and if you cannot see Paimio as a whole, you can enjoy here his chair made in 1931 of laminated birch and pressed plywood. Of the same period are Elsa Elenius' ceramic vase, and Göran Hongell's blue crystal vase for Karhula Glassworks. Aalto's most celebrated design was the 'Savoy' vase (now made in many sizes, colours and textures) produced from 1954, its sinuous lines intended to represent the forms of Finnish lakes and shores, forms already evident in his architecture and experiments in bending wood for furniture. Similar natural roots invigorate the vase 'Chanterelle' designed by Tapio Wirkkala for Iittala Glassworks.

Bertel Gardberg's stainless steel cutlery 'Carelia' (1957) made by Hackman proved timeless in its classic simplicity and, never out of fashion, remains in production today. I bought a set to use at home, and it graces our dining-table more than any heavy silver ever could. If I had to choose one element of Finnish design above all others to celebrate the genius of the country, it would be the series of 'i' glasses designed by Timo Sarpaneva (1954-64) for Iittala, intermediate in price between costly limited editions and mass-produced goods for everyday use. The colours of the ricepaper-thin glasses are lilac-grey, smoky-grey, blue-grey and green-grey. 'The rim of every glass object', declared Sarpaneva, 'must be as thin as the blade of a knife'.

A special display was devoted to the 'Marimekko Phenomenon'. Founded by Armi and Viljo Ratia in 1951, the company, with a factory in Herttoniemi and a supportive financier in the Union Bank of Finland, expanded with incredible speed and zeal, appealing to the younger generation with a dazzling range of clothes and fabrics for interior design. During the 1960s a utopian village was planned near Porvoo, and Aarno Ruusuvuori's pilot house for Mari village (1967) perfectly reflects the new forms, colourism, free interiors and unisex, uniage clothes within a natural enviroment. Jörn Donner, having to be in his own words 'a cold-blooded financier in order to be an idealist' with a group of reformists applied the brakes to unlimited expansion into soap and glass, houses and furniture, retreating pragmatically into the single (if abundantly varied) world of textiles. Donner summed up the inconsistency of the original Marimekko goals: 'to sell to individuals whose individuality, as a result of uniformity, would increase rather than decrease'. The owner-founder bond was finally broken in 1984, but by then Armi Ratia had realized much if not all of her original dream, taken from the ethos of the nineteenth-century novel *Seven Brothers* by Aleksis Kivi, and its heroines Anna and Venla: 'Marimekko is the forest path between the practical Venla and the ethereal Anna projected into the highways and byways, homes and whole living environment of this changing world.' Total design has meant that Marimekko's innovative photographers have influenced how television and film producers 'see'. Unisex clothes have by and large (though it is hard to quantify this) helped to make Finnish men and women more responsive to each other than hitherto. Brighter colours have increased the pleasurability of work and home environments. Armi's emotional, intuitive style of management created a sensational impact in a country used to formal relationships. 'Here I sit and try to sniff what the world wants. How it wishes to dress. Sometimes I get that itchy feeling and ... Either it succeeds or it doesn't. Sometimes one's too early. Sometimes too late.' She made it a rule to pick up five pieces of rubbish a day *at least*. 'I know the whole world, but I don't remember anybody'. Again, 'It's difficult being a woman when men are so stupid.' And the immortal line: ' We sure look after our staff, even if it's only a snack with the coffin.'

Suomenlinna

Italy, France, Germany, Spain, England: castles and fortresses spring to mind almost as the cardinal features of man's relationship to landscape. But in Finland one can travel hundreds of miles without encountering a vestige of dread portrayed in bricks and mortar; crags dominated by snaking walls; mottes and baileys; moats and donjons. We come across the castle of Turku in surprise; the fort of Hämeenlinna with astonishment in a peaceful landscape of lakes, fields and forests.

Mainland Helsinki shares the pacific nature of the country as a whole; you will scour its parks and streets in vain for a castle. 'Finland's fortress' (which is what 'Suomenlinna' means) must be sought in the bay, where it covers six islands, but grass covers them, a Doll and Toy museum lures children in the summer to Iso Mustasaari, cafés, Walhalla Restaurant and the Nordic Arts Centre combine to present an almost theatrical representation of a fortress, an impression strengthened by the Summer Theatre between Café Piper and the submarine *Vesikko* on Susisaari. Suomenlinna is linked hourly with Market Square throughout the year by ferry, and summer waterbuses ply with extra stops (Tykistölahti and King's Gate) from May to August, the journey taking about 15 minutes. Guided tours from Tykistölahti information kiosk take about 1½ hours, covering Susisaari and Kustaanmiekka (in English at 12.30 and 2.30 from 1 June to 31 August). Allow ample time to wander in the Ehrensvärd Museum (Susisaari, 3 May to 30 September, 10–4 or 5; 1 October – 30 November weekends only, 11–3) and the Armfelt Museum (Kustaanmiekka, 12 May to 31 August, 11–5.30; September, weekends only). On Susisaari you can also visit the submarine *Vesikko* (1931–3), (10 May–31 August), the Jetty Barracks Gallery and the Gallery Barracks, belonging to the Nordic Arts Centre, and on Kustaanmiekka a Coastal Defence Museum in a vaulted powder room (10 May–31 August, 11–5).

In the eighteenth century, Finland still lacked adequate roads and its small population formed isolated hamlets away from the few fortified towns (Turku, Hämeenlinna, Loviisa). The Russian army could occupy Swedish-held Finland only by marching infantry along the one good, coastal road, and bringing its supplies on rowed galleys along the treacherous southern shores. Large Swedish ships could not enter the archipelago, so Helsinki seemed vulnerable especially by sea. By land, the Swedish rulers strengthened Olavinlinna, and Loviisa on its eastern side with granite fortifications, after the loss of the Karelian isthmus and Ladogan lands.

In 1748 the Swedish crown entrusted the construction of a new military fortress in Helsinki Bay to a young artillery officer, Augustin Ehrensvärd. It was called Sveaborg, echoing Göteborg (Gothenburg) on the west coast of Sweden; in Finnish, Viapori, and it was originally intended to include a mainland base, but Swedish resources had been stretched so far and so thinly that the landward base was abandoned and all money and efforts devoted to the six islands. Ehrensvärd designed and oversaw the whole operation, using men seconded from the army, and money contributed by Sweden's ally France. Ehrensvärd died in 1772 (and is buried here) but the work continued unabated until completion in 1787, the irregular fortifications of local stone using the contours of the islands to best advantage. Four of the six islands have self-contained forts, and the complexity of the fortifications was intended to confound invaders; an aim frustrated, in the sense that an incompetent commander, Admiral Cronstedt, surrendered to the Russians in 1808 after three weeks of ineffective bombardment. Three islands were given up at once, and the others after a month, the Russian flag being hoisted from 8 May 1808 until 1918. Nobody can say with any certainty even today why the Swedish garrison gave up despite superiority in numbers, tenfold superiority in cannon, and sufficient supplies. Of 6,750 men, the Swedish-Finnish army lost six dead and thirty wounded. It is said that the Russians printed forged newspapers showing that the rest of the defensive forces had already surrendered, and smuggled the papers into Suomenlinna. If so, Cronstedt's naïveté seems hardly credible.

While Suomenlinna remained in Russian hands, Anglo-French forces attacking Russia during the Crimean War bombarded the fortress in August 1855 incessantly for forty-eight hours. The attacking fleet pounded the bastions, and caused immense damage with fire rockets, the defending army proving incapable of retaliating with its antique artillery. Old Sveaborg was seen to be virtually useless, and a new line of defence was constructed with huge sand embankments covered by cannon, and supported by many ammunition vaults. During World War I, the Russians built forts on the outer islands, and used Viapori as a garrison area, training base, and factory area for ordnance and maintenance. In 1919 Viapori was annexed to independent Finland, changed its name to Suomenlinna, and was turned into a camp for prisoners of war. The last troops left in 1972, since when the islands have returned to their original, peaceful state. The many civilians who live there have heating from the mainland by means of a tunnel under the seabed, and the Nordic Arts Centre was established in 1978.

Do not miss an extraordinary feat of engineering: the drydock in an enclosed bay, created in the 1780s and so large that up to fifteen frigates could be laid up during the winter.

The Armfelt Museum, a branch of the National Museum of Finland, consists of five rooms from the estate of Count Carl Alexander Armfelt (1850–1925) at Joensuu Manor, Halikko (southwest Finland, between Salo and Turku). Though the Armfelt collection has no historical connection with Suomenlinna, the upper rooms of the Carpelan bastion on Kustaan-miekka closely resemble the age, size, and basic design of corresponding rooms at Armfelt's Halikko home. The White Room has Empire-style furniture from the time of Count Magnus Armfelt (1792–1856). More than 600 fine pieces in the Porcelain Room include Meissen, Chinese and Japanese wares. The Study shows Count Carl Armfelt's collections, such as weapons and paintings. The Library contains Count Armfelt's private library in its original mahogany bookcase. The Blue Room equates with the blue sitting-room at Joensuu, in Gustavian and Empire style.

After sandwiches and coffee at the Piper Café amid demure blond children, 'playing nicely' on grassy slopes at the highest point of the archipelago, I entered the Good Conscience bastion to take my seat for the performance (starting at 6.30) of Molière's *Don Juan*, translated into Finnish by the Theatre Group 1986, and performed on most evenings from 11 June to 17 August, with two performances on Saturdays, Kari Heiskanen taking the title rôle. A play you know can be enjoyed in any language, and the best *King Lear* I have ever seen was acted in Georgian. The director, Arto af Hallström, had welded a fine production from disparate musical, dramatic,

Suomenlinna. Summer Theatre in the Good Conscience Bastion

and choreographic elements to minimise the disadvantage of being without a stage. The most elaborate effect was the whitened living image of the Commendatore, portrayed by Esa Tulokas; as the summer's day slanted from bright to dull grey, tarnished silver, I reflected that this splendid event, like Mozart's *Don Giovanni* I had witnessed at Baalbek, enhances life by the turning inside out of dramatic convention. Art is what is performed indoors; life happens outside. Except that illusions may become more powerful than reality, as Pirandello teaches us in *Sei personaggi in cerca d'autore;* the same rigorous mystification deepens our perceptions in Beckett's *Waiting for Godot.* As I stepped on to a waiting waterbus returning to Kauppatori (Market Square), I pinched myself to make sure I was not dreaming. (And I am still not sure of the answer).

Korkeasaari

Finland's most ambitious zoo, established in 1889 on a once barren rock acquired by a company of retailers in 1882 to run a restaurant, is on 'High Island', or Högholmen to use its exact Swedish equivalent.

Accessible by bridges from the Porvoo road across Kulosaari and Mustikkamaa, Korkeasaari is however best approached by the ferry departing from Meritullintori at the eastern end of Aleksanterinkatu, not far from Kauppatori, during the summer months (May through September) every half hour during zoo hours: 10–4 from October through April, 10–7 in September, and 10–8 from May through August. The ferry trip takes about fifteen minutes.

No matter how long you spend in Finland, you will never see all these animals in the wild, and many in Korkeasaari zoo are rare animals from other countries, such as wild asses and Siberian tigers. You can pick up the regular *Zoo News* leaflet to find out which animals have young: during my own visit I saw newborn Himalayan tahr, Alpine ibex, chamois, yak, wapiti, Whitetail deer, European forest reindeer, snow leopards and baboons. Foals had been born to Przewalski's mares in three successive years: a formidable coup, bearing in mind the rarity of this Central Asian species.

The big cats live in quarters too small for them: I felt particularly sorry for the Amur leopards, jaguars and lions lying in eternal indolence on their back. By contrast the screeching peacocks roamed at will and the Lesser Panda gazed at me myopically, at least halfway to contentment. The Alpine ibex delicately stripped bark from branches cast down before it, and I came within a foot of an elk gnawing bark off branches just behind the fencing. After seeing the elk, you descend to the shore for snow geese, whooper swans, and the Maritime Museum open on the islet Hylkysaari, a thoroughly

Korkeasaari. An elk feeding

worthwhile side excursion between 10 and 3 every day in summer (2 May through 31 August) but only at weekends during the rest of the year.

Most enchanting of all? The playful wolverines, and then the delicate fallow deer with her young. Two Kodiak bears from Alaska dozed in the sun, then even more unexpectedly I came across emus, wallabies, opossums, and kangaroo. Bactrian camels eyed me with hauteur. The great grey owls and eagle owls, just fed with white mice, snatched with beak and talons at their tiny prey.

Past picnicking families, I made my way to the kiosk for a cup of coffee before taking the next ferry back to Kauppatori. Everyone relaxed in the sun, for they could barely remember those long dark days of winter, when perpetual snow and ice make up in their whiteness for the great black bowl of the sky, hour after hour, week after week.

The little zoo ferry chugged past the Sally Line boat *Sally Albatross* of Mariehamn (Åland), and on the other side *Mariella* of the Viking Line.

Pihlajasaari

'Mountain Ash Island' consists really of two islands joined by a footbridge. Purely recreational, it has nothing to interest the traveller, but if you just want to sunbathe between 1 June and the end of August you can take a picnic on a motorboat from Laivurinkatu, and in about 15 minutes you arrive at the jetty near the beaches. Cooking facilities can be found on the smaller inlet over the footbridge; in the other direction you will find bathing huts, a kiosk, and a restaurant, open only in the summer.

Seurasaari

'Seura' is the Finnish word for company or society, and also the title of one of the leading weekly magazines, 'saari' meaning island. In fact a bridge has long linked Seurasaari to the mainland, and bus number 24 leaves roughly every quarter of an hour from Erottaja (at the southern end of Manner-heimintie) all the year round, or if you prefer, you can take a motor boat from Kauppatori from June through August.

The island was first leased in 1889 to a company who turned it into a public park with licensed restaurant. The Open-Air Museum began with the Niemelä tenant farmhouse in 1909, since when nearly a hundred buildings have been acquired from all over Finland, then lovingly re-erected and restored in the Museum, which covers a third of the island.

Admission includes a guide service, given daily except on Wednesdays in English at 11.30 and 3.30. All the buildings and the restaurant are open in June, July and August from 11.30 to 5.30, with more limited opening in May and September. Folkdance performances may be seen several times a week in the summer at 7 p.m. and remember the traditional celebrations here on Midsummer Eve. Music and vespers may be enjoyed on Wednesday evenings here at 7 in Karuna Church. The restaurant is open from noon to late evening from 18 May to 31 August; snack bars, a buffet at the Antti farmstead, and kiosks for icecream, coffee and soft drinks can be found on the Meilahti bridge and in the festival grounds.

Near the entrance, look for the tar boat from Paltamo (Kainuu) dating from the early years of the century. It was used for taking 25 barrels of tar down the Oulu River to Oulu port. Tar was always a valuable export, and indeed Helsinki has its own 'Tar Island', the causewayed Tervasaari (north of Katajanokka), with a Finnish-style restaurant. During the seventeenth, eighteenth and nineteenth centuries, vast quantities of tar were required by Europe's ships.

You can see a watermill, windmills, sawmill, church boats, and a replica of a cottage used by the writer Aleksis Kivi (1834–72) during the summer and autumn of 1863, when he finished the plays *Kullervo* and *The Village Shoemakers*.

The little group of Lappish buildings near the late 18th-century parsonage from Iisalmi, Northern Savo, comprises a barn and turf-roofed cottage from Nuorgam, and a tree store from Petsamo, built atop a high tree stump to keep meat and fish safe from wild animals, especially wolves. Take the right-hand path from the parsonage, and you will come to the Antti Farmstead, from Satakunta (Southwest Finland), where folk-dance evenings are held. This can stand for any typical Finnish farmstead plan, with outbuildings such as a woodshed, granary, and sheds for sleighs, carriages, wagons and tools outside the main complex. Around the farmyard are grouped two vestibules; the first leading to a guest-room, sitting-room and main room, and the second leading to the same main room, the master bedroom, daughter's bedroom, and kitchen. A fish-cellar and central 'uncle's house' separate the farmyard complex from the barnyard complex, with its sauna, sheep-barn, piggery, cow-barn, cowfeed-barn, ox-barn, oxfeed-barn, and stable. The separate sitting-room would have been used only for high days and holidays, the kitchen being occupied by the family for all meals as well as during the preparation of food, and the main room throughout the rest of the day and night. After the main work of the day, the women would spin and weave on one side of the room, while their menfolk would carve wooden utensils, or work on a new sleigh. In Eastern Finland bread was baked every week, but in Western Finland bread was made only twice a year: in spring and autumn, the oven holding up to sixty loaves at a time. After cooling, loaves hung on breadpoles to dry, then stored in the grain-barn until needed. The sitting-room would be used to entertain visiting clergymen or travelling schoolmasters, for festivals, and to celebrate weddings or mark funerals.

Seurasaari's rocky shore and wooded hillocks conceal many other surprises, such as the Niemelä tenant farm from Konginkangas, Central Finland, which in fact displays the peasant life of eastern Finland throughout the eighteenth and nineteenth centuries. The oldest room is the sauna, where the first tenant lived, Lasse Turpeinen (1721–1806), who supported his family by fishing. Then his son Heikki was granted the right to grow crops on the farm, and the family lived here for six generations. When the farmstead buildings were moved to Seurasaari in 1909, the open-air museum effectively began.

The principal building from Niemelä consists of the sauna, the vestibule with the dairy at the back, and the main room, dating from 1844, which in place of a chimney had a hole in the ceiling through which smoke would eventually disappear, after having filled the room. In the coldest weather the farmer's horse, his most precious animal, would be brought into the house to take warm feed: hence the horse-trough beside the door. Cooking, eating, sleeping, and light work in the evenings were all carried out in this main room, heated by a stone fireplace-oven. Minor buildings are scattered higgledy-piggledy in a rough semi-circle: boathouse, piggery, threshing barn, cooking shelter, stable, toolshed, netbarn, and other barns. Of

Seurasaari. Niemelä Tenant Farm

Karuna Church (1686), with Ari from Jyväskylä

particular interest is the conical pole-tent, used for cooking and distilling spirits, not very different from the North American wigwam, with earthen floor and open stone fireplace. Ari, the history student from Jyväskylä who showed us round in impeccable English, told us about the worst harvest in Finnish history, causing 100,000 people to die of hunger in 1867–8; bark-bread was the only solid food that many country folk could get for many months.

Seurasaari teems with playful squirrels; two of them scrambled into the eaves above the porch as we entered the seventeenth-century church from Karuna, in Varsinais Suomi, or 'Finland Proper', as the lääni surrounding Turku is known in Finnish. Like almost every Finnish church, Karuna has a separate bell-tower, built in 1767, with a wooden beggar outside into whom the better-off could unobtrusively slip coins intended for poorer parishioners. The church itself was constructed in 1685–6 with funds offered by Baron Arvid Horn, Lord of the Manor of Karuna, and dedicated to S. Mary Elizabeth, the name of Horn's second wife. In a remodelling of 1773–4, the baroque long church was remodelled, with arches added to the windows, straightening of the gables, and a vaulted ceiling replacing the flat original. Church paintings in Finland are generally undistinguished, and those in Karuna are no exception: from the vestry door to the pulpit you can make out Christ preaching; the Sacred Conversation; Crucifixion; Holy Communion;

Adoration of the Magi; Scourging of Christ; Tribute Money; the Heavenly Kiss; the Broad Way and the Narrow Way; and the Flight from Sodom. The characteristic church-ship (a votive offering from a sailor safely returned from a hazardous voyage) comes from Pulkkila, Northern Ostrobothnia. A few of the many paintings which once covered the church walls can be seen today: look for instance at the wall near the pulpit.

Two church boats are housed near the shore; these were used by communities who lived some distance from their nearest church, and the 1897 example from Virrat (north of Tampere) accommodated a hundred adults and children. With fourteen pairs of oars, it is over 21 metres long.

On a warm summer's day you could happily spend three hours more wandering from Sulkava tar pit to the Karelian farmhouse, Duchess Zinaida Yusupov's stable, Professor Florin's 19th-century summer house, and Selkämä farmstead. But on no account miss the Savitaipale country shop, near the Antti farmstead. As elsewhere, the rural shop provided a focal point for spreading news from far and wide, verbal and also printed after newspapers began to be disseminated in the nineteenth century. Announcements in church would sometimes draw villagers' attention to stocks which would perish if not sold quickly. Credit would be offered to villagers before their crops could be sold. A backroom allowed the shop assistant to sleep on the premises, where bookkeeping was done during slack periods. What kind of stocks would be held by a Finnish country shop? Nothing that could easily be bartered by farmers, such as meat, dairy products or grain; but certainly oil and oil lamps, soap, leather boots, felt boots, herring, spices, tobacco, dried fruit, fishing tackle, tea, coffee, needles, simple domestic pottery and cutlery, and metal farm tools. Finnish design and fashions have become so relentlessly up-to-date and stylish that it comes as quite a shock to discover how recently the simple life ruled supreme throughout the country. Even now, Finnish cities seem almost entirely unspoilt to Parisians, Romans, Berliners, and Mancunians, but one must recall the idyllic scenes of empty squares and empty streets on prints and drawings of Helsinki, even just a few decades ago. The Finns regard Helsinki as their great metropolis, a Mecca for jobhunters where unemployment remains virtually unknown.

I left Seurasaari for the Friends of Finnish Handicrafts permanent sales exhibition at Tamminiementie 3 (open 9–5 weekdays and 9–3 on Saturdays; closed on Sundays), where between 11 and 2 in the summer you can see craft demonstrations in this charming old villa. The emphasis is on textiles, especially *ryijy* tapestries and rugs which are hung on walls much as you would hang an abstract painting: the motifs were originally traditional but now range to the geometrical and abstract expressionist, reflecting in short all the modern movements: op art, pop art, and abstraction. Standards of taste involving simplicity, truth to material, and subtle colour-blending have never been higher. Enjoy the permanent exhibition of *ryijy* rugs, with

Friends of Finnish Handicrafts. Räppanä, designed by Lea Eskola

outstanding works by Uhra Simberg-Ehrström, Lea Eskola, Ritva Puotila, Leena-Kaisa Halme, and Mirja Tissari, among many others. I brought a linen place-mat for 70 Finnmarks, dark brown and rough to the touch, like plain wood on an old sauna, and admired a double-weave wall-hanging for 320 FM.

A little way up the road at Tamminiementie 6 (Wednesday through Sunday, 11 to 6.30), I explored the Bäcksbacka Collection in Building A of the Helsinki City Art Museum (Building B being devoted to the Becker Collection), accessible from central Helsinki by bus 8 from Railway Station Square, 24 from Erottaja (by the Swedish Theatre), 36 from Simonkenttä, and tram 4. Most of the works are by Finnish artists, beginning with Magnus Enckell (1870–1925) and his *Wounded Nymph*. Enckell the mystic joined the Parisian artistic circle called Soleil d'or, and fell under the spell of Plato, Swedenborg, Baudelaire, and the Catholic mystic Joséphin Péladan. 'Only here', he noted, 'did I learn to understand what art is and how deep my roots are in it'. He revered Michelangelo, and in a painting at the Ateneum in Helsinki, *Awakening* (1984), he seems to respond to Ferdinand Hodler's *Sommeil*, shown in Paris in 1891. Rejecting the old Finnish national art of landscapes and inward-looking portraits or still-lifes, Enckell constantly explored fresh themes, from his dark period to more colourful post-Impressionist works. We shall encounter the apotheosis of Enckell's vision, and that of Hugo Simberg (1873–1917), in their creation of the frescoes for Tampere Cathedral, conceivably the most beautifully coherent of all *art nouveau* buildings.

Other masters represented in the Bäcksbacka Collection include Marcus Collin (1882–1966), Alvar Cawén (1886–1935), Jalmari Ruokokoski (1886–1936) and Ragnar Ekelund (1892–1960). A large selection from Collin's oeuvre concentrates on Finnish and French outdoor themes, such as *Drinking Companions, Douarnenez* and *Sickbed, Hattula. Winter Street Scene, Helsinki*, splendidly atmospheric, will remind British connoisseurs of Vorticist works by William Roberts and Edward Wadsworth. Cawén's *Sleeping Child*, from the Becker Collection, uses white angles of sheets and pillows in a memorable *tour de force*. Ekelund's uneven landscapes include an interesting attempt to capture *Notre Dame* and an evocative *Suburban Street*. Ruokokoski is represented by good portraits, notably that of the artist Tyko Sallinen (1879–1955).

Ellen Thesleff (1869–1954), in Paris at the same time as Enckell, exemplifies the vigorous part played by women in Finnish art, and I greatly enjoyed works from the Laaksonen Collection by three other women: Elin Danielson-Gambogi (*Two Women*), Fanny Churberg (*Still Life with Fruit*), and Helene Schjerfbeck (a haunting *Portrait of a Young Girl*), as well as minor works by Edelfelt and Gallen-Kallela.

If you want to study Akseli Gallen-Kallela (1865–1931), in Helsinki there are the frescoes in the National Museum and paintings in the Ateneum; at Kalela near Ruovesi (north of Tampere) stands his own first house, lovingly tended by Aivi Gallen-Kallela and her mother; but since the studio-home of Kalela has been closed (except by appointment) the most important place to experience the artistic personality of the national painter is at the studio-castle of Tarvaspää. To get there, catch a tram 4 to Munkkiniemi, then (between 9 and 3 Monday through Friday) the 33 bus to Tarvo, followed by a country walk in Leppävaara. In ten minutes, through silent woodlands, you come to the 1850s villa inherited by Akseli's wife Mary. The family moved there in early 1907, but the old Alberga manor house (now adapted with great sensitivity as a patrician café) soon proved inadequate for the ambitious Gallen-Kallela, who designed his new studio and built it before leaving in spring 1914 for the Venice Biennale, where he was given his own section. In 1915 the family moved back briefly to Kalela, and in 1916 he produced a self-portrait for the Uffizi. In February 1918 he spent two weeks at the Vilppula front, then Supreme Commander Mannerheim gave him control of the Mint, Cartographic Department and presses, finally appointing him *aide-de-camp* in 1919. From 1920–22 he busied himself with illustrations for the epic *Kalevala* and supervised its printing at Porvoo. Lengthy stays in Chicago and Taos led to more *Kalevala*-inspired works, then from 1926 to

1928 he completed the four frescoes we now see in the National Museum, and more *Kalevala* paintings emerged in the three years before his death from pneumonia in Stockholm, on the way home from lecturing in Copenhagen.

The Gallen-Kallela Museum at Tarvaspää is open from mid-September to mid-May on Tuesday through Saturday, 10–4 (Sunday, 10–5), and during the rest of the year on Tuesday through Thursday, 10–8 (Friday through Sunday, 10–5). The view from the north towards the studio gives the impression of an enchanted castle atop an inaccessible rock, whereas from the gardens or from the south the atmosphere changes to one of Mediterranean loggias, expansive windows and 'ancient' walls covered with ivy. Secret tunnels and magic doors were crafted into the original design, which incorporated central heating by steam, later converted to hot water. The ground floor consists principally of a great studio, with a skylight facing north to provide a uniform light free of shadows; this leads to a small graphics room late adapted to a kitchen, and a high round hall intended as a sculpture and music room. Objects from the artist's travels in Kenya in 1909–10 were displayed in the upper room and the lower tower room, while the upper tower room remained sacrosanct as his 'ivory tower' where he could think untrammelled and work on his *Kalevala* illustrations.

After the artist's death in 1931, the family lived on for some time at Tarvaspää but later left their home there, with its resonance of such activity, and it stood abandoned until its purchase in 1959 by the Akseli Gallen-Kallela Museum Trust.

On my visit, a special exhibition had been mounted to show some of his 'Masterpieces from Private Collections', ranging in date from *Girl with White Collar* of 1883 to *The Taos Home* of 1925. If they are not all masterpieces, since after all his output was too prolific to permit uniform excellence, then at least one salutes with respect such oils as *Eero Järnefelt at Work* (1888), *Imatra in Winter* (1893) and *Mary on the Shore* (1908). Yet it is for the upper tower room displaying prints and reliefs that I cherish my deepest memories of Tarvaspää. Its simple pine bench and simple table were designed by the artist: no other furniture disturbs the monastic purity of this silent chamber, with views to east, north, west, south through panes of glass that protect one from the fiercest winter gales, while allowing the luxury of gazing on all the world. Elsewhere, I admired in particular the compass mosaic inscribed *Iterare cursus cogor relictos* ('I shall return to my footsteps') in the antechamber; the famous 'Flame' tapestry in the autochthonous *ryijy* mode, created for the Paris Universal Exhibition of 1900; the *'Bad Conscience'* stained glass roundel of 1897; the striking posters such as the daring Bil-Bol lithograph of 1907; and the authentic masterpiece in oils, *Mary in a Rocky Landscape at Vehmersalmi* (1893).

Tarvaspää. Gallen-Kallela Studio-Museum (Courtesy of the Akseli Gallen-Kallela Museum Foundation)

On leaving, I encountered to my astonishment a gardener, wheeling a barrow, whose rugged and determined face seemed the living image of the Lemminkäinen painted by Gallen-Kallela. I remembered Kirby's version of that passage in runo XXXIX of Elias Lönnrot's reconstruction of the *Kalevala* which so obsessed Gallen-Kallela throughout his later years. The heroes Väinämöinen and Ilmarinen accept the reckless, jovial Lemminkäinen as a third companion to rescue the magic mill, the Sampo:

> 'Said the lively Lemminkäinen,
> "O thou aged Väinämöinen,
> Take me with you as your comrade,
> As the third among the heroes,
> When you go to seize the Sampo,
> Bear away the pictured cover.
> Perhaps my manly sword may aid you,
> In the combat may be useful,
> As my hands may bear you witness,
> And my shoulders witness to you".'

I thought back to Gallen-Kallela's portrait of Lemminkäinen's mother, who bears the face of his own beloved mother, and then of all the mothers of the Finnish countryside who provided Lönnrot with the raw material of monotonous songs (that is, in the rhythm later made familiar to Anglo-American readers of *Hiawatha* by Longfellow) celebrating a pre-Christian past. I thought of the mothers of Finland addressed by Marshal Mannerheim's letter hung up in every Finnish church; of the mothers whose menfolk died in wars against invading Swedes, invading Russians, and in Civil Wars and two World Wars; of the Virgin of the Air's descent into the sea where, fertilized by the winds and waves, she becomes the Water-Mother and creates bays and capes, depths and shallows of the ocean, and creates too Väinämöinen, unborn inside his mother's body for thirty years until he bursts forth into the sea, then on to the dry land. Legends and heroic deeds mingle in the folk memory of Mother Finland; even today I find the tenderness and meticulous hygiene of Finland essentially feminine. Women not only outnumber men: they have attained high positions in almost every field, and present a brilliant example of feminism triumphant, a lesson for all societies where women have been forced back by male chauvinism. Helsinki is called 'the daughter of the Baltic', not the son. Sports are essentially amateur, without the ruthless masculine single-mindedness that has led to unscrupulous professionalism or shamateurism in many other nations. Fashion, design, and domestic architecture can be considered major strengths of Finnish culture, and they too are rooted in feminine taste, though many practitioners are of course men. In Scandinavia generally women occupy a place more central in society than elsewhere; but in Sweden and Finland more especially they have entered almost every profession and occupation and dominate many, such as dentistry and librarianship, even if banking, industry and politics still reserve their highest positions for men.

Every day but Saturday you can visit the small but highly significant Burgher's House (Ruiskumestarin Talo, in Finnish) between 12 and 4 in the afternoon, with an extension to 8 p.m. on Thursdays. The Burgher's House is situated unexpectedly at no.12 Kristianinkatu; with a typically tasteful touch, the girls who act as guides are dressed in period costume, the period being 1817–18. It had been intended to rebuild the city in stone, after the devastating fire of 1808, but 'housing associations of the poor' to be set up for that purpose predictably came to nothing, and by 1811 permits were being issued to enable the poor to rebuild in wood. Kristianinkatu 12 was built for the widow of a seaman, after whose death the property passed to a counsellor, an assessor, and a sequence of burghers, shipmaster, carpenter, and quartermaster, until in 1858 it came into the hands of Alexander Wickholm, later to become city bailiff, then his daughter Augusta Nevalainen, and finally her daughter, the dancer Martta Bröyer (1912–74), who sold it to the city as part of the City Museum in 1974. Full restoration to its present glory was carried out between 1978 and 1980, and the house generally looks within how it might have been in about 1850, when the owners might have wanted to give an impression of comfort, and of 'rising in the world', or upward social mobility in jargon now current. The house was built with newly-cut logs on a natural stone base varying from 170 cm high on the street side to only 30 cm high in the courtyard. A cellar runs underneath the house for roughly its whole area; look for the larder just inside the door. The entrance hall leads off through separate doors to the bedchamber, the kitchen, and straight on to the drawing-room, or *sali*. Narrow stairs lead up to an attic. All stoves are 20th century in date, except the original brickwork stove in the room behind the kitchen. The Wickholms, Alexander, Erica, and their children, belonged to the new middle or upper middle class, with a three-bedroom house. Their home would today be considered over-furnished, so the present appearance is not representative of what the Wickholms would have displayed for their own gratification to selected guests. They possessed two sofa sets, one of which has 12 chairs, 14 plain chairs, 8 tables, 8 bureaux and cupboards, a rocking-chair, an armchair, bookcase, pipe-rack, two wash-tables and a bedside table, plus five mirrors, 23 paintings and nine lamps. Today the floors are bare, but the Wickholms would have covered them with rugs or linen carpets. A similar overabundance applied to domestic utensils, tableware and linen: sixty-two pieces of silver cutlery and a coffee set of German silver. Domestic chores included spinning, weaving and quilting, while the inventory also showed an ironing-board, mangle, and starching-frame for curtains. Since the Wickholm moveables were auctioned off in 1898, the furnishings and utensils we see today in the house-museum are not authentic, but do emanate a warm feeling of 'belonging', seizing the *gemütlich* Biedermeier style of the 'gentlefolk', gently satirised by Turgenev in a Russian context, and transforming it into a homely clutter that we read of in so many middle-class dwellings described by Dickens.

We are in the northern sector of Kruununhaka now, and a turn to the water will bring us to Siltavuorenranta. Instead of crossing Pitkäsilta ('Long Bridge') towards the City Theatre and City Administration Building, cross Unioninkatu towards Kaisaniemi Park, site of the Botanical Gardens of the University of Helsinki (1833), a marshy area drained in the early 1830s. Ahead now stands the National Theatre designed by Onni Tarjanne (1902) with a sculpture of the novelist and playwright Aleksis Kivi created by Wäinö Aaltonen in 1939. If one discounts (controversially perhaps, but with some justification) the sculptors of the earlier generation: Ville Vallgren (1855–1940), Robert Stigell (1858–1907) and Emil Wikström (1864–1942), then Aaltonen is the first major sculptor to emerge in Finland. His bronze Kivi may impress a visitor who has just arrived from the Railway Station, but if you have just come from Tampere you will probably prefer the bronze figures on the Häme Bridge there. His marble relief 'The Goddess of Liberty Crowns Youth with Laurel' for the Great Hall of Helsinki University was destroyed in a bombing raid in 1944, but a plaster cast of the work can be seen in the foyer of Helsinki University's Small Hall. Aaltonen once declared that he had come to understand sculpture only by contemplating the shape and texture of Finnish granite and, if he did not achieve Henry Moore's unique mastery of pure form, symbolism, and truth to material, such works of the World War I period as 'Head of a Girl' and 'Boy in Granite' made their own idiosyncratic impact. Perhaps his Paavo Nurmi bronze seems over-rated now, if one sets aside the emotional thrust engendered in sporting nationalism.

Opposite the National Theatre is the Ateneum Art Gallery building of 1887 by Carl Theodor Höijer, near which you can see a figure of the painter Albert Edelfelt by Ville Vallgren.

The Ateneum building has had to be vacated for basic repairs (1984–9) so I saw a small proportion of only the best examples of Finnish art from the 18th century to the present day, other major galleries in Helsinki being the Sinebrychoff Art Gallery (European old masters, mainly 18th-19th centuries) and the Amos Anderson Art Gallery (contemporary art). Since the Ateneum has no catalogue on sale, it is perhaps worth drawing attention to some exceptional paintings, beginning with Isak Wacklin's *Portrait of a Man* (1757), a representative oil by an artist who studied in Stockholm, like most of his compatriots before the Finnish Arts Association was founded in 1846, followed in 1848 by the opening of the Art School in Helsinki. Even so, from the 1850s there was a steady stream of Finns studying in Düsseldorf, a route diverted to Paris, in the main, from the 1880s. Freer brushwork and warmer colours mark the portraits by Gustaf Wilhelm Finnberg (1784–1833); his younger contemporary Berndt Godenhjelm (1799–1881), a lawyer who worked for the Tsar, has a pleasant self-portrait. Robert Wilhelm Ekman (1808–73), another graduate of the Stockholm Academy, has technically brilliant, if deliberately 'academic' posed figures of an *Italian with a Child in his Arms* (undated) and an *Italian Flower-Girl* (1845) at odds with modern sensibilities in roughly the same way as are Pre-Raphaelite aesthetics.

It is Werner Holmberg (1830–60), dying so young of tuberculosis, who complies with his own desire 'to show the world that Finland too can create her own school of art', for he almost single-handed provided a Finnish 'Barbizon school', idealising (as Constable did in the *Hay Wain*) his native countryside, so that others could follow, and 'see' their landscape as the raw material for works of art. After all, the landscapes of Rembrandt's Holland are no more romantic than *A Croft in Häme* or *A Hopfield in Häme* that shimmer in the ebullience of Holmberg's brushwork. I particularly enjoyed his *Road in Häme* (1860) for its symbolism of the rejuvenation of peasant life in Finland with the laying down of new, wider roads to promote communication between village and town, farm and seaport. *Storm over Näsijärvi* typifies the constructive dialogue between his winters in Düsseldorf art school and his summers back home.

Others who studied in Düsseldorf became landscape painters, among them Hjalmar Munsterhjelm (1840–1905) and Berndt Lindholm (1841–1914), depicting shore scenes to better effect than their forestscapes, which almost by definition spoil the intended effect of vastness by lack of sufficient scale on a canvas intended for a bourgeois home. Fanny Churberg (1845–92) took private lessons in Düsseldorf, since the academy remained closed to women. In Paris she saw the Barbizon school and at once recognized the affinity of French landscape painters to the natural potential of Finnish scenes, and exploited that potential in such works as *Before the Storm* (1872) and *Moonlight* (1878). She must be credited with having founded the Friends of Finnish Handicrafts in 1879, a society run by women (except for a couple of years) ever since. The Finnish 'Iris Room' at the Paris Universal Exhibition of 1900 won a gold medal, attracting the world's attention to the excellence of the Finnish commingling of art, craft, innovation and good taste, rivalled nowhere but in Japan.

Düsseldorf genre painters achieved almost equal success: Karl Emanuel Jansson (1846–74) in his *At the Vestry Door*, Arvid Liljelund (1844–99), and Adolf von Becker (1831–1909), who studied in Paris but continued to idealise aspects of peasant life in the 'Düsseldorf' manner.

Victor Westerholm (1860–1919) is often thought of as the last Düsseldorf artist and the first of the Parisians. The Antell Collection in Helsinki Ateneum possesses a number of his youthful German and Dutch landscapes.

Lakeland Kuopio's main claim to fame in pictorial art is as the birthplace of the other brothers Wright: not the aviators, but the painters Magnus von Wright (pronounced Vricht, 1805–68), Wilhelm (1810–87) and Ferdinand (1822–1906). Magnus is perhaps best-loved nowadays for his watercolours of themes drawn from Helsinki life, but his brothers won eternal fame (and the obloquy of the avant-garde) for their bird paintings endlessly reproduced on greetings-cards, embroidery, and coasters. You will find them everywhere you go, like the popular undercurrent in British homes preferring Gainsborough's *Blue Boy* to Turner, and Frans Hals' *Laughing Cavalier* to Vermeer: a tug of the obvious, the 'easy'. Here is the Finnish *mies* in the street mouthing 'I may not know much about art, but I know what I like.'

Yet things were to change radically with Albert Edelfelt (1854–1905), who showed Finns that Paris would become the next centre of world art. After recognising that patriotic historical painting had reached a dead end with his

Queen Bianca (from a fairy-tale by Topelius) and *Duke Charles insulting the Corpse of Claus Fleming,* Edelfelt looked around him, applying the techniques of open-air naturalism he had used in *The Luxembourg Gardens* (1887) to Finnish scenes like *Suru* (1894; the melodious title resembles 'sorrow' and that is what it actually means). In the foreground a girl covers her face in grief, while a pondering man casts an unseeing glance beyond the frame and below it, the whole set in a horizontally fenced midground, in front of an endless expanse of conifer trunks, to a lake or river, and a farther shore and sky. The extravert von Wrights have given way to the introvert Edelfelt in a single generation: Finnish art will never be the same again.

Finnish nationalism rose in the 19th century under Runeberg, Lönnrot, Snellman, Topelius and others, and to avoid the suffocating influences from Sweden, and equally unwelcome overtures from their huge Russian neighbours, Finns turned to the 'authentic' Finnish voice of the Karelians who had preserved *Kalevala* in oral tradition. The superhuman ambience of gods and heroes, limitless wilderness and lakeland, provoked a 'Karelianism' which concentrated perhaps too obsessively on landscapes and characters associated with the national epic. (The Estonians have the same epic, which may be earlier, but this quibble is tactfully ignored by foreigners.) Thus, Sibelius wrote much of the music for which he is remembered on *Kalevala:* and such writers as Eino Leino and Juhani Aho also made great play with Karelian ideas. Edelfelt, that many-sided artist, explored Karelian subjects too, as in his portrait of the rune-chanter Larin Paraske. His more 'official' portraits are equally fine: the singer Aino Ackte and the brilliant characterisation of Louis Pasteur. Then there are the pastels of Parisian girls, the romantic Italianate *Christ and Mary Magdalene,* the *Madonna in the Rose Garden*, and finally *The Founding of Turku University, 1640* mural for Helsinki University destroyed in a bombing raid in 1944. Edelfelt spent the summers in Finland *(View from Kaukola Ridge,* 1889–90) and the winters in Paris, with his model Virginie (*Parisian Girl,* 1885), a conveniently pleasant pattern followed by many of his successors. Technically and aesthetically such a division of lives produced the best of both worlds, as it did in the rather different case of Elin Danielson-Gambogi (1861–1919), a greatly underrated artist, whose *Self-Portrait* and *View of Lake Massaciuccoli* are in the Ateneum. Helene Schjerfbeck (1862–1946) – ill for much of her life, and lame – found content and inspiration in France between 1880 and 1886, then spent some time at St Ives after her engagement had been broken, painting *The Bakery* (1887), and *The Convalescent* (Paris Salon, 1888) now in Pohjanmaan Museo, Vaasa. The works in the Ateneum display her sensitivity to a painting as a painting, 'not just air or nature', as she once said. *The Door* (1884) evokes an atmosphere of ecclesiastical simplicity, in understated greys and browns. She retired with her mother to Hyvinkää (halfway to Hämeenlinna) in 1901 and *The Seamstress* (1903–5) emerged during this period of isolation, the needs of housework and caring for her mother conflicting with the demands of her art. Her mother's Shaker-style rocking-chair makes a hard structure bearing the sinuous but unsexed forms of the seated figure: (black clothes, almost white hands and face, a scissors-band proffering a sudden green line culminating in the glint of the downpointed scissors. Then comes the vibrant *Still Life* of 1930, small but echoing, where passion meets restraint.

Eero Järnefelt (1863–1937) became a first-rate landscape and portrait artist. Though my favourite work of his is the *Girl Reading* (1909), the Ateneum has a famous landscape, *Lake Shore with Reeds* (1905), suffused with autumnal sadness, a lone chair unoccupied, dwarfed by asymmetrical treetrunks. See also Järnefelt's sympathetic portraits of Dr Tekla Hultin and Matilda Wrede.

The highly significant figure of Gallen-Kallela will be examined in more detail at Tarvaspää (this chapter) and at Kalela (Tampere chapter), but while in the Ateneum you must 'retrace his footsteps' to 1884, for the French naturalist-style *Boy and Crow*, to 1891, for the Aino triptych (in its second version), and to 1897, for the characteristic *Lemminkäinen's Mother*, in his best *Kalevala* mode, overtly symbolistic. The poet Lemminkäinen has failed in his attempt to master death by shooting the swan of Tuonela, Kingdom of Death. 'He is lying on the ground', wrote Gallen-Kallela, 'greenly pale beside the black water, from which the swan, with a taunting lift to its neck, is swimming away. The golden shimmering rays of the sun give the mother hope, and she sends a bee to fetch balsam from the source of the rays.' If you know the portrait of his mother in Stockholm's National Museum, you will recognise her again here, as the poet-hero's own mother, a theosophist he called 'my wise, intelligent and contemplative mother'.

Amid this celebratory nationalism, I pause. The reason is that, for me, the greatest Finnish painting of all, here in the Ateneum, is Gallen-Kallela's glorious nude *Démasquée*, illuminated by warm Parisian sunshine as she sits on a settee. The mood slips as you study the work from quizzical to turbulent, calm to ardent: the quintessential woman poised between *agape* and *eros*.

A relatively feeble Gauguin landscape (*Hiva Oa*) of 1903 reminds us that Gauguin taught, for a short time in 1894, the landscape artist Pekka Halonen (1865–1933), who went to Paris in 1891 with Magnus Enckell and Ellen Thesleff. While they joined the Symbolists, Halonen leant towards the theosophical and nationalistic, participating in the Karelian revival trumpeted by Gallen-Kallela. Puvis de Chavannes' monumental art, such as *Winter* for the Paris Hotel de Ville, influenced many Scandinavian artists, and Halonen perhaps above all, as you can see from the *Washing on the Ice* and *Lynx Hunter* commissioned for the Paris Universal Exhibition.

Juho Rissanen (1873–1950) took Gallen-Kallela's contoured forms to their ultimate extent in early water-colours, then in 1908 he took up oil-painting, an interesting example in the Ateneum being *Woman Sifting* (1908).

Magnus Enckell (1870–1925) is a complex figure who started off by affirming that 'there are no colours at all in nature' and ended as a colourist. From an impressionist background in Finland, he was struck by Puvis de Chavannes, Plato, Swedenborg and Baudelaire, by the Italian masters in his tour to Italy in winter 1894–5, and by Böcklin. Then he swerved towards post-Impressionism, under the influence of Bonnard, and with a group of like-minded artists formed the 'Septem' group to introduce French impressionist colourism into Finland: Thesleff, Thomé, Alanko, Per Åke Laurén, Oinonen, Åström and Ollila. Enckell can best be studied in Tampere Cathedral, but the Ateneum has a fine *Awakening* (1894) which harks back in its austere and even sublime mysticism to the monumental works of Michelangelo such as the slaves in rock, or the *Sommeil* of Hodler.

The November Group, expressionist in tendency, arose at roughly the same time as the Septem Group and was led by Tyko Sallinen (1879–1955), whose large group composition *Holy Jumpers* constitutes the main example of Finnish expressionism, as Alvar Cawén (1886–1935) represents Finnish cubism, as do in at least some ways Marcus Collin (1882–1966) and Ragnar Ekelund (1892–1960). Ekelund excludes people in a misanthropy demonstrated for instance in the *View from a Bridge* (1922).

Surrealism made an impact in Turku during the 1930s, following which Finnish artists felt completely liberated from playing a nationalistic rôle, for Finland's identity and autonomy have been protected from further encroachment by her neighbours.

Enckell worked with Hugo Simberg (1873–1917) on Tampere Cathedral, following Simberg's study of fresco techniques in Italy. Simberg studied under Gallen-Kallela, deriving from his mystical and Symbolist preoccupations, and from the isolated environment of Ruovesi that love-awe relationship with nature that affects so many northern artists. Small watercolours like *Autumn I* and *II* and the magical, elfin *Frost* twist apparent technical naïveté into the raw substance of primitive art so admired in le Douanier Rousseau, whose work is recalled by Simberg's almost humorous *Death and the Peasant* (1895) and *The Garden of Death* (1896). The latter may have been influenced by Andersen's treatment of the theme in *Historien om en Moder*. Since almost too much has been made of Simberg's symbolist fancy, it is salutary to return to the masterly portraits of *Auntie* (1898) and the artist F. Basilier (1904); the charming boy straining to raise the crown of life (1905) is a study for the extraordinary frescoes in S. John's Cathedral, Tampere.

Nearly opposite the Finnish National Opera, at Bulevardi 40 you will come to the foreign old master collection of the Fine Arts Academy called the Sinebrychoff Art Museum. The nucleus of the museum was the collection formed by Paul and Fanny Sinebrychoff and willed to the State in 1921. The Sinebrychoff fortune, partly inherited and partly earned, derived from shares in industry and banks, and land in Otaniemi and Tapiola, but principally from the family brewery. The original museum contained three rooms: the Empire, the Gustavian and the Dutch, then a fourth opened when the whole was renovated in 1960. In 1980, the whole building was converted into a museum, its holdings enhanced by the foreign old masters of the Ateneum. The Sinebrychoffs' own collecting interests centred on Swedish portraits, even now the envy of Stockholm's National Museum. Seventeenth-century works included the *Charles XII* by David von Krafft, two portraits of Queen Christina by David Beck, and the portraits of men, bombastic to a fault, by David Klocker von Ehrenstrahl. Eighteenth-century works acquired at auction in Stockholm against lower bids from Swedish collectors and institutions include *Jean Martin du Ron*, by Carl Fredrick von Breda, the fashionable *Portrait of a Boy* (1774) by Pehr Krafft the Elder, and the undeniably fetching *Portrait of a Young Lady* (1780) by Alexander Roslin. Specialising in pictures of Sweden's monarchy and nobility drew the Sinebrychoffs into the field of the miniature, and their collection became the second largest in the Nordic countries, with 350 pieces, including examples by Niclas Lafrensen the Elder and Younger, Peter Adolf Hall, and Jacob Axel Gillberg, as well as non-Swedes such as Pierre Signac (1623–84), Giandomenico Bossi (1765–1853), Alexander Cooper (1605–60), and the Finn Elias Brenner (1647-1717).

When Osvald Sirén took over from H. Bukowski, A. Matsson and Axel Durling as the Sinebrychoffs' adviser, he found them more than thirty Dutch and Flemish paintings, including *The Artist's Two Daughters* by Cornelis de Vos, and Salomon van Ruysdael's atmospheric *Landscape with the Ruins of Egmond Castle*. The gallery must have seemed hysterically lopsided to visitors from abroad in earlier generations, but now one can enjoy works by Lucas Cranach the Elder (*Portrait of a Young Lady*), French works (Corot and Daubigny), English portraits (Raeburn and Reynolds), minor Spanish works (*Ecce Homo* by Ribera and a *Still Life* by Bartolomé Pérez), Rembrandt's *A Monk Reading* (authenticated by Borenius), and Italian paintings from the collection of Eliel Aspelin-Haapkylä: Ugolino da Siena's *S. John the Baptist* being the pinnacle. Old Eastern art and icons have their special room, and elsewhere furnishings have been unobtrusively restored to offer an authentic feel of an aristocratic home filled with art. Major collections of western graphics and 650 Japanese woodcuts have no adequate display as yet, but at least the present uncluttered atmosphere is more conducive to appreciating the select few masterpieces on show than was the old crowded gallery of the 1910s.

The Finnish national revival of the 19th century was due to a handful of intellectuals who realised that their future was neither with Sweden, nor with Russia, crying 'Let us be Finns!' These names included Lönnrot and Pacius, Snellman and Topelius, but none was more honoured than Fredrik Cygnaeus (1807–88) who in 1872 willed his collection of 19th-century Finnish art to the nation, on whose behalf it is now administered as a branch of the National Museum. Opening hours of the Cygnaeus Gallery are 11–4 from Wednesday to Sunday, and 6–8 on Wednesday.

The building itself, as so often in Finland, offers its own reward, for the paintings were intended by the collector to be placed very much where they are today. You will be familiar with most of the painters from the Ateneum, but this is another excellent opportunity to evaluate the von Wright brothers, their contemporaries and their successors, in addition to works by Alexander Lauréus (1783–1823) and Gustaf Wilhelm Finnberg (1784–1833). Two hundred new works of the period have been acquired, in addition to the original two hundred, the latest (1986) being a *German Landscape* by Werner Holmberg, to complement the evocative *Finnish Birches* (1858) already on show. Other major artists, in chronological order, include Holmberg's pupil

Helsinki. Cygnaeus Gallery in winter (Courtesy of the National Board of Antiquities)

Munsterhjelm, Berndt Lindholm, Fanny Churberg, Albert Edelfelt, Helene Schjerfbeck, and Eero Järnefelt.

Cygnaeus' home in Kalliolinnantie 8 is situated so close to the Mannerheim Museum (at no. 14) that the two museums should always be seen together, the latter being open on Friday and Saturday from 11–3 and on Sunday from 11–4; otherwise by appointment. From Turku, you should make a point of visiting Louhisaari Manor at Askainen, birthplace of the Marshal of Finland. In Helsinki, the Embassy quarter is the setting for the home that Carl Gustaf Mannerheim occupied from the dissolution of his marriage in 1903, with all the collections accumulated in a lifetime of political, military and travelling exploits. A video recaptures his journey along the Silk Road from July 1906 to August 1908, riding the same horse throughout, and returning from Peking by the Trans-Siberian railway. By then he had already distinguished himself in the Russian Army during the 1904–5 war against the Japanese. In 1911, Mannerheim was promoted to Major-General and given command of the Uhlans stationed in Warsaw. During World War I he led a brigade and later a division against the Austrians. When the Russian Revolution broke out Mannerheim, now 50, returned to Finland and, after the declaration of independence, he was appointed Commander-in-Chief of the armed forces, leading the White Army against the revolutionary Red Guards and Bolshevik troops still in Finland. He rejected the Senate's pro-German policy, and resigned, winning the support of the Allies and returning as a regent in 1918. He lost the country's first presidential election in 1919, however, to K.J. Ståhlberg, and retired to private life, where he worked for the Red Cross and in child welfare. He was named Field Marshal in 1933 and, when World War II broke out, he was again appointed Commander of the Defence Forces, leading the country during the Winter War of 1939–40 and the Continuation War of 1941–4, as a result of which he was appointed President of the Republic by Parliament at the end of the war, but poor health compelled him to relinquish the post in March 1946, and he died in Montreux in 1951 at the age of 83.

A man of action indeed, as you can see from the proud equestrian statue near the City Museum on Mannerheimintie, but a glance at his magnificent library is enough to reveal his breadth of interest, his thoughtful internationalism tempered with sufficient national self-interest to forge a revered statesman into an effective politician. Here are the Army and Navy Lists in a library with a view over the South Harbour unspoiled even today; Sven Hedin's travels in Southern Tibet; good Lamaistic silk paintings of the 19th century; a uniform designed by Gallen-Kallela. The dining-room has antique Spanish chests flanked by French mirrors. Three chandeliers and two large bowls come from Venice; four candlesticks from Bohemia; two vases from China. The drawing-room is equally eclectic: a French eighteenth-century clock; tablecloths from Morocco and India; Italian lamp-sconces; and Oriental antiques such as a prayer-wheel. The Orient dominates the Marshal's study: temple tapestries from Tibet, a tile from the great Mosque of Samarkand, a table from Peking on which are displayed a variety of Buddhas, carpets from China and the Caucasus; a good library of books in a dozen languages, including Russian, Swedish and Polish.

The upstairs hall, reached through an openwork Italian wrought iron gate has a painting by Gallen-Kallela of the artist with a leopard kill, and a variety of the Marshal's weapons. Guests were lodged in the blue room, noticeably more 'comfortable' than the Marshal's own room, with its narrow camp bed. Then come the daughters' room, small drawing-room, and upstairs library, which house the more formal parts of the museum. Together, the home of Mannerheim, with the objects he acquired, make an unforgettable impression on the foreigner trying to understand what manner of man could have achieved so great a respect despite having so little overt political power. His *Memoirs*, translated by Eric Lewenhaupt, appeared in 1953.

The National Opera was originally built to house the Russian Theatre, and was made over to the Opera in 1919 after Independence. The opera company has long outgrown its old home, and a new opera house is planned for the shore of Töölönlahti, not far from Aalto's Finlandia Hall. You will see the Swedish Theatre regularly if you use the bus services, for many routes intersect at the small square called Erottaja, at the southern end of Mannerheimintie. Completed in 1866, to a design by N.L. Benois, it was entirely renovated by J. Eklund and Eero Saarinen in 1936.

Between the National Opera and the Swedish Theatre, between Lönnrotinkatu and Bulevardi, stands the oldest surviving church in Helsinki, consecrated in 1826 and appropriately known as Vanha Kirkko (Old Church), designed in neo-classical style by Engel as a provisional place of worship while he built the Church of S. Nicholas in Senate Square, known since 1959 as the Cathedral. Vanha Kirkko's furnishings were brought from the former Church of Ulrika Eleonora, once on Senate Square. Engel also designed the stone gateway for the park, which was a graveyard commemorating victims of the plague of 1710.

Vanha Kirkko seems elegant and intimate, compared with the imposing neo-Gothic S. John's Church to be found southward, at the end of Yrjönkatu. Consecrated in 1891, Johanneksen Kirkko is the work of the Swedish architect A.E. Melander, and enjoys capacity audiences for sacred music such as the S. Matthew Passion of Bach, performed in Easter Week, with a Walcker organ. The altar painting is by Eero Järnefelt, but I felt uncomfortable in this, the largest church in Helsinki, which dwarfs the human spirit without the excuse of being appropriate to its age, unlike the

National Romantic Kallio Church, designed by Lars Sonck and consecrated in 1912. You can find the Kallio Church (*kallio* means 'rock') by walking across Pitkäsilta, and straight up Siltasaarenkatu: at the top of a hill the granite tower springs like a jack-in-the-box above the Helsinki skyline, in the workers' quarter. Kallio Church is spoiled by its disproportionately small apse. Sonck is also responsible for the Church of Mikael Agricola, again aesthetically damaged by lack of proportions, here between the rectangular tower and needle-thin spire: to make your own judgment of this church (consecrated in 1935), walk south from Johanneksenkirkko along Laivurininkatu into Tehtaankatu.

Functionalism, that boon to office-workers, has not produced many outstanding churches, and that in Käpylä is regrettably no exception to the rule. Designed by Eero Sutinen and consecrated in 1930, it reflects, true enough, the picturesque surroundings in its small scale, but it jars unhappily against the adjoining congregational hall, and its little round window conflicts with the proportions of bell-tower and matchstick-like cross. Martti Välikangas, designer of the varied grouping of Käpylä's domestic buildings, in a suburb north of Helsinki, later confessed that 'when Käpylä's houses began to be completed everyone, both authorities and the general public, agreed on the ugliness of the buildings.' The Olympic Village in Käpylä, designed by Hilding Ekelund and Välikangas, was started in 1939 and the job eventually finished despite the cancellation of the 1940 Olympics with the outbreak of World War II. The eventual total of 165 houses contains apartments of two or three rooms with kitchen and bathroom, the earliest examples having standard fittings. Like a small Tapiola, the village has its own schools, kindergarten, library, restaurants, shops and saunas.

The first church to arise in Helsinki after World War II was Markus Tavio's Meilahden Kirkko (Church of Meilahti), in the northwestern suburb close to Töölö. Lacking any sort of connection between tower and nave, Meilahti Church falls short of architectural distinction, but socially and ecclesiastically its importance cannot be denied, for it is the first church in the capital to create work centres within, and to incorporate two sanctuaries: one for the Swedish-language congregation of Mejlans, as they say, and one for the Finnish congregation of Meilahti. Multi-purpose churches are now the rule throughout Finland.

The best of Helsinki's latest churches must be considered among the most distinguished of all. From 1968 we have the church of Kannelmäki, a northern suburb, by Marjatta and Martti Jaatinen, its best feature a soaring, sloping roof with a slender vertical window letting in a mysteriously tall light reminiscent of Jacob's ladder. From 1969 there is the Rock Church (Temppeliaukion Kirkko), using its bedrock in a manner familiar to sculptors as 'truth to material', with a magnificent use of natural light in a

Helsinki. Temppeliaukio Church, designed by Timo and Tumo Suomalainen

low dome that cinemagoers might feel has something in common with the 'extra-terrestrial' vehicle in *Close Encounters of the Third Kind*. While I was absorbing the extraordinary atmosphere of this church, half grotto (like the Church of the Nativity in Bethlehem), half concert-hall, a singer of popular religious songs was accompanying herself on the piano, emphasising brilliantly the insecurities of her vocal technique in acoustics which made me long for a choir to partner the organ. Every whispered interruption from floor or gallery shot down the concert, which emerged bright as a new pin, like the clarity of Pavarotti at Verona's Arena. Timo and Tumo Suomalainen's Rock Church is cruel beyond imagination to unskilled singers: how exquisitely it must display the style and security of a great voice!

Malmi's new church (by Kristian Gullichsen, 1981) could hardly be more different. The Rock Church gives the impression of a wide, low, open field; the church of Malmi reverts to the old view of a church as a fortress, mixing with the modern view of a church as communal meeting-place. The Evangelical-Lutheran community in Finland may be numerically strong, counting more than ninety per cent of the population, but the secularist swing of the pendulum noted throughout Europe since World War II has affected Finland equally, and to attract a sizeable congregation one must offer physical comfort (heating, air conditioning, parish hall, club room, kitchen and store). The architect commented wryly: 'We may well ask

48

whether the requirements of practicality and multipurpose functionality have acquired such a dominant position among the goals of church architecture nowadays that it is impossible to build a church that looks like a church.' One might enquire, 'What then does a church look like?', and Gullichsen's response lies in clever lighting, rows of columns, stone walls, cloisterlike arcade, barrel vaulting, but perhaps above all in the vertical stress that looks back to Gothic, even if some details, like the central yard, hark back only as far as Alvar Aalto.

From Helsinki bus station the buses number 192, 194 and 195 will take you northwestward to Kuusisaari ('Fir Tree Island'), on the opposite shore of Laajalahti from the Gallen-Kallela Museum at Tarvaspää. At Kuusilahdenkuja 3 you can find the modern house created by Viljo Revell (1910–65) for Marie-Louise and Gunnar Didrichsen. Revell designed Toronto's City Hall, Vaasa Civic Centre, the Industrial Centre in Helsinki, and the Vatiala Funeral Chapel in Tampere. Since the lovely house and grounds remain private property, they are open to the public (except by discretionary prior appointment) only from 2–4 on Wednesdays and Sundays.

Helsinki. Malmi Church, designed by Kristian Gullichsen

Downstairs, the Didrichsens show choice examples of Olmec and Maya art from Mexico and Guatemala, and Mochica wares from Peru. Amlash, Luristan and Hittite bronzes have been expertly chosen, and the Chinese antiques display equal connoisseurship. Marie-Louise Didrichsen gives the same impression of artistic brio and exaltation that one received from Peggy Guggenheim in Venice. The first painting the Didrichsens acquired after their marriage was Pekka Halonen's *The Meal* of 1899, and their taste continued for many years to reflect traditional Finnish ideas and ideals: Edelfelt, Gallen-Kallela, Järnefelt, and no fewer than 14 examples by Helene Schjerfbeck dating between 1910 (*Girl in Rocking-Chair*) and 1940 (*Cyclamen in Bowl*). Deepen your awareness of painters seen in the Ateneum: the Enckell of the *Landscape: Portofino* (1920) is not the Enckell of *Purgatory* (1923), and unfamiliar aspects of Cawén, Ruokokoski and Saarinen emerge.

But the enthusiasms of the Didrichsens cross the generations and their taste has evolved with the passing decades to celebrate the paintings of Ole Kandelin, Ahti Lavonen, Alpo Jaakola, Juhani Linnovaara and especially Reidar Särestöniemi's Finnish landscapes, and the sculptures of Eero Hiironen, Eila Hiltunen, Mauno Hartman, Kain Tapper, and Arvo Siikamäki.

Kuusisaari. Marie-Louise and Gunnar Didrichsen in their art gallery home designed by Viljo Revell, beside a sculpture by Henry Moore

The bronze *Reclining Figure on a Pedestal* (1960) was the first large Henry Moore to arrive in Finland: since then the Didrichsens have acquired seven other Moore bronzes: the *Flower* (1951) the two-piece *Knife Edge* (1962), *Mother and Child* (1963), the *Atom Piece* (1964) and a working model for the three-piece *Reclining Figure Draped* (1975); a maquette for *Twin Heads* (1976) and a maquette for *Reclining Figure Distorted* (1978); and a small marble version of *The Archer* created in bronze to be set outside Toronto City Hall. Sculptures of varying quality are scattered about Helsinki's parks and squares, but most offer monumental bombast, derivative eclecticism, or worst of all, that twee sentimentality marring the Market Square fountain, 'Havis Amanda', made by Ville Vallgren in 1908. I propose that eighty years of Havis Amanda should be brought to a decent end with its replacement by a work of art, such as a work in wood by Mauno Hartman. The Didrichsen collection of Finnish and foreign sculpture makes an object-lesson in how to place objects in space, and in the choice of works that would grace any national gallery, such as Jean Arp's bronze *Demeter*, and fine examples by Marini and Giacometti, Hepworth and Chadwick, Picasso and Richier, Calder and Siikamäki. The integration of house, garden, museum-building and objects in two and three dimensions creates an indelible impression.

Plan your visit to coincide with the opening hours of Villa Gyllenberg (very close, at Kuusisaarenpolku 11, open 4–8 on Wednesdays and 2–4 on Sundays, but closed throughout July).

Villa Gyllenberg, built in 1938 for the stockbroker Ane Gyllenberg and his wife Signe, now belongs to the Gyllenberg Foundation, and was opened to the public in 1980, together with a new gallery. The focus of the collection is on Finnish painting of the last two centuries, though you will find sculptures by Wäinö Aaltonen, Essi Renvall and Aimo Tukiainen. The paintings include work by Albert Edelfelt, Akseli Gallen-Kallela, Eero Järnefelt, Helene Schjerfbeck, Magnus Enckell, Jalmari Ruokokoski, Tyko Sallinen, and Juhani Linnovaara. Opening hours are 4–8 on Wednesdays and noon to 4 on Sundays (closed throughout July). Here too gardens strike a happy balance between cultivation and the natural state, enjoying views of water on three sides.

The Helsinki Metropolitan Area comprises not only the city of Helsinki, with a population of 484,000 (1986), but also Espoo (with 156,000), Vantaa (141,000) and Kauniainen (7,700).

Among the chief points of interest in Espoo in addition to the Gallen-Kallela Museum at Tarvaspää, are Tapiola garden city, the fifteenth-century stone church, and the Glims Farmstead Museum in Karvasmäki (bus 109 from the bus station) for those without a chance to see Seurasaari. Vantaa is the site of the largest Finnish airport.

If you take the southern ring road from Helsinki, follow the signs first of

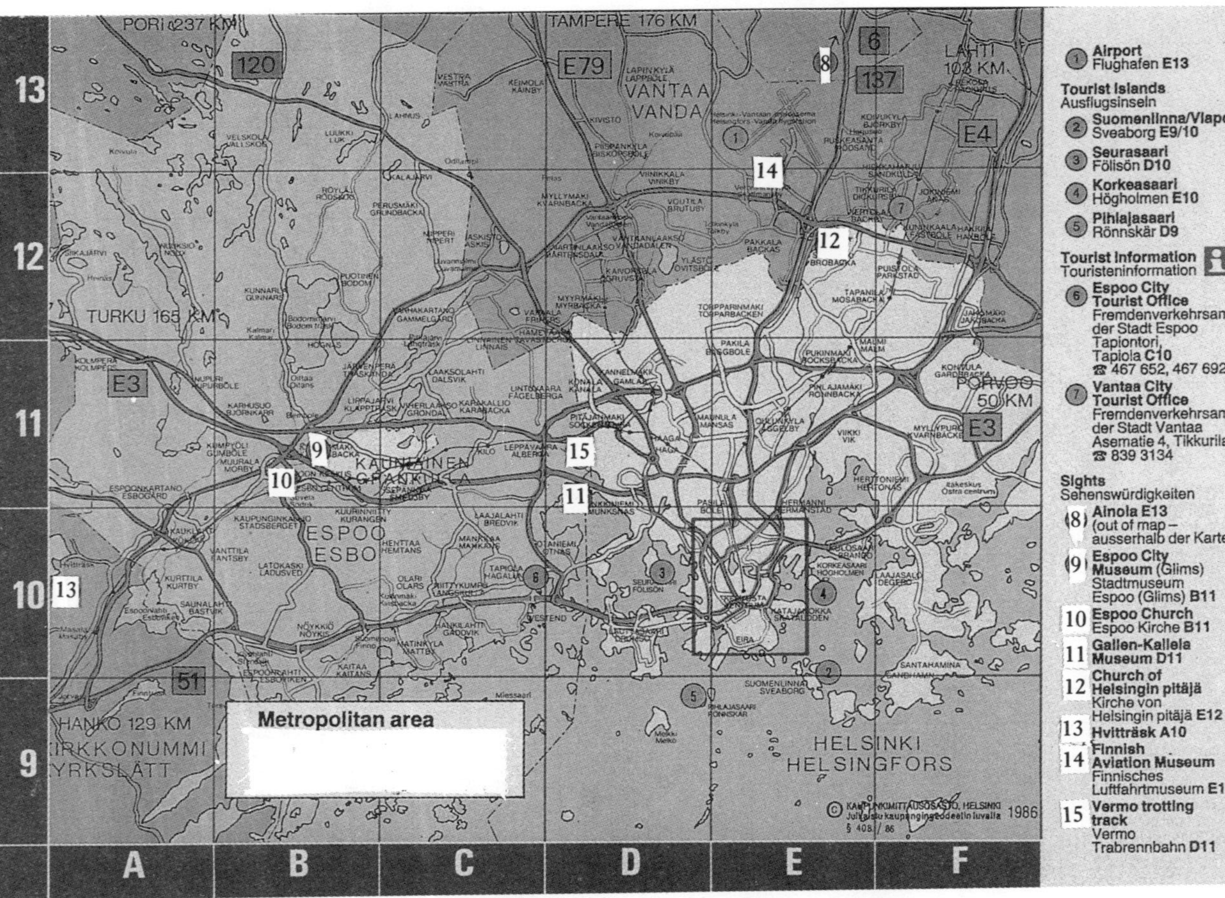

Airport
Flughafen E13

Tourist Islands
Ausflugsinseln

2 Suomenlinna/Viapori
Sveaborg E9/10

3 Seurasaari
Fölisön D10

4 Korkeasaari
Högholmen E10

5 Pihlajasaari
Rönnskär D9

Tourist Information
Touristeninformation

6 Espoo City
Tourist Office
Fremdenverkehrsamt
der Stadt Espoo
Tapiontori,
Tapiola C10
☎ 467 652, 467 692

7 Vantaa City
Tourist Office
Fremdenverkehrsamt
der Stadt Vantaa
Asematie 4, Tikkurila F12
☎ 839 3134

Sights
Sehenswürdigkeiten

(8) Ainola E13
(out of map –
ausserhalb der Karte)

(9) Espoo City
Museum (Glims)
Stadtmuseum
Espoo (Glims) B11

10 Espoo Church
Espoo Kirche B11

11 Gallen-Kallela
Museum D11

12 Church of
Helsingin pitäjä
Kirche von
Helsingin pitäjä E12

13 Hvitträsk A10

14 Finnish
Aviation Museum
Finnisches
Luftfahrtmuseum E12/13

15 Vermo trotting
track
Vermo
Trabrennbahn D11

all to Otaniemi, built on a cape (which is what 'niemi' means: the Swedish 'näs', and the Scottish 'ness') jutting out into Laajalahti ('Broad Bay'). Otaniemi possesses the Helsinki University of Technology with a main building (1964) and a library (1970) by Alvar Aalto, and the 'Dipoli' or second polytechnic, the first a National Romantic building in Helsinki now used by the Student Union. Dipoli's Summer Hotel and Youth Hostel are open from 1 June to 31 August, whereas the Strand Hotel in Dipoli offers accommodation all year round. Otaniemi is not only the main centre for advanced technology for the whole of Finland, with the Technical Research Centre and Keskuslaboratorio Oy, but it also has a tiny Paper Museum, the Geological Survey of Finland, the National Computer Centre, and colleges for the Fire Service, Police, and the Coastguards. Alvar Aalto's other buildings in Otaniemi include the Sports Hall and Guesthouse (1952), shopping centre (1960), and the water tower (1971). Dipoli Congress Centre (1966), next to the Summer Hotel, is the work of Reima Pietilä and Raili Paatelainen whose towering masterpieces we shall see in Tampere.

Tapiola ('Tapio' being the pagan god who protected trees) is a garden city planned by the Housing Foundation on virgin forest in the 1950s and 1960s, and it is still growing and changing, like any living organism. Sirkka Jääskeläinen, who has lived in a flat there for many years, expressed herself well content with the pure air and relaxed lifestyle of Tapiola, within easy commuting distance of Central Helsinki. Originally planned over 670 acres for 16,000 inhabitants of all age groups and wage groups, 54% of the city's area is green belt. Over 90% of mixed high- and low-rise housing units are now owner-occupied, and plans are to expand the centre of Tapiola to serve a population of 40,000, with new multi-storey car parks and new shopping centres, with a cultural centre to be built by Espoo Municipality. As in other garden cities, such as Welwyn and Letchworth, the aim was to provide homes in the heart of natural surroundings, with a low density of population and a high level of services; in other words, to preserve the human scale in the spirit of E.F. Schumacher's dictum that 'Small is beautiful'. The same spirit of 'the unobtrusive' governed the design of Tapiola Church (1965) by Aarno Ruusuvuori. Inspired by the anti-baroque impulse which stirred minimalism in all arts, from Webern and Wittgenstein, Ruusuvuori has chosen a nest for his church behind a screen of dark green pines, claiming 'the church cannot compete with the shimmering façades of the massive tower blocks in the surrounding landscape, so the building is merely a dark shadow behind the pines. The proximity of other public buildings has led to the internalizing of the church as far as possible. Looked at from without, it has become a world shut in by walls.' He has eliminated all baubles and gargoyles of earlier churches, exposing rough bricks, grey concrete and a greenish-black marble altar. The only light (and how powerfully it shines at midday!) pours in through a huge window in the west wall.

Tapiola. General View (Courtesy of Tapiola Housing Foundation)

I took the lift up to the highest point in Tapiola, the 13-storey Central Administrative Tower (1961), to survey the buildings from an eyrie before examining their impact at closer quarters. Aarne Ervi was the architect of this Tower; the controlling intelligence behind the fascinating mixture of urban and rural that makes Tapiola a constant surprise: Ervi also designed the Tapiontori ('tori' means 'square') of 1959–61, the Heikintori (1961), swimming baths (1965) and Tapiola Garden Hotel (1974) within the Sokos chain. I contrasted the 1959–61 high-rise apartment houses of Viljo Revell with the Suvikumpu housing by Reima Pietilä (1967–9), and the Sokos Department Store of Pauli Lehtinen (1979) with the local Stockmann (1981) by Bertel Gripenberg. But the life of Tapiola should be sought not so much in its monuments, ponds, sculptures and waterfalls, as in intimate relationships between homes and shops, footpaths and cycle tracks, overhead pedestrian walkways, new covered footpaths, and Otsolahti harbour for boats which sway and drift at their moorings.

In Finland, with a population of barely five million, Espoo has quietly become the fourth largest city, 12% of its inhabitants being Swedishspeakers. The term 'city' it acquired in 1972 fits oddly, when you realise that ninety-five lakes and 165 Baltic islands form part of the 'city' and that its farming community seems as important as ever it did with a population as low as 10,000 before World War II. You can explore the wilderness of Lahnus, or the Andorra-style enclave of Kauniainen within its borders, or the beautiful Leppävaara Public Library and nearby race-track for trotting.

Yet 'new' as Espoo might seem to the superficial glance, in fact its church, erected close to the so-called Royal Road that ran from Turku to the east, dates from 1458. Typically of mediaeval stone churches in eastern Uusimaa ('New Land'), the decorations on the west wing pediment have cross, aperture and mock aperture motifs. Originally rectangular, with three naves, the church was made cruciform in 1821, when most of its mediaeval features were swept away or covered up. A century later, the architect Armas Lindgren removed the nineteenth-century north-south barrel vault, and covered the building with a dome. The mediaeval paintings were uncovered, and sixty frescoes can be seen in restored glory today, following further renovation by Professor Ola Hansson (1982), who replaced the wooden floor by traditional bricks. The old 17th century altar remains in the east wing of the sanctuary; the new altar stands where it probably stood in the original foundation. Hours of visiting are 12–6, except that Swedish services take place at noon on Sundays, following Finnish services at ten.

Vantaa has a small Aircraft Museum, and Espoo a Car Museum consisting of about 150 vehicles, including fire-engines, mopeds and motorbikes. For the latter, take a 249 bus from the bus station to Viherlaakso, then a 67 bus to Pakankylä Manor. Opening hours are 10 to 6 between July and August, and in April, May, September, and October between 10 and 6 on Saturdays and Sundays only.

Glims Farmstead Museum, Glimsintie 1, can be reached by bus 109 from the bus station; visiting times are 12–6 daily except Mondays in the summer, and 12–4 from 1 October to Mid-May. If you feel that Seurasaari lacks homogeneity, almost even authenticity despite its brave efforts, then Glims will satisfy you, for the buildings stand very much as they were in the nineteenth century. The main room is a large farmhouse *tupa* or living-room with an open-range oven. The back room was used as the main bedroom, and the other room has a grandfather clock made in Suomenlinna. The main building, with an exhibition room and offices, dates from the eighteenth century, like the storehouse, now displaying woodworking tools and other objects of daily use. Stables for nine horses hint that they came into full use when the farmhouse became an inn, most recently in 1900. The building for vehicles is local, but the threshing-house, with its exhibition of tools, comes from Rastaala.

Town-planning in Finland may seem revolutionary, but many of the striking offices, houses, supermarkets and libraries that we see today derive from the vision of Eliel Saarinen, as articulated in his plans for Munkkiniemi and Haaga (north of Central Helsinki) in 1915, and Greater Helsinki in 1918. Saarinen believed that the correct type of growth for Finnish towns was to establish independent settlements near the city, and one was suggested on the site of modern Tapiola and Otaniemi. Pragmatism necessitates that ribbon development take precedence over utopian planning for the next thirty years, however, and it was only in the late 1940s that Saarinen's vision found active support in Heikki von Hertzen, managing director of the Finnish Population and Family Welfare League, and later director of the whole Tapiola scheme. The League bought the Hagalund Manor lands in 1951, and the Housing Foundation asked Otto I. Meurman to rethink his low-rise housing plans for the area, with the architects Aarne Ervi, Aulis Blomstedt, Viljo Revell and Markus Tavio to plan the first stage, bearing in mind the cardinal principle of allowing the natural environment to dictate form, purpose and colour as far as feasible. Rocks, headlands, trees and lakes presented a landscape in which a sensitive planner could humbly subsume his own personality in that of the environment. 'The most important aim of town planning,' noted von Hertzen, 'is to create an environment *biologically right* for man, the subject and object of human activity.' When one looks at London or Lille, Chicago or Detroit, the inescapable conclusion is that man has been cowed by the buildings: he is a wage-slave, and his environment has been razed flat to make him *economically* more successful at the expense of his spiritual self. Aarne Ervi, winner of the first prize in the competition to plan the centre of Tapiola, emphasised the family-oriented vision of von Hertzen: 'We wished to retain a living contact with nature. We also desired to create a number of units of human dimensions which could combine to form a whole. On the site of an old gravel pit we built a pond, which became the central focus of the whole area. Our banning of traffic in the central square was essential, and exceptional.'

What happened? Migration to Helsinki continued, but Helsinki itself, hemmed in by the Baltic on three sides, could only move north and outwards on the fan of highways. So Espoo had to grow, becoming a borough in 1965 and achieving city status in 1971, but of its four regional centres only Tapiola possessed all the potential for harmonious growth, having acquired the significant new business building, Heikintori, in 1968. A new plan, completed in 1969, envisaged the enlargement of Tapiola by 15,000 square metres of new public buildings, 60,000 square metres of new shopping areas, and 75,000 square metres of new office space.

Critics of Tapiola attacked the original concept for 'wastefulness' of land, when a great deal of low-cost housing was needed for many new immigrants to the city, and ideologically opposed extension of the garden city ideal on the grounds that the original garden cities in Europe had not been emulated in countries where they had been tried. So the new plan of 1969 proposed a two-level traffic scheme, with a uniform building height three storeys above the pedestrian level, and covered heated public spaces. A 1974 plan modified the 1969 proposals by reducing traffic areas, decking, the rate of construction, and the number of heated public spaces, and the architect Timo Penttilä's office designed a variety of high tower blocks. Some of the atmosphere of a garden city has been lost, with the increase of traffic, the high-rise buildings, and aspects of the new centre such as the concentration of offices and department stores, but Ervi's plan – though diluted – will shortly be completed with a cultural centre for concerts and plays, and a determination to retain those bungalows and wooded walks that made Tapiola piquantly unique.

The evolution of architectural styles in Tapiola (stressed on the first syllable, like 'Helsinki' and indeed most other words in Finnish), can be illustrated neatly by two developments designed by Reima Pietilä and Raili Paatelainen (now Raili Pietilä). Suvikumpu (literally 'Summerhill', reminiscent to English ears of that other great experiment, the school of A.S. Neill) is a series of buildings, each with 140 apartments, created on a fortress hill the Russians built to protect Helsinki during World War I. Suvikumpu was created in the 1960s following the 'fifties aesthetic of closeness to nature and the *genius loci* principle, coupled with eclectic considerations of early 'twenties modernism, before the Bauhaus. The estate flows upward in steps like a ziggurat seen from one side, but with the human element overshadowing the religious. The *in situ* concrete frame was complemented by surface materials such as plaster, concrete and board facing. The architects were not ashamed of using such naive or romantic concepts as applying green paint on concrete and board to echo the grass and leaves in the wooded environment. Suvituuli ('Summerbreeze') by contrast was designed in the 1970s to be built in lightweight concrete with shell slab intermediate floors but, during construction in the 'eighties, materials changed to sandwich units and hollow slab, involving some alterations to the original design. Both remain highly successful in their different ways in that most challenging field: social housing.

In 1896 three young architects established a joint office in Helsinki. Herman Gesellius, Eliel Saarinen and Armas Lindgren, having graduated from the Polytechnic in 1898, were selected to create the Finnish pavilion for the Paris Universal Exhibition in 1900, which caused a tremendous stir, and brought Finnish design to the forefront of world attention. On the shores of Hvitträsk ('White Lake' in old Swedish), they found a tranquil wilderness west of Espoo, and designed a house each, linked by a large

Hvitträsk. (Courtesy of Hvitträsk Foundation)

studio, the ensemble reaching completion in 1904. Lindgren's wing was sold to Saarinen in 1905, when Lindgren moved back to Helsinki: it burned down in 1922 and was rebuilt in a different style by Eliel Saarinen's son Eero. Gesellius died in 1916, when Saarinen took over the rest of the complex as guesthouses for his friends and fellow-architects.

Saarinen's original home is now a museum, Gesellius' home a restaurant, and Lindgren's home a hotel for six guests. Hvitträsk is a triumph of the Art Nouveau which swept across Europe in the early 1900s, and should be seen by every visitor to Finland with an interest in the development of aesthetic style. You can reach Hvitträsk by buses from platform 62 at Helsinki bus station, and by electric trains marked E, L or Y from Helsinki Rail Station: ask for Luoma and walk 2 km, or Masala halt and take a taxi.

Your *frisson* of delight on first seeing this home-studio will be deepened on minute examination of the interior. Saarinen designed all the furniture himself. The colour-coordinated fireplace bricks and tiles were designed by Louis Sparre and made at Porvoo in the Iris Factory which Sparre had founded. Akseli Gallen-Kallela painted the ceiling frescoes in the dining-room, and designed the famous 'Flame' rug (this is one of six copies, the original being lost), all other rugs being woven by Loja Saarinen. The round chandelier in the sitting-room has twenty-four candles, to bring luck throughout the whole day, one candle for each hour. Beams from Karelia give this main room its informal title. The little adjoining dining-room, with a fairy-tale rug, is adorned with a window-painting, *The Proposal*, showing the features of Matilde Saarinen (his first wife) between Saarinen and Gesellius. She is glancing furtively at Gesellius, and in fact divorced Saarinen and later married Gesellius. The second Mrs Saarinen proved a match for her husband in both energy and creativity: a textile artist, pianist, gourmet cook and gardener. Upstairs you can explore four ingenious split levels. The first belonged to Eliel and Loja Saarinen themselves, with a charming flower room, breakfast room, balcony, bedroom with handmade linen wall-coverings, and a bathroom with the first bath in Finland not to stand on legs. The second level belonged to the children, Eeva-Liisa (Pipsan) and Eero, who both became architects too. Here is the loveliest view of the lake, another bathroom, and a playroom considerately provided with rounded corners on every pillar or table. Hvitträsk's third level was for guests, and the fourth for the principal maid, Lidia. A path down to the lake leads to a sauna designed by Reima Pietilä amid magnificent natural scenery, yet only two dozen km from Helsinki. One might think that the art of life had been perfected and time could stop. But ambition plays strange tricks, and in 1923, Saarinen and his family took up residence in Cranbrook, Michigan, returning to Hvitträsk every summer until 1949, when he sold the houses to Anelma and Rainer Vuorio. He died in 1950 and is buried here. The Vuorios' conditions of purchase entailed leaving everything in its place. In 1969 a private foundation took over Hvitträsk, which opened as a museum in 1971, and ten years later passed into the hands of the Finnish State. *Si monumentum requiris, circumspice.* Not only here, but at the National Museum and Railway Station in Helsinki. New Yorkers will find echoes of Eliel Saarinen's great (but never built) design of 1922 for the *Chicago Tribune* in the New York Telephone Company of 1926, Beekman Tower Hotel of 1928, and Chanin Building of 1929. Eliel worked with his son Eero on the General Motors Technical Institute, and Eero himself was responsible for the CBS Building and the TWA Terminal at JFK Airport in New York, the Arch of St Louis, and Dulles International Airport in Washington.

Hvitträsk Museum is open from 10–8 in summer, and 11–7 in winter: it should be seen by anyone staying more than three days in Helsinki.

The foremost musical pilgrimage in Finland, apart form Savonlinna's opera festival, can be by train, from Helsinki to Järvenpää, or by bus from platform 1 at Helsinki bus station to Hyrylä-Järvenpää, a distance of 38 km from Helsinki to Järvenpää, and a few hundred metres by foot from the road fork to Ainola. Jean Sibelius lived here with his wife, Aino (hence the name), and three daughters, from 1904 until his death in 1957. Born in Hämeen-linna, he published nothing after 1929, though he worked every day. The last twenty-eight years of his life he lived the so-called 'silence of Ainola' in idyllic surroundings which we recognise elsewhere in Finland at Hvitträsk, for example, or Kalela.

Born in 1865, 'Janne' Sibelius married Aino, sister of the painter Eero Järnefelt, in 1892; it was Eero who discovered this delightful setting and Lars Sonck who was commissioned to design a home worthy of it. Sonck's brilliant versatility can be estimated from the diversity of his achievements: Helsinki's Kallio Church, S. Michael's Church in Turku, S. John's Cathedral in Tampere, and no less a creation than the Presidential Summer Palace of Kultaranta, near Naantali! The three upstairs rooms, always closed, are the bedroom, guest-room and study. Visitors to the house (closed on Mondays; open May-September between 10 and 6, except on Wednesdays (12–8); at other times phone 287 322) are shown four rooms and a kitchen downstairs. The drawing-room has a winter landscape by Pekka Halonen (1915), Eero Järnefelt's portrait of his sister (1907) and a fine drawing of 'Janne' by Albert Edelfelt (1904). Electric light came to Ainola in 1918, but no electric heating or running water was provided here until three years after Sibelius' death. Green, the composer's favourite colour, dominates not only his estate but also his dining-room, with a table designed by Aino herself. The long library, with comfortable armchairs and a stove ceramic-tiled gives the impression of being more for show than for use. Gallen-Kallela's *En Saga* (1894) hangs on the back wall. The room was originally intended as a nursery for the three little girls, but later on in life Sibelius preferred to work on the ground floor, where he also slept. It is in this bedroom that he died. For some reason I found Ainola's kitchen the most affecting room in the house. Aino proved a staunchly loyal and self-sacrificing wife, even at the height of Janne's womanizing and boozing, his manic depressions, and his hypochondria, so candidly documented in Erik Tawaststjerna's definitive biography. She rescued him from debaucheries at the Kämp restaurant in Helsinki, 'where he would be lost for days at a time', and yet still found time to win first prizes for apple-growing at the Agricultural Exhibition in Tuusula. Aino grew tomatoes in a greenhouse in the 1940s, and all the bread eaten in the home was baked in this kitchen. She cleared most of the stony ground around the house to make gardens and an orchard; it is she who designed the sauna (1905). One cannot underestimate the stability Sibelius derived from the solidarity of the Järnefelt family, writing incidental music (later recorded as *Valse Triste*) for the play *Kuolema* by his brother-in-law Arvid and entering discussions with his brother-in-law, the composer Armas. For all his human faults, Sibelius learned eventually a great tolerance in musical values: 'When you have lived as long as I [he lived to be 91], and have seen one tendency after another being born, blossom and die, you are inclined to take up a less decided position. You prefer to search for what is good, wherever you can find it.'

Järvenpää. Ainola. The Library of Jean Sibelius (Courtesy of Ainola Foundation)

But there is something more to 'the silence of Ainola'. In the surrounding woodland, lilies of the valley scattered like candles luminescent but unlit-seen from above- in a darkened church. They are Finland's national flower, small and apparently threatened by great birches around them but really autonomous, unaffected. One can always hold one's head up high if it does not reach the level of the executioner's axe. A writer with whom I spoke in Budapest told me, 'I must write the truth even if it is never published; especially *because* it can never be published.' Under threat, in a state of nervous tension, one can create works of passion like poems of Rozéwicz, the plays of Havel, the novels of Solzhenitsyn. But, in the earthly paradise of Ainola, where does the creative artist discover those seeds of anguish and frustration that fecundated in a deaf Beethoven or a persecuted Radnoti?

Finlandia (1899) was composed by Sibelius at a time when the Russification of Finland had reached new levels of intensity, and a plan to follow up *Kullervo* with a full-scale *Kalevala* opera was realised only as far the overture which we know as *The Swan of Tuonela*, but the Sibelius remembered today is the symphonist, whose last major work, the Seventh, dates from 1924. Receiving a state annuity, and in a situation of material comfort, adored by a patriotic public, could it be that, despite all the well-publicised gossip of hard drinking and extra-marital affairs, the 'silence of Ainola' signifies the death of creativity by contentment?

Taking the high road from Helsinki to Vantaa Airport, beyond Oulunkylä you come to the village of Tuomarinkylä, which dates back at least to the 15th century. The manor has been in existence since the mid-18th century, and the present manor building, commissioned by Johannes Weckström in 1790, typifies early neo-classical buildings of the time, and in 1986 was fully restored as a branch of Helsinki City Museum. Of the four original outbuildings, one was demolished early in the present century. The southeastern building (now a café) contained a ballroom, salon, and two guest rooms. In 1845 the manor passed into the hands of the Kavaliev family until 1917, when it was bought by Helsinki City, though Kavaliev lived in the main building until 1957, and it opened as a museum in 1962. The form and colours of the building's exterior look as they did late in the 18th century, and the rooms have been rearranged as they were in the 1840s.

A park laid out to the south of the main building in 1781 has also been restored, with its regular paths and terrace. The manor hill rose during the Stone Age, about 1500 B.C., and by the first century A.D. the land around the hill was already above sea-level, and the Vantaa river channel allowed access to the sea. By the time of Helsinki's foundation in the mid-16th century, Tuomarinkylä possessed 23 inhabitants who made their living from farming, fishing and boatbuilding. Traders took furs, timber, tar and leather to Stockholm and Tallinn in return for corn and salt. Weckström planted kitchen gardens with vegetables and herbs, while Kavaliev's main interest lay in exotic plants, for which he created his own nursery and experimental garden. In the spring you can see Asian squill (*Scilla sibrica*), spring anemones, and the Lesser Celandine (*Runuculus ficaria*). Rare plants still seen today include the thistle *Echinips exaltatus*, the Caucasian stonecrop (*Sedum aizoon*) and the great Norway spruce (*Picea abies*).

If Tapiola's garden city answered one planning need, beginning in the 1950s, a generation on there are different planning needs, and a solution is offered by the laconically-named Itäkeskus ('Eastern Centre') which forms the gateway to Porvoo and Eastern Finland. The population of the eastern suburbs had risen to 120,000, but the inhabitants of these hurriedly-built post-war housing schemes still needed to commute to central Helsinki for jobs and services. A special problem lay in the fact that a six-lane highway separates the two halves of the inhabited area.

The first solution, bearing in mind the immense traffic problems, was to build a metro line to the east, which would empty into a central station connecting both areas by a pedestrian bridge, covered against the elements. The next was to create in the same complex a multi-purpose building with offices and shops which would attract local people to work and shop without having to leave the nucleus, a parish centre and a shopping centre, all independent of the traffic system. A brilliant sky-blue sculptural monument, like a summer temple rather than a summer cottage, was made by Hannu Sirén to form the centrepiece of a square facing the parish centre and the multi-purpose building. Though the public library and church may seem aesthetically undistinguished, they are certainly functional and convenient. The multi-purpose building by Björn Krogius includes a library, adult education rooms, halls for concerts and plays, an exhibition area, coffee shop and hobby facilities for young people, as well as a créche. The church and parish centre by Veli-Pekka Tuominen has also been functioning from the mid-1980s: the cross by the altar seems apologetically tiny; the ambience, plain and Quakerish with one main light-source from the left of the altar, struck me as overbearingly secularistic.

You will see Itäkeskus if you travel to Porvoo by road. But you can see Porvoo by sea as well. From 15 June to 24 August, m/s *Queen* departs from Koleraallas, Market Square, at 10.30 on Tuesdays, Thursdays, Saturdays and Sundays. The return trip takes 6½ hours, including two hours in Porvoo itself. If you have less time, m/s *King* and m/s *Katarina* operate roughly every hour from 11 to 4 between June and August. This costs less than half the Porvoo cruise and takes only 90 minutes. The *King* provides a canal cruise with a circuit of Suomenlinna; *Katarina* offers 'Helsinki by Sea'.

I took a bus from the bus station in central Helsinki, arriving an hour later in the central bus station of Porvoo, an unremarkable square between Piispankatu and Rauhankatu. Yet, after Turku, Porvoo claims to be the oldest town in Finland, with a stronghold on the river (Borgå, its Swedish name, derives from *borg*, 'castle' and *å*, 'river') dating back at least to 1200, to protect the fine river and harbour-entrance, the best anchorage between Helsinki to the west and Loviisa to the east. Start by taking the main street, Mannerheiminkatu, towards the river. On the bridge, you can look down to the row of old wooden storehouses, lovingly restored, where salt and other merchandise brought by sea was stored on arrival. The Cathedral's steep roof rises brown into the cloudy blue sky, and that is the heart of Old Porvoo (8 on the map). I headed south straight for the house where the national poet lived from 1852 to 1877. Johan Ludvig Runeberg (1804–77) wrote solely in Swedish, but his *Tales of Ensign Stål* (1848) celebrated the 1808–9 War against the Russians in narrative poems which possess the same treasured place in Finland that Scott's narrative poems possess in Scotland. Nothing has been disturbed in Runeberg's sparsely-furnished scholar's bedroom. Or in the library, amply provided with Finnish and Swedish books current in his lifetime, with a good number of German and French authors, with George Eliot and with Sir Walter Scott. Porvoo people commemorate his birthday every February by lighting candles in their windows. Runeberg's house (1 on the map) is a museum-shrine open throughout the year, as is the collection of sculptures by one of his sons, Walter, in an adjacent house (4 on the map).

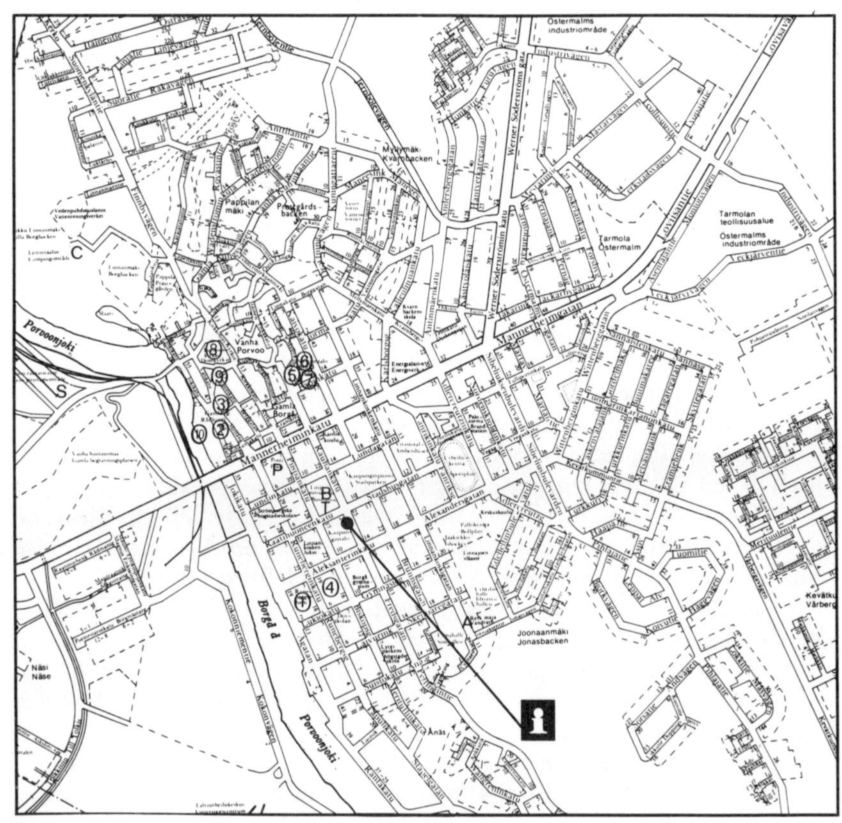

Porvoo. Town Plan

A	Youth Hostel	① J.L. Runeberg's House
B	Bus Station	② Historical Museum
C	Camping	③ Edelfelt-Vallgren Museum
P	Post Office	④ Collection of Walter Runeberg's Sculptures
S	Railway Station	⑤ Natural History Museum
T	Taxi	⑥ Hunting and Game Protection Museum
		⑦ Art Gallery ⑧ Cathedral ⑨ Gamla kaplansgården
		⑩ Dollmuseum

Picturesque old Porvoo has a cluster of interesting showplaces left off Kaivokatu: Porvoo House, with a Natural History Museum, Hunting Museum, and Art Gallery (5–7 on the map), but your steps lead ever upwards towards the Cathedral. Like Helsinki, Porvoo has its Linnanmäki (Castle Hill), and here too there is virtually nothing left. But traces of a thirteenth-century church survive in the present Cathedral's north wall and northwest corner. The structure dates to the fifteenth century but the interior was reconstructed beginning in 1729, after Viipuri had been lost to Russia in the war and episcopal status was transferred to Porvoo. Under master-builder Johann Friedrich Schultze the interior was remodelled, with fine new double galleries of the 1760s, their original colouring restored in

64

Porvoo. Old Riverside Storehouses

the 1970s. The organ front dates from 1799, but the organ itself is a new instrument by Veikko Virtanen (1978). The crucifix above the altar is a baroque work of the early 18th century. Porvoo Cathedral is perhaps most revered in Finnish history for a vow made on 29 March 1809, when Tsar Alexander guaranteed that Finland would be allowed to retain its religion and constitution intact. Walter Runeberg's statue of the Tsar was unveiled in 1909. You might request the privilege of seeing the 13th-century Sifridus Chalice, so-called from the Latin inscription by the German silversmith who made it (for Osnabrück). It has found refuge at last in Porvoo, having been taken to Viipuri as war booty. If you are not particularly interested in the Doll Museum (10 on the map), you should now see the Historical Museum and Holm's House (1762), an art gallery named for Edelfelt and Vallgren (2 and 3 on the map). The Historical Museum at the end of Välikatu, reputedly the oldest continuously used street in Finland, is situated in the old town hall, and here you can see random components of old Porvoo. Inside the entrance hall stand 19th-century sledges used by Tsar Alexander I and Tsar Nicholas I, tangible reminders of the Russian occupation. Furniture from the 18th century includes a wistfully silent clavichord from Stockholm. On an upper floor my eye was taken by a Swedish Gustavian desk of the late 18th century, which once belonged to Näse Manor in Porvoo. In the Diet meeting rooms tin soldiers of 1790 froze in re-enacting battles long lost. Among the bric-à-brac of dead men are a range of bookbinders' tools used between 1863 and 1914. On the top floor a display of military costume, crossbows, cannonballs, pistols and swords is offset by the weapons of peace: embroidery, children's toys. Then I explored the nearby Art Gallery. I had grown to love Albert Edelfelt, in the Ateneum at Helsinki, and eagerly scanned the spine of his library: Topelius, of course, Runeberg, Lönnrot's *Kalevala*, but then the pleasurable surprise of Molière, too. Old tiled fireplaces have been preserved here and in the Historical Museum, but the most interesting feature must be the works of Alfred William Finch (1854–1930): not only the ceramics and paintings, but the lithograph series depicting Old Porvoo. Finch, of Belgian ancestry, moved in 1897 to Finland where he became head of ceramics at the influential Iris Factory, and later taught graphic art at the Art Association. Originally, Porvoo sloped from church to riverbank, then a bridge was erected in the 15th century, and the township throve despite Gustavus Vasa's preference for Helsinki's relative proximity to Sweden. Porvoo's inhabitants were ordered to emigrate to Helsinki, so that the settlement diminished to only 360 inhabitants in 1639. This figure rose to 1,033 by 1759, and over 2,000 in 1805. Several fires devastated Porvoo, but the citizens tenaciously retained their mediaeval street plan, despite the fire of 1760, after which most of old Porvoo was again rebuilt. Then Tsar Nicholas ordered Carl Ludwig Engel to make a new plan for Porvoo in 1832, following which new Porvoo rose, south of Mannerheiminkatu, a neo-classical town. The Town Hall, on the market square, (Raatihuoneenkatu) was designed by F.A. Sjöström in 1893. Other distinguished buildings in this sector include the Bishop's Palace in Kirkkotori designed in 1927 by Valter and Bertel Jung, and Juhani Pallasmaa's Jäntti art collection premises in the WSOY office, Papinkatu 19, as recent as 1984. I sauntered along River Street (Jokikatu), the summer boats lolling, moored against Porvoon-joki's banks, blond Finns eagerly talking to each other about a rock concert in Helsinki, and sucking ice-cream cones as passionately as any Russians in Odessa.

The Road to Turku

The temperature on the Yhdyspankki (United Bank) building read 22°C one July afternoon at 4.30 as our luxury route bus slid out silently from rank 33 at Helsinki bus station. Our smart male driver concentrated on the road as a beautiful conductress in neat white blouse and black shirt welcomed us on our 165-km drive to Turku. We sped along Mechelininkatu and Paciuksen-katu with the carefree abandon of freemen leaving urbanites chained behind: the Toad of Toad Hall syndrome. In half an hour the bus streamed through countryside deeply wooded on both sides of the motorway, reaching Saukkola at 5.20 and Lahnajärvi, for a twenty-minute break, at 5.30. The water-gardens here, with a chute for children, open in summer from 10 to 8, and the consumption of ice-cream seemed to rise despite the gradual drop in temperature. I bought a litre of strawberries for 8 FM. We reached the little town of Salo (17,500 inhabitants) at 6.05, and loitered in the town, picking up parcels and standing about, like the carter in *Peter Grimes*. Old wooden buildings waited for someone to tell them about the invention of stone. Unobtrusive police in light blue stood with arms crossed, hoping for outlaws. But without many prospects, for crime is so insignificant in Finland that every police patrol car has pinned up in it a sheet of paper with the registration numbers of *all* the stolen vehicles not yet traced. The glorious evening padded about like a familiar teddy bear, warm, golden-brown, affectionate. We arrived in Turku at 7 p.m., each passenger courteously waiting for the others to disembark first: tactful, patient, even-tempered, conscious of the space and privacy due to others: Finns are the quiet ones, the Japanese, of Europe.

TURKU

In the first centuries of our era, immigrants from Eastern Europe and the southern Baltic settled the river-valleys of southwest Finland, a movement of peoples that has led this part of the country to become known as 'Finland Proper' or Varsinais Suomi. Gradually these settlements evolved into small towns, trading with each other and with other communities inland and overseas. Because the hinterland has always been sparsely populated, and relatively poor in commercial terms (possessing only furs, meat and antlers), towns like Turku (and Naantali, Rauma, Pori, Vaasa, Kokkola, Oulu and Kemi farther north) expanded and enmeshed their economy and trading patterns with Sweden, and with the Hanseatic League, especially following immigration from Sweden beginning in the eleventh century. Erik, King of Sweden, made it his business to colonise (and probably to bring Christianity) to his Swedish and Finnish subjects, according to Porthan's legend, with the 'First Crusade' of 1155. The Finnish bishop of Åbo (as Turku is still known in Swedish) acted as Sweden's delegate also in civil matters, though resistance to the invaders (who spoke a language entirely different and came from a completely alien racial stock) persisted for centuries. Across the Vänäjoki ('Little River') I came to the earthworks of Koroinen, with its complex of church and bishop's castle, once excavated, but now again covered up. The first church here dates from 1220–45, during the bishopric of Tuomas, then Bero became bishop from 1249 to 1258 and Ragnvald I from 1259 to 1266, and Kettil from 1266. Pope Gregory IX agreed to the transfer of the Bishop's see from Nousiainen to Koroinen in 1229, the year which Turku celebrates as the founding of the city because no documents testify to earlier settlement. A stone church built shortly afterwards was consecrated in 1300 as the Cathedral. A citadel to protect the growing settlement sprang up in the later 13th century. Apprehensive of surprise by Finnish insurgents from the rear, or even Russian invasion from the direction of Novgorod, the Swedish rulers of Turku did not place their fortress on a hill dominating the river Aura (near the Cathedral), but chose instead an island in the river mouth, equally effective to keep watch over the approach of threats from the west. An extended compound offered space as

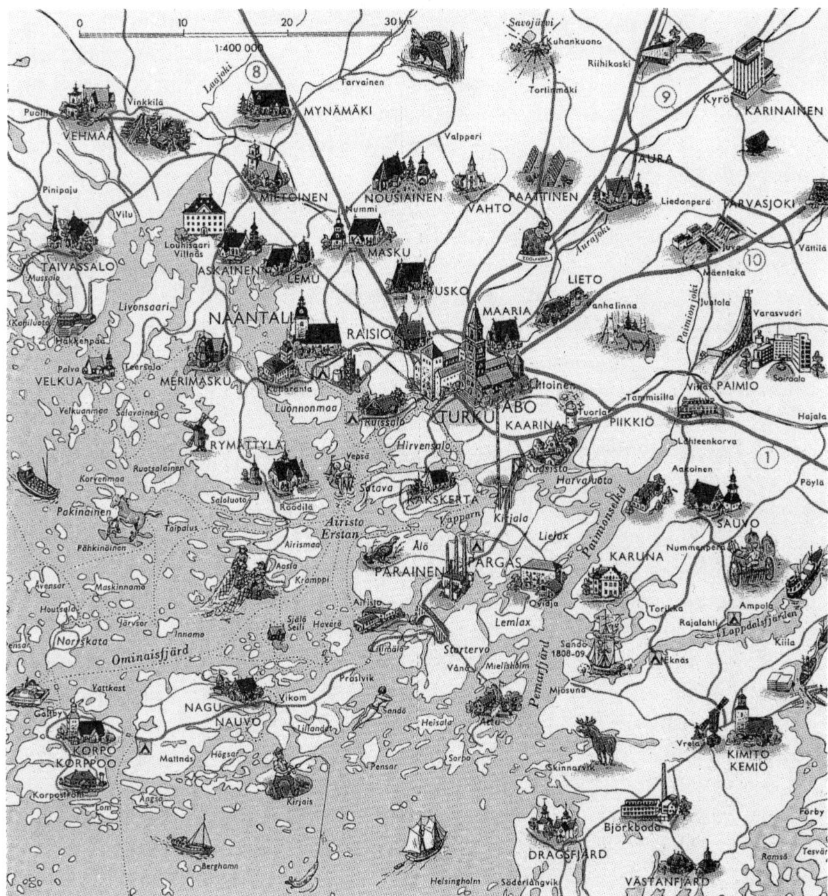

Turku. Environs

a refuge for townspeople under possible siege. In 1414, the first bridge was built across the Aura, and Turku spread across the western bank as well, though the growth of the town was slow, and at this period consisted only of a few wooden huts and houses under the shadow of the Cathedral. As we were driving northeast to Lieto, a fox darted through the woods to our left, a silent lord, sharp-eared, and Janáček's music opening *The Cunning Little Vixen* sang in my heart. We were on our way to Vanhalinna ('Old Castle'), but these woodlands could have been Moravian; they could have been Janáček's whistling Forester, cricket, gnat, grasshopper, frog and badger. Finland's bracken crackled and rustled with teeming life as summer opened its portals. Seven km from Turku we came to the prehistoric hill overlooking the Aura valley. It is owned by Turku University, whose historians have found evidence of habitation from 300–1300 A.D., before the construction of Turunlinna. A museum showing farmyard implements is open only on Sundays between 10 and 3. (Buses for Vanhalinna leave Turku bus station from platforms 8 or 9).

Ecclesiastical rule ended in 1280, but the Golden Age of Turku began within thirty years of the end of the Roman Catholic age, ended in 1527, by decree of Gustavus Vasa. He appointed his eighteen-year old younger son, Prince Johan, as Duke of Finland in 1556, and presented him with Turku Castle as a ducal residence. Gustavus Vasa sent Swedish builders and artisans to extend the castle, provide it with massive earthworks, and replace the simple crenellations with great halls and smaller chambers, with flat ceilings and wide, light windows contrasting with the Gothic vaulting and dark rooms of the mediaeval part. Imagine the splendid scene, on Christmas Eve 1562, when Duke Johan (later King Johan III), brought his Polish bride, Princess Catherina Jagellonica, to their Renaissance court, with its tournaments and banquets. Yet within eight months his brother Erik XIV had invaded the castle from Sweden, besieged Johan and after three weeks dispatched the young couple into captivity in Sweden, together with all the robes and costly objects brought from Poland and elsewhere in Europe. A few years later Erik himself was held prisoner in Turku Castle, and later sieges in 1597 and 1599 were carried out by Karl, brother to both Erik and Johan, the latter ending in the massacre in the town hall square on 10 November 1599. Land uplift, still active today, gradually increased the area occupied by the castle and its immediate domain, but the bailey was given its present form between 1576 and 1588. It burned down in 1614 and, though rebuilt, little of its former glories remained and it found menial use as a storehouse, with the exception of the chapel. A new chapel was built in the top floor of the south wing in 1705–6, and two carved 'royal chairs' were added in it during the visit of Gustavus III in 1775. Red was the colour of the castle's great ladies. The girl-attendants at Turku Castle today wear plebeian blue, and with the appropriate hairstyle and footwear might have stepped out of eighteenth-century kitchens with steaming platters in their hands for the table. After the time of Gustavus III, Turku's bailey was converted into a prison, acting as such until the provincial prison was established elsewhere in 1891. The Lord-Lieutenant's residence had been removed from castle to town as early as 1698 and the castle henceforth remained peripheral to life in Turku, much as Windsor or Hampton Court might be considered from the vantage of Buckingham Palace, or Runnymede from the Houses of Parliament.

The restoration of the Castle, completed in 1961, serves a dual purpose:

City Tourist Office
Käsityöläiskatu 3, 20100 TURKU 10, (921) 336 366
Tourist Information, city centre
Aurakatu 4, (921) 152 62
Tourist Information, harbour
Silja Line Terminal, (921) 303 563

Line Terminal, Tourist Information
Line Terminal
Castle and Historical Museum
Church
Ferry ('Föri') over the Aura
aara Football and Ice Hockey Halls
ay Station
Police Headquarters
Hostel
bus Quay
' Museum Ship
Catholic church
en Joutsen' sailing ship
Church
aara Swimming Baths
sh Hologram Gallery
Tourist Office
allery
Office and telecommunications
ies
Aaltonen Museum
palinna Windmill and open-air
er theatre
s Field
rnment Offices
Theatre
gical Museum
Station
gogue
dox Church
et Place
ish Theatre
t Hall
palinna Swimming Stadium
Mormon) Church
aistentori ("Puutori"), buses for
tali

35 City Hall and Tourist Office
36 Qwensel House and Pharmacy Museum; waterbus quay; SW Finland Tourist Association
37 Concert Hall
38 Finnair terminal
39 City Library
40 Sibelius Museum, Kingelin Summerhouse
41 Cathedral
42 Åbo Akademi (Swedish-language university)
43 Maritime Museum and Astronomical Collection
44 Handicrafts Museum
45 'Ett Hem' museum house
46 Vartiovuori open-air summer theatre
47 University of Turku (Finnish-language university)
48 Student Village
49 Ikituuri Congress Centre
50 Turku University Central Hospital ("TYKS")
51 St Mary's Church
52 Scouting Museum
53 St Catherine's Church
54 Kupittaa Sports Hall
55 St Henry's Well
56 Kupittaa Ice-Hockey Hall
57 St Henry's Church
58 Chapel of the Resurrection
59 Chapel of the Holy Cross
60 Turku University Botanical Gardens
61 Ruissalo Recreation Park
62 Hirvensalo Skiing Centre
63 Metsämäki Racecourse
64 Varissuo Athletics Hall

0   500   1000 m
1:15 000

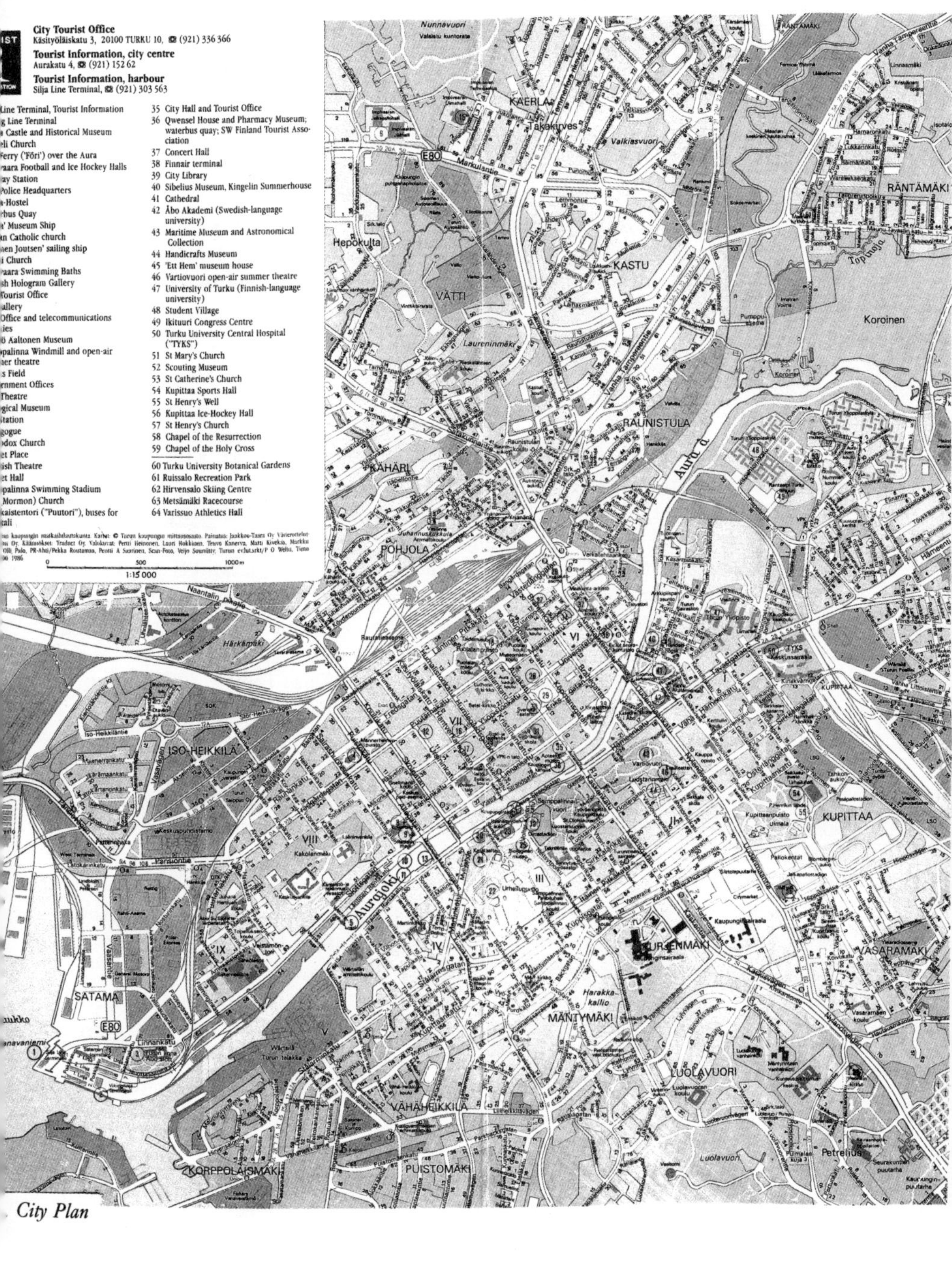

City Plan

much of it is made over the museum which has expanded here since 1881, and the rest serves as living banqueting halls, council chambers, and a chapel where services and ceremonies are still held. Every August a dozen banquet evenings are held in Turku Castle, with dishes of the period, and musicians and servitors in traditional costume. The menu is: salted Baltic herrings with mustard sauce and mushroom salad, chicken legs, currant soup, smoked pork chops and baked roots, cheese pie, fruit and sweetmeats.

The modern entrance-hall served as a store-room. Just before you enter the porter's lodge, after the broad staircase, look left on the far side of the door: here is the oldest stairway, of the 14th century, built within the original wall.

Delightful paintings *al secco* (of 1530, uncovered in the early 1930s) show a Renaissance couple; symbolic human figures, one armed, with cap and bells, and the other gazing into a mirror; and a scene from the Battle of Pavia, 1525.

Next you see the Sture Church, named for Sture the Elder, who held the castle in fief from 1472 to 1499, and created this church, originally rib-vaulted, in the 1480s, but the rib vaulting collapsed in the fire of 1614 and was replaced by barrel vaulting. Here is a treasury of mediaeval sculpture, such as the Job with Sores from Lieto, and a splendid S. George, Dragon, and Princess, reminiscent of the group in Helsinki's National Museum. Sture Church was abandoned when the castle's third church was consecrated in 1706, on the top floor of the south wing.

The first church no longer exists, according to Knut Drake. It was made of wood and situated above the Lord's Cellar (not open to the public).

The so-called 'Nuns' Chapel', formerly believed to have been the first church in the castle, took its name from the tradition that the Polish princess Catherina Jagellonica would have worshipped here, with Roman Catholic priests. The chapel, heavily restored, has the first star-vaulting seen in Finland. A vent in the floor, once opened, allowed heat to rise into the chapel from stoves on the floor below. Splendid sculptures include a seated Madonna and Child by the Master of Lieto (*fl.* 1330) presumably from Visby or elsewhere in Gotland. The standing S. Olaf from Rusko Church dates from the 1290s and is by a master called Väte from Gotland. Light falls flatteringly on a late 14th-century standing Madonna and Child from Rusko.

Now we come to the magnificent King's State Room used from the early 14th century to 1556. State guests were received here, and honoured with banquets. The monumentally thick exterior wall has no windows and two niches, one being the royal lavatory. Above the King's State Room you can see the quarters for the royal children, where Johan lived from 1556 to 1558 before his new suite of rooms on the top floor became ready for occupation. Through a narrow dressing-room you proceed into the West Tower, with the Ladies' Sitting-Room, which you can imagine with its open fireplace (demolished in the 18th century), its walls covered in rich and colourful tapestries, and without the present great window of 1585, the date when the castle's gallery first permitted lateral communication between the several wings. Now you come to the mediaeval scriptorium, where wall-niches would have held scrolls. It is possible that the names on the walls are not those of scribes, but of guests at a later period when the room became lodgings.

Here in the South Wing the Great Guard Room and vaulted Constable's Chamber correspond to the King's State Room and the King's Chamber in the North Wing. Below the Constable's chamber, concealed at last in deserved obscurity, lies a dungeon ten yards deep, six yards long and three yards wide: here, if anywhere, can the world's most horrific nightmare come true.

In the Great Guard Room assembled the castle's garrison, then you enter the Great Staircase tower, designed by Duke Johan after tearing down the mediaeval curtain-wall and the fortifications on the walls, to make way for windowed halls, an almost physical rejection of the 'Dark Ages' and a trumpet call for the coming Renaissance, when religious obscurantism and feudalism would begin to make way for first hesitant moves towards the modern world, moves exemplified by the transformation of the archers' and cannoneers' gallery into Duke Johan's banqueting hall (1550s-1706), before its final incarnation as a church for the castle and vicinity. Two royal pews were added in 1775, for the visit of Gustav III of Sweden and Queen Sofia Magdalena. Though the church was destroyed by the great fire of 1941, the pulpit is of earlier date (1757) and comes from a village church in Varsinais Suomi. The interior has been faithfully restored following the original design, and the touching addition of the votive ship adds a note of rural charm to the sober grayish-blue interior.

The scale of Johan's castle emerges as you enter the King's Hall, which takes up only the eastern sector of the North Wing. The ceiling was reconstructed in 1946–61 after Swedish models, but the walls are preserved. An eighteenth-century Gobelin tapestry adorns one wall, but all the other tapestries are copies. The finest painting, on loan from the Ateneum, was painted in Paris by Albert Edelfelt in 1878. It depicts *Duke Karl Insulting the Corpse of Claes Fleming,* a scene taking place in the Sture Church in 1597 after Karl's unsuccessful rising against Sigismund, who ruled after Johan. Count Fleming died while battle raged around Turunlinna, Death his only conqueror. In Edelfelt's painting the coffin is surrounded by mourning retainers and the gallant Count's widow, but the scene is roughly interrupted by the Swedish Duke Karl, who pulls the warrior's beard, sneering 'Had the Count been alive, his head would not have rested safely on its shoulders as it does now!' To which his widow rejoined: 'If Claes Fleming had been alive, Your Highness would not be here now!' The western sector of the North Wing has the Queen's Hall, also dating from the late 1550s, with a restored fireplace and ceiling. A Flemish tapestry of the late 16th century depicts the Queen of Sheba, and other tapestries show scenes from the life of Moses. The Queen's Chamber offers no hint of the life here in some eight eventful months of the Polish princess: her portrait on the wall is a copy donated by the Polish Government. We are constantly reminded, by the paucity of early originals, that no more than about eighty objects survive from Finland before the year 1500: it follows that extreme love and care are lavished on everything old, on authentic antiques, and that you might as well not even start looking for shops offering such rarities, as you might in Germany or Spain.

A permanent exhibition of costume, silver, glass, ceramics and porcelain will be found in the renovated attic of the North Wing, while the South Wing attic displays Finnish textiles in all their splendour and quiet good taste, from *ryijy* to embroidery, scarves to samplers. I enjoyed a comprehensive view of Albanian folk arts in a temporary exhibition, and then, once outside again, explored in greater detail the courtyard of the Inner Ward, reconstructed (with the demolition of additions) to its likely appearance in the early 14th century. See the staircase turret (1549–50) with a stone, bearing the arms of Sten Sture, which is believed in folklore to wall up the skeleton of a robber. The Outer Ward, reached through a gate in the East Tower, has a vaulted gateway with pointed arches preserved in its mediaeval form.

Eva Dziedzic, a charming vivacious polyglot, infectious in her many enthusiasms, told me how her Seaport Hotel had grown out of an old warehouse by the shore, immediately beside the rail buffers and a hundred yards from the Viking Line and Silja Line terminals. Five carriages pushed by an engine rolled to a halt, a clanging bell having warned pedestrians out of its overgrown way. Expensive, luxurious, but relying on good taste and simplicity, ingenuity and spotless cleanliness, the Seaport Hotel has cost 18 million FM to prepare so far (it opened in June 1986) and another 6 million are to be invested in it. Of its eighty rooms and four suites, four are for the handicapped, and ten for non-smokers. One men's sauna and one women's sauna are already in, with massage and solarium facilities; conference rooms and banqueting halls are being prepared. For breakfast next morning the ample buffet included coffee, tea, milk and orange juice; three different kinds of bread or toast you make yourself, savoury hot porridge, corn flakes, cheeses and cold meats, and several kinds of jam, honey or marmalade, with hard-boiled eggs in plates labelled '2 minutes', '4 minutes', and so on. In central Turku I have felt equally home in the traditional *Gemütlichkeit* of the

Turku. Kauppatori. Orthodox Church with vendors of peas and strawberries

Hamburger Börs on Kauppatori, and the modern Marina Palace, Linnankatu 32. You could try the Cumulus on Eerikinkatu, the Henrik on Yliopistonkatu, the Park Hotel on Rauhankatu or the Ritz or Seurahuone, both on Humalistonkatu. Summer Hotel Domus Aboensis can be found on Piispankatu, and Rantasipi hotels are outside the city centre at Ruissalo, by the yacht marina (bus 8 from Kauppatori), and Ikituuri.

After exploring the castle and seaport area, you can walk, or take a bus, up Linnankatu ('Castle Street') along the western bank of the river Aura, taking not the first three bridges (Martinsilta, Myllysilta, and Auransilta) but the fourth, Tuomiokirkkosilta, turning north before reaching Åbo Akademi. On this height stands Turku Cathedral, and near it the Town Square, the centre of Turku between the 14th century and the Great Fire of 1827. Imagine how it looked, after the first bridge was built across the Aura in 1414. At the centre of the Town Square stood the Town Hall, around which clustered little wooden houses, with alleyways between them instead of the great modern avenues in modern Turku. It was in fact a small Hansa town like all the rest: Danzig, Riga, or Visby. Alleyways that still survive are Karjakatu, beside the Town Hall, and Luostarin Välikatu that stood on the way from Stockholm to Viaborg/Viipuri. Some mediaeval cellars have survived, but fires long ago destroyed every vestige of the wooden houses, and the rise in land level forced shipping downriver, so that today nothing but a rowing boat can navigate upstream.

While the rest of Turku was being rebuilt in grid-fashion to plans by Engel, the Town Square also took on a neo-classical façade but most of the buildings retained their private character, like the old Town Hall of 1736–7, which belonged to the police force until the mid-1980s. I took a pizza in the evocative Ravintola Pinella, named for Nils Henrik Pinello. In 1863 he moved his pavilion to its present site, a terrace supported by Doric pillars overlooking the river Aura. Coffee, tea, and light meals were taken there by men of letters, such as Topelius and Lönnrot, Cygnaeus and Wecksell, and the artists Sjöstrand and Ekman. The Pinella is still one of the most popular summer restaurants in Turku, and I cannot forbear to recommend the salmon-trout recipe known here as 'Luutnantti Adoniksen Unelmakala', called 'Lt. Adonis' Dream-fish', the Adonis in question being the handsome Julios Pinello, son of the founder.

Finding high ground in Finland is like finding a needle in a haystack, so here on Unikankare ('Sleep Knoll') it is hardly surprising to find Turku Cathedral, above an ancient Finnish burial ground, dominating the city and its river. The first wooden parish church rose in the 13th century, but of course nothing remains of this edifice, and of its earliest stone successor all that can be seen is one gable (marked for clarity) in the wall of the modern vestry. After side-chapels had been added, the interior became so dark that the roof was raised and new windows let in at the sides and above the altar, the work being completed by Pietar Kemiöläinen in 1466. Fires, pillage and vandalism have wrought havoc over the centuries. One such terror was the devastation caused by the Danish captain Otto Rud, who plundered Turku over a period of five days, and robbed the Cathedral of all its treasures. Eventually, the chalice and paten found their way to the parish of Ejby, on the island of Själland, which returned them to Turku in 1925. Then there was the capture of Bishop Henry's remains by the Russians, during the Great Hatred: to this day they have not been returned. Finally, the Great Fire of 1827 caused heavy damage to the fabric.

In recent decades the Cathedral has been restored by Armas Lindgren

Turku. Cathedral, towards the mouth of the Aura (Courtesy of Turku City Tourist Office)

and Juhani Rinne (1929) and by Pitkänen, Laiho and Raunio (1976–9), the latter including a new 81-register main organ, a new museum, and restoration of the bells for use.

As a national shrine the Cathedral remains supreme, and should be visited with due reverent quiet one would accord to S. Patrick's or S. Pietro in Vaticano, an atmosphere aided by the dominant high white light, and the numerous inpressive funerary monuments. From here the solemn Christmas Peace is broadcast every year at noon in a simple, moving ceremony: then Finland's Christmas properly begins. The Cathedral dedicated to the Virgin Mary and S. Henry is open 9–7 on weekdays, 9–5 on Saturdays, and 2.30–4.30 on Sundays. The main points of interest are described in anticlockwise order from the main west door. All Souls' Chapel (15th century) has the sarcophagi of General Stålhandske (d.1644), Commander of Finnish Cavalry during the Thirty Years' War, and his wife Kristina. The Mayor's Choir, dedicated to the city, is the burial vault of distinguished citizens, but the most significant object is a 14th-century crucifix. In the old southern choir tower you will find the tiny, exquisite Tigerstedt-

Wallenstjerna Chapel, with its lovely portal and a mediaeval decorative window looking to the Chapel of S. Bartholomew. The latter, and the Chapel of S. Catherine (Kaarina in Finnish), together comprise the Chapel of the Holy Cross, and both date from the 14th century. The 15th-century S. Laurence's Chapel is distinguished for one of the great Baroque sculptural ensembles: the marble monument of Field Marshal Åke Tott and his wife, Christina Brahe, standing imperious in death as in life, the work of Peter Schultz (1678). The High Altar disappoints by comparison, both for the *Transfiguration of Christ* (1834) by the Swedish court-painter Fr. Westin, and for the overrated frescoes (1850–4) by R.W. Ekman. Next we come to the sarcophagus of Karin Månsdotter, queen of Sweden's Erik IV, a work of 1867 by Theodor Decker; the relief on the wall is said to be an authentic portrait of the Queen. Beyond this Kankainen Chapel is the vestry, into whose walls are let the Chapel of S. George,with the 16th-century reliquary of the Blessed Hemming, and the Altar of Henry, patron saint of the Cathedral, and S. Erik. The altar is yet another reminder of the all-pervading influence of Carl Ludwig Engel, and dates from 1836.

The main feature of the Corpus Christi Chapel is the wrought-iron railing of 1425, though it is worth noting that burials here include Bishop Magnus II Tavast (d. 1452), the Scottish colonel Samuel Cockburn, and Field Marshal Evert Horn (d. 1615) and his wife Margareta.

Do not miss the northern porch, of the 1490s; the votive ship is recent, a model of the barque *Turku* presented in 1968. Next is S. John's Chapel, a christening chapel of the 1440s with exceptionally beautiful murals on the vaults. Last of all you see the mediaeval Finnish limestone font, restored in 1978. The Cathedral Museum (opening at the same hours) displays miniature models of the Cathedral (early 14th century and after the 1827 fire), the celebrated Ejby Chalice and Paten (Turku, 1480s) and other church silver and gilded copper, wooden images of the 14th century (a birch bishop and an oaken S. Catherine of Alexandria from Visby, and an oaken *Pietà* from North Germany, and others of the 15th century from Lübeck, all in oak: S. Anthony by Johannes Hagen, and two works by the school of Berndt Notke: a man's head and S. Anne with the Virgin and Child. Ceremonial church utensils from the post-Reformation period include silver baptismal bowls, silver candlesticks, and gilded silver spoons. Among the textiles are chasubles and chalice cloths of the 17-18th centuries. The residence of the Archbishop of Turku can be seen not far from the Sibelius Museum.

Of the many wonderful churches in Turku itself, you might consider seeing Kaarina, or S. Catherine's (1351), Maaria, or S. Mary's (15th century), Michael's (1905), Martin's (1933), the Chapel of the Resurrection (1941), the Chapel of the Holy Cross (1967), and S. Henry's and either

Engel's neo-classical Orthodox Church (1846) on the Market Square, open 10–3 on weekdays and 12-4 on Sundays, or the highly successful Catholic church of S. Birgitta (1966).

Kaarina, grey without and red-brick within, will enchant those who love intimate village churches of the Turku archipelago. Like the Cathedral, it rose on a Bronze Age cemetery. A wooden sculpture of the patron saint has recently returned from the National Museum after restoration, but the mid-17th century reliefs of Simon, Bartholomew, John, Jesus and Peter round the pulpit are poor provincial work by Mathias Reiman of Turku. The oldest part of the church is the sacristy, with its heavy door leading into the church, which was plundered and burned by German pirates in 1396. Reconstruction soon afterwards saw a single row of columns replaced by a double row, the vaults renewed, a new single window created between the bricked-up door in the north wall and bricked-up choir-gable windows. Galleries added in 1735 were removed in 1926, when the floor was restored to its original level. The original railings from the gallery are painted with scenes from the miracles of Christ by Jonas Bergman (1759–60). The votive ship by Johan Tolander (1820) came from the village of Nummenkylä. Don't miss the mediaeval pillory and choir chair in the west entrance porch. The text on the pulpit reads 'Titt ord är min fötters lychta och ett lius på minon wägom', 'Your word is the lantern for my feet, and the light for my way'.

Near Kaarina is the Ikituuri Centre, in the Student Village. The multi-purpose building, designed by Jyrki Tasa, Kari Raimoranta and Matti Nurmela, opened in 1977 as a public bath, congress centre, activities hall, hotel and two restaurants, post office and bank. Accommodation for four thousand students includes 1,100 rooms turned into a summer hotel, run by the Centre. 150 of the rooms serve as hotel rooms year-round. The architects' achievement is to integrate the student village into a sweep of landscape capped by S. Catherine's.

Across the Aura, if you can possibly find the time, do visit Mary's church, at the trivium where Koroistentie enters Maunu Tavastin katu and Vanha Tampereentie. The modest proportions of Maaria resemble those of Kaarina; the most delightful detail of this 15th-century church is an affecting 14th-century crucifix. Little has been done to wreck the original mediaeval inspiration within this little grey stone edifice, except for a routinely sentimental painting of the Crucifixion which could well be silently removed.

Maaria reopened after restoration in 1984, and can be visited between 12 and 3. Wäinö Aaltonen (1894–1966) is buried in the graveyard. The vestry displays the earliest gravestone found so far in Finland: that of Ingegerdis (d. 1290), and an elaborate memorial to Pehr Kalm, Linnaeus' favourite student, whose fame rests comfortably on his three-volume topographical study of America. The church was originally dedicated to S. Dionysius. A big fire destroyed much of the mediaeval wood in 1876. More paintings were uncovered during restoration in the early 1980s: the finest ship can be seen in the gallery, but my favourite image is a fox with a fish on its tail.

But the greatest glories of Turku's architecture are its recent religious buildings, beginning in 1905 with the imposing Jugendstil and neo-Gothic S. Michael's in an airy open space between Puistokatu and Sairashuoneen-katu. Breathtakingly large, the interior seats 1,800 parishioners, with deft side-lighting making up for the softer light filtering through splendid stained-glass windows by Hilkka Toivola and Otso Karpakka. Slightly less impressive from the exterior, but equally fine within, is Martin's Church, off Martinkatu. Broad where Michael's is high, whitelighted compared with Michael's golden glow, S. Martin's has great barrel vaults framing a great altar fresco taking up the whole of the flat recess behind the altar. This *Crucifixion* by Gunnar Wahlroos and Totti Sora conquers problems of perspective and colour by misty background and restriction to a few bold tones: blue-white, flesh-brown and subtle pastels.

When G.E. Kidder Smith noted a generation ago, in *The New Architecture of Europe* (1962), that 'Finland is by many considered the most architecturally interesting country in Scandinavia, and one of the finest anywhere', he was thinking mainly of Saarinen father and son, Alvar Aalto, Viljo Revell, Aarne Ervi, Kaija and Heikki Siren, Johan Cedercreutz and Helge Railo. But he makes especial mention of the Chapel of the Resurrection (1941) by Erik Bryggman, and one can readily understand why. It is situated southeast of the city, like the Chapel of the Holy Cross and Bishop Henry's church. The exterior, within the great new cemetery, has attracted criticism because of ill-defined forms and lines, but the interior, with gently curved ceiling, sensitive placing of the small altar organ, and profound sensibility towards light at both upper and lower levels make this church a gem of Finnish religious building. I disliked the extraneous low reliefs by Jussi Vikainen, but the yellow lighting by Paavo Tynell in the vestibule is a *tour de force*, like the 'tree of life' on the pulpit, and imaginative use of plants, such as white lilies on the altar, and sixteen cacti, ten between the congregation and the windows, and six beside the altar. Natural lighting is supplied by five windows over the great picture window, and four others on the opposite side. Rough peasant-style benches are placed oblique to the main altar and the tender rounded arch. A tribute should be paid to the designer and builder of the great white organ in the gallery. A mood of tranquillity (perhaps even bliss?) could be maintained by strolling within the cemetery garden. Do not miss the patriotic monument by Jussi Vikainen, commemorating the dead in World War II, inscribed 'Rakkaus ei koskaan häviä', 'Love never vanishes'.

If you have never visited a crematorium, or mortuary chapel, then make an exception for the Chapel of the Holy Cross (1967), by Pekka Pitkänen, Ola

Laiho, and Ilpo Raunio. Three conjoined chapels of different sizes offer overwhelming spirituality by purity of colour (white), of line (horizontal) and space (empty). Concealed lighting in ceilings and pillars adds to the emotion of calm and peace. Flowers? Only white lilies are permitted. The large chapel has an organ in the gallery, and ascetically uncomfortable benches. Iconography is limited to a plain low cross accentuating the horizontal. The middle chapel's window is proportionately larger, with the same silent cross. In the hierarchy of death, the small chapel has a tiny organ, artificial wall-lighting assisting natural illumination from a huge window occupying more than half the length of one wall. The pines surrounding the Holy Cross Chapel were planned and landscaped down to the last detail, the whole conveying an oddly majestic view of man's fate and aspirations. My most lasting memory of the Holy Cross Chapel is Essi Renvall's symbolic sculpture *De Profundis*, the hand of God holding an oyster, and a pearl within the oyster.

If you enjoyed the Orthodox section of the old central Helsinki burial ground, you will relish the old burial ground here in Turku, with the eighteenth-century tombs of the shipbuilding Crichton family.

The road into Turku, the Uudenmaantie, takes you from the cemetery to Peltolantie in about 1 km. Turn left there and you will come to the Church of S. Henry (open 12–3), in the fashionable new suburb of Petrelius, a landmark in recent architecture. The church is set in a park, with wide vistas towards it, but heavy traffic dictated special restrictions on planning which affected the lighting and dimensions of the main room. S. Henry's is one of the most beautiful, harmonious and practical churches I have seen, and the fact that it dates from 1980 augurs a brilliant future for the new wave of Finnish architects and sculptors. The elevation shows a range of clean rectangles, with tiny rectangular windows proposing a solution like a Mondrian monochrome or a Japanese squared paper door. The 600-seat church interestingly forms only a small part of the ensemble, which Pitkänen, Laiho and Raunio designed to cater for the handicapped too, every component being on ground level. A parish room and large club room can be partitioned off when services are not in progress, and there is a relatively huge lobby area, as well as daytime club activities, in four separate club rooms. The plan in fact presents a slight resemblance to Alvar Aalto's celebrated 'Aalto' flower vase, unexpected curves and corners adding a perpetual sense of surprise. The main bearing structures are walls and pillars of reinforced concrete, but the façades, partition walls, cladding and floors are in warm red brick. The window frames and outer doors are painted steel, and birch has been used for interiors and veneer to coat the chipboard drop ceilings. Virtually every aspect of S. Henry's excites, from the magnificent abstract sculpture by Eero Hiironen beside the altar, to the op art of Raino Utriainen in the vestibule. The view from the gallery seems even more brilliant, with dazzling effects of light on the asymmetrical organ within the asymmetrical hall. Even the location of the simple message of the cross atop a brick corner seems to exult in the leafy surrounds of Petrelius.

The first Jews in Finland came from Russia during the time of Tsar Nicholas I in the first half of the 19th century. Visits to the Turku Synagogue can be arranged by prior appointment (tel. 12 557 between 10 and 12) and the Synagogue itself is located at Brahenkatu 12, very near the bus station. With Finnish independence, in 1917, Jews were offered rights of citizenship but were not allowed to form an official congregation. A wooden house was used by the unofficial congregation before the city gave Jews the present site in 1902 outside the centre. The city architect Johan Hindersson made drawings and the building was financed by selling 160 seats, the front costing more than the back. Turku Synagogue was officially taken into use in 1912, August Krook being responsible for the Jugendstil interior.

Catholics can attend Mass at 10.30 a.m. and 6 p.m. on Sundays, and at 8 a.m. on Mondays, Fridays and Saturdays, and 6.30 p.m. on Tuesdays and Thursdays, at S. Birgitta's, Ursininkatu 15A, located halfway between the Tourist Office in Käsityöläiskatu and S. Michael's. There are 3,700 Roman Catholics in Finland; 430 of these live in Turku. The nuns, from Italy, Mexico, and India are all learning Finnish. Their parishioners are mainly Polish, German and Italian. The red-brick exterior is quirkily asymmetrical, without a great deal of style, and ruined by an unfortunate wire, while the tasteful brick interior seems at odds with the agitated stained glass and a vulgar tapestry best ignored. The total collapse of Catholicism in the Nordic countries following the Reformation has not been followed by any significant revival anywhere. Finland - properly the Helsinki diocese - consists of only five parishes. In *A History of Finland* (1965), John H. Wuorinen notes that 'the Christian faith and at least some of the practices associated with the Christian creed and church had spread to Finland long before the alleged crusade of the mid-1150s' reported uncritically by Henrik Gabriel Porthan, who died in 1804. Y. Koskinen's *Suomen Kansan Historia* (1869) relied on Porthan's conclusions, yet Wuorinen stresses that the only 'sources' for the 'crusade' described by Porthan and his followers 'turn out to be legends of saints compiled in Sweden well over a hundred years later, toward the end of the thirteenth century, and a rambling Finnish folk poem dealing with Bishop Henry and his death which dates from about the year 1400 or possibly earlier. *The legends do not describe the undertakings of King Erik and Bishop Henry in Finland.*' The first document from the Church of Rome referring to Finland dates from 1172, in which Pope Alexander III chides the Finns for being remiss in according their priests the honour due them. It does not (and neither does any other record of the time) refer either to S.

Erik or to Bishop Henry. Even the famous Swedish *Erikskrönika* has no information on the matter. We must therefore deduce that Swedish secular or ecclesiastical authorities, seeking to justify their colonisation of the unwilling Finns, invented a convenient legend which they then perpetuated.

The last Catholic bishop of Finland died in 1522, and Catholics were forbidden to practise their faith until the country was annexed by Russia in 1809. The Catholic parish to Turku is dedicated to S. Birgitta (1302–73) and the Blessed Hemming, Bishop of Turku from 1338 to 1366. The present church was built in 1966 to the designs of A.S. Sandelin.

New Turku, like new Helsinki, falls into a grid pattern following the plans of Engel approved in 1828. But Turku had a previous town plan, which survived until the Great Fire of 1827, dating back to the time of Per Brahe, Governor-General from 1637–40 and 1648–51. Penetrating eyes, lively features and evident good humour characterise Brahe's portrait in the Historical Museum. He travelled throughout much of the country, despite the difficulty of poor or non-existent roads. Though a Swede, he foresaw the necessity for Finns to possess their own university, a proposal accepted in 1640. Its premises were the old Grammar School, but few felt inhibited by unsuitable buildings, and the new Academy attracted not only promising students but also teachers and scholars from Scandinavia and the rest of Europe. Turku Art Museum displays a sketch by Albert Edelfelt envisaging the ceremonial procession from the Academy's new home to the Cathedral. The right panel of the triptych shows professors, with Per Brahe striding proudly in the centre panel, towards the onlooking burghers, awaiting near the Cathedral. Åbo Akademi's old main hall is mainly the work of the Swedish architect C.C. Gjörwell (1766–1837), but the Piedmontese-born Carlo Bassi (1722–1840) must be credited with directing the construction and much of the interior decoration. The rectangular hall, in Swedish neo-classical style, has a barrel vault and red granite columns (dividing the hall into three) hewn from Vartiovuori. Narrative reliefs by Erik Cainberg show the epic hero Väinämöinen playing the kantele, the arrival of Christianity in Finland, the Reformation personified by Mikael Agricola's handling his Bible translation to Gustavus Vasa, and three scenes from the story of Åbo Akademi itself. After the Great Fire of 1827, the university moved to Helsinki in 1828 and the modern Åbo Akademi was founded in Turku in 1918 as a centre of research for the Swedish-speaking minority (about 6% of the population), though it changed from private status to state control as recently as 1981. At any one time Åbo Akademi has about 4,250 students and 240 staff. What did Finns do about higher education before the enlightened age of Per Brahe? Their preferred seat was Paris, the first Finns there being mentioned in 1313, forty-one Finns obtaining masters' degrees up to 1485. Next, they found their way to the Charles University in Prague, founded in 1348, fifteen Finns receiving Prague degrees between 1382 and 1404. Uppsala was founded in 1477 and Copenhagen in 1479, but German universities generally found greater favour among young Finns wanting to travel beyond the confines of the North: to Leipzig, Erfurt, Rostock and Greifswald.

Below the Cathedral, two museums face each other across Piispankatu. Ett Hem, 'A Home' in Swedish, is situated at no. 14, and is open daily except Mondays from 1 to 3; the Sibelius Museum at no. 17 is open daily except Mondays from 11 to 3, and on Wednesdays also from 6–8 p.m.

Mr and Mrs Alfred Jacobsson donated funds for the Biological Museum in 1902 and participated in the founding of Åbo Akademi (Turku's Swedish University) in 1918. Finally, in 1925 they willed their home (hence the name) to Åbo Akademi, and after Alfred's death in 1931, the museum opened in 1932 at Hämeenkatu 30, and remained there until 1939, but the building was partly evacuated during World War II, subsequently condemned, and demolished in 1955. The contents were removed to the present 'home' (designed by the same architect) and dating to the same years, 1831–2) and 'Ett Hem' reopened in 1965, compressing the contents from the original eighteen rooms into eight. The first, in Biedermeier style, is named for Helene Jacobsson's grandfather, Abraham Kingelin (1788–1849), a leading industrialist in the city. The sofa and chairs come from Turku (1840), and the distinguished paintings are by Helene Schjerfbeck (*Portrait of a Man*, 1879), and Hjalmar Munsterhjelm. Alfred's study has Russian-style furniture and books from the library, including Jugendstil bindings. The drawing-room, focus of the home, features Albert Edelfelt's glowing *Midsummer Evening* (1883) inappropriately framed. Helene's room has fine landscapes by Victor Westerholm and other works by Gallen-Kallela and Elin Danielson-Gambogi, the latter represented also by portraits of *Walborg Jacobsson* and *Kerstin Jacobsson* in the bedroom, after which comes the boudoir. The baroque-style dining-room has an interesting exhibition of pewter, and old Finnish rugs on the walls. The porcelain room also displays glass, silver, Japanese *ukiyo-e* woodcuts and the history of the former residence.

A great contrast to 'Ett Hem' is the spacious modern Sibelius Museum designed by Woldemar Baeckman (1968). The composer never lived in Turku, though he conducted performances of his music by Turku Musical Society. The Museum which bears his name consists of an exhibition of musical instruments and the teaching section of Åbo Akademi's music department. The instruments were donated by the shipowner Curt Mattson, and by Professor Otto Andersson, who also gave his valuable collection of books and scores. Dozens of original Sibelius MSS have been supplemented by photocopies of scores in other libraries, and by the extensive collection of

Sibelius MSS owned by Adolf Paul. The auditorium puts on thirty concerts a year, and on Wednesdays the 150 seats are packed out for recitals by Finnish and international recitalists. Visiting the exhibition anticlockwise, you come first to musical boxes and accordions, drums, then members of the zither or Finnish *kantele* family from Turku, Sammatti and Taivassalo, America and the Soviet Union, guitars and lutes, a lyre from Ethiopia, and a one-stringed gusla from Yugoslavia. A charming French monochord (invented by Pousset, 1882) has a secret compartment for cosmetic boxes in the back of its chair. Among the violins is one by Johan Lindström of Turku dated 1796; another made by Otto Selling of Stockholm in 1836 belonging to Baron Axel Carpelan and often played by his close friend Sibelius. Finnish birchbark horns can be compared with one from Norway. Chinese mouth-organs, Rumanian pan-pipes and an Israeli ram's horn are followed by a Tibetan temple trumpet, Italian bassoon, French clarinet and Czech French horn. A fine range of pianos includes square pianos by Hiekisch of Porvoo, Granfeldt of Turku, Lindros of Helsinki, Malm of Turku, Rothman of Kuopio, and Palmgren of Helsinki. Here are psalmodikons from Rauma, Parainen, Laitila and Turku. The last section is devoted to organs, a harmonium from Tampere, a pianino from Helsinki, and a positive organ from Sauvo.

Beside the Sibelius Museum stands the Kingelin Summer House, dating back to 1830, open from 10–6 between mid-May and mid-August.

Shopping in stylish, fashion-conscious Turku is as easy as in Tampere or Helsinki. Shops are generally open from 9–5 Monday to Friday, and 9–2 on Saturday, but department stores generally stay open till 8 in the evening. The covered market near the Swedish Theatre corner of Kauppatori opens at 8 and closes at 5, except on Fridays (6) and summer Saturdays (1). But perhaps the most endearing of all is the open market, for which the best times are shortly after 7 a.m. and every evening from May to September between 4 and 8. Conventional shops are found in the Market Square area, Yliopistonkatu, and Eerikinkatu. The best antiquarian bookshop is Qvariaatti, Hämeenkatu 16. I loved Sylvi Salonen's handicraft shop at Kauppiaskatu 10, where you can buy kits to make your own rugs and wall-hangings, or you can buy ready-made art rugs with up to a hundred different colours each and up to ten thousand naps each: Sylvi also has 100% woollen blankets handwoven, as well as shawls and ponchos. Do not miss the Pentik Shop here, with magnificent ceramics, woodcraft and leather goods, at Yliopistonkatu 25, and jewellery at Jorma Suominen's. Finnish music can be brought at Musiikki Helin, Kauppiaskatu 13, and handmade decorative bags at Nahka-Ateljé Rita, Läntinen Pitkäkatu 22. The finest department store, near Hotel Hamburger Börs on Market Square, is Wiklund, where you can see the best of Finnish design under one hospitable roof: don't forget the 10% tax-free concession for foreigners.

Turku Art Museum has a splendid home, designed by Gustaf Nyström (1904) in a charming setting, in Puolalanpuisto, at the head of Aurakatu, near the rail and bus stations.

Nyström taught both Lars Sonck and Eliel Saarinen, so his influence can be considered incalculable, but this Jugendstil building is truly outstanding, ranking with his Market Hall. Opening hours are 10–4 on weekdays (and also 6–8 on Thursdays) and 10–6 on Sundays. Turku Art Museum ranks second to the Ateneum in Helsinki for its collections of Finnish art, much of the credit being due to the artist Victor Westerholm, its first curator and an important teacher. Traditional landscapes by Westerholm include the excellent *Valley of the Kymi River* (1901), but of this period possibly the most stimulating example of Finnish landscape is a nervously chromatic *Karelian Landscape* (1899) of Pekka Halonen, with a clear antecedent in Gallen-Kallela's *The Great Black Woodpecker* (1893), both shown at the Hayward Gallery in London (1986) in the exhibition 'Dreams of a Summer Night'. Gallen-Kallela's remarkable pair of works in tempera, *The Defence of the Sampo* (1896) and *Joukahainen's Revenge* (1897) form a fascinating contrast; the former all colour and raging violence, the latter with a simple palette of yellow-green-grey, and contained passion set in vast distances. Here are Gallen-Kallela's *Old Woman with a Cat* (1885) and his fine portrait of Maxim Gorki (1906). A pure, pallid *Self-Portrait* (1915) by Schjerfbeck contrasts with a portrait of an old woman painted in old-master style by Hugo Simberg in 1898, when he was 25. An Italian landscape by Elin Danielson-Gambogi (1861–1919) contrasts with a muted *Café Interior* (1884) by Albert Edelfelt.

I picked out *At the Toilette* by Gunnar Bernatson (1854-95), and, from later generations, a gouache (1979) by Juhana Blomstedt (b.1937), and *Hot Day*, a metal sculpture by Tapio Junno (b.1940).

Nobody else interrupted my afternoon in Turku's gallery; no attendants stamped suspiciously up and down. On my way down the steps, I was reminded that Turku is twinned with Leningrad by a bus-troupe of solemn Russians, processing out of their chartered bus, and ceremoniously laying one tulip each (just bought on the market) beside Lenin's bust in front of the Art Museum. They filed silently back on to the bus, without entering the gallery at all.

Westerholm, teaching at Turku Art School, then on the ground floor of Turku Art Museum, had among his pupils the sculptor Wäinö Aaltonen (1894–1966), whose museum at Itäinen Rantakatu 38 was opened within a year of his death. The plain, airy, functional gallery, designed by his son and daughter-in-law Matti and Irma Aaltonen, houses not only a wide variety of Aaltonen's sculptures and paintings, but also changing exhibitions of works by other modern Nordic artists. He worked in cubist style between 1924–30, but abstraction lured him back repeatedly, even if commissions for stolid monuments stunted his originality. You can see his works outside the National Theatre in Helsinki (Aleksis Kivi), inside the Parliament Building (five works in the series 'Work and the Future'), the University of Turku ('Genius directs Youth'), outside the Concert Hall (the equestrian statue 'Friendship Sealed') and on the Häme Bridge in Tampere. I like best the gentle marble relief 'Contemplation' (1921), and the 1924 *Self-Portrait* with handwriting on a page concealing the painted face: the legend reading 'Would that my heart were stone, a rock cut with a vast and smiling face, time flowing by. Alas, alas! It is not so! Wrenched it is with pain, galled at the roots by sorrow, yet experiencing such hellish joy'.

Behind the Aaltonen Museum stand the Windmill Hill, and Summer Theatre, with the Biological Museum very close at Neitsytpolku 1. The old-fashioned little museum, donated to the city by Consul Alfred Jacobsson and his wife after they had visited Stockholm, consists of twelve dioramas showing various natural habitats throughout Finland, including Lapland, and will interest anyone not seeing a great deal of the country in person. I particularly enjoyed the scene depicting Ruissalo in spring. Ruissalo is a summer resort with a recreation area (National Park) and the University Botanic Gardens. The Biological Museum is open 10–6 from 2 May to 30 September, and 10–3 in the winter; the Botanic Gardens with their eight conservatories can be visited daily between 8–3, except 10–12 on Saturdays and 11–3 on Sundays. In Ruissalo I love the villas: over a hundred shoreside mansions built after 1847, reminiscent of Russian *dachas* for the simple reason that the nobility satirised to such gentle effect by Chekhov and Turgenev would have summered here too. (It was only later that I discovered to my huge delight that Turgenev's play *Myesyats v derevne*, of 1890, which we know as *A Month in the Country*, was playing throughout the summer at Tampere's revolving theatre, and I should see it there). Ruissalo Nature Reserve, found in the east of the island, shimmers in spring with wood anemones and lilies-of-the-valley amid ancient oaks and pines. To reach Ruissalo, with its two swimming beaches, nature trail, keep-fit track, and camping site, take bus no. 8 from the Market Square.

Anyone keen on trees would be advised to wander in the gardens of Turku Biological Museum: the varieties of tree include spruce, Siberian fir, Douglas fir, Arolla pine, Weymouth pine, European larch, Colorado spruce, yew, maple, Amur maple, oak, silver birch, sallow, wych elm, bird cherry, ash and rowan.

Walking away from the Aura, that is turning right out of the Biological Museum, look at no. 42 Sirkkalankatu, once voted the most beautiful house in Turku by readers of *Turun Sanomat*. Crossing Kaskenkatu, you will come to the museum with something for everybody: the Handicrafts Museum on

Turku. Ruissalo. Summer Villa

Luostarinmäki, or 'Cloister Hill'. This sector, south from Vartiovuori Hill, remained country fields until the late 18th century. After the fire of 1775, new housing was needed and the artisans settled here until about 1808, when all the lots were filled with wooden houses. Occupants then included carpenters, masons, watchmen and labourers. Many came from outside the city, and brought their animals, so byres, and cowsheds adjoined the simple wooden houses with one or two rooms. Gradually further rooms were added, as families grew or lodgers moved in. After the 1827 fire, pressure on Cloister Hill and the other few sectors of the city unaffected by fire increased to the point where virtually all houses had to be extended, the only exception being house no. 174. The owner or landlord had an open fireplace and baking oven; the other rooms were heated by tiled stoves and tenants could

88

Turku. Luostarinmäki. Handicrafts Museum

use the oven for bread and other food. When Turku was rebuilt during the Empire period, Luostarinmäki was ignored, and houses passed to poorer families who could not afford proper maintenance or modernisation. Early in the present century Sirkkalankatu replaced the most dilapidated district of Luostarinmäki. Many of the seventeen remaining houses on the hill were preserved, and the museum, with renovated homes and workshops, opened as a museum in 1940, on the model of Skansen in Stockholm and Den Gamle By at Århus in Denmark. None of the houses had been modernised or painted so, like the Burgher's House in Helsinki or the Amuri district in Tampere, Turku's Luostarinmäki offers the visitor an authentic view of the past.

Each self-contained house and outbuildings are built round a central courtyard, and separated from its neighbour by a fence or building. Animals were kept in sheds, and other sheds for wood and stores would ring the courtyard. A ladder and hook had to be available by law. 'Witches' brooms' of bound twigs are found everywhere to sweep steps, but here 'suopursu' – roots of swamp plants – are bound up as sweeping brooms.

The first craftsman attracted here was the combmaker Emil Ahlrot, and the second Fredrik Renfors, maker of wicker baskets. Some of the descendants of the original inhabitants still lived in some of the houses taken over and preserved, so they were able to describe how the houses looked before, what utensils were used, and what animals were kept. Craftsmen visit a dozen of the workshops to practise their skills throughout the summer, and during a special late August Handicrafts Week. These include lithographic printers, tinsmith, shoemaker, potter, tobacco-maker (tobacco plants grow outside), coppersmith, wigmaker, seamstress, baker, weaver, goldsmith, ropemaker, sweep, brassfounder, carriagemaker and tailor. By and large the costumes worn are those of the turn of the century, and they make a great impression on the 'time-warped' visitor, but this magnificent museum offers many more dazzling cameos. For example, one can buy ABCs in Finnish and Swedish printed here on a heavy Leipzig, the proofing presses being antiques from Berlin and Vienna – even the bag into which the booklets are placed is printed here. But bags are relatively modern so when you buy some local sweets, for example, they are wrapped in cornets of paper squares. The violinmakers Jukka and Carlo Bergman have fitted out a workshop, and I greatly enjoyed the gilder's, who made frames for mirrors in rococo and Gustavian styles; here are the plaster-of-paris moulds, magic of the art. House 173 was made by a carpenter in 1798, but subsequent generations of the same family, who lived here until 1938, were sailors, A parlour/sitting-room is situated on one side, and a kitchen/living-room on the other. Breadpoles hanging from the ceiling bore loaves baked with a hole in the middle; spills in a holder lit the room; the open dresser displays mugs and wooden dishes brought home in trunks by homecoming sailors. A loom is sometimes used by a weaver even today. Outside once stood a byre where a cow and a goat would have been kept, grazing on the turf on the roofs in the summer, and fed hay for the rest of the year. If you ascend to Ms Fridén's room, you will see a notice of 1834 proclaiming that the clerk's widow performs several kinds of needlework: her wares on show include hats and bonnets, gloves and ladies' clothes.

You might come across Risto Aaltonen making a candlestick or Mauri Uusitupa demonstrating the art of the wheelwright, Leo Honkasalo cobbling shoes or Kirsti Vuorinen weaving ribbon in house no. 168.

Alvar Aalto's buildings in Turku date from 1928–30: they are the Varsinais Suomi Agriculture Cooperative Building at Humalistonkatu 7b,

Turku. City Hall. (Courtesy of the City Tourist Office)

not far from the Hologram Gallery on Yliopistonkatu; the Standard Apartment block at Läntinen Pitkäkatu 20, on the other side of the Art Gallery; and the *Turun Sanomat* building to the south of the Standard building, at Kauppiaskatu 5; a pilgrimage within easy walking distance.

Finland's burgeoning reputation for library planning and architecture, culminating in the new Tampere Central Public Library, can be supported by looking at the library of Åbo Akademi, Finland's Swedish Academy (Erik Bryggman, 1935, extended by Woldemar Baeckman, 1957) very close to the Cathedral, and by Aarne Ervi's excellent work for the Finnish-speaking Turku University (Turun Yliopisto) on the hill called Vesilinnanmäki (Water Castle Hill), approachable from Henrikinkatu, behind the Cathedral.

A short walk from the Kauppatori ('Market Square') will bring you to the City Hall and Tourist Office, on the west bank of the Aura. Beside the tourist office of Varsinais Suomi (Southwest Finland) stands the house called Quensel or Qwensel: 'v' and 'w' are interchangeable in library catalogues and throughout most proper names in Finland, and the name is pronounced Kvensel. In 1694, Wilhelm Johan Quensel moved from Stockholm to Turku as associate judge of the Court of Appeal, but fled back

91

to Sweden during the Great Hatred, returning only after the Treaty of Uusikaupunki (1721). Quensel House dates from shortly after this, and subsequent owners have included Counsellor of the Court of Appeal Johan Lostierna (for forty years from 1723), Professor Josef Gustaf Pipping, the father of surgery in Finland (1785 to 1816), and the merchant shipper Nils Fredrik Tjäder, who added the shop, now used as an apothecary's shop.

This part of town, 'Gentry Corner', was occupied by noblemen, administrators, and officials of the Court of Appeal, and this patrician house can be compared with the plebeian homes on Cloister Hill. The fittings of 1858 in the apothecary's shop come from the Old Pharmacy in Oulu, as do the doors, the fine mahogany furnishings in Empire style, and the pictures of Hygeia, goddess of health, and Aesculapius, god of medicine. The materials-room behind the shop is also furnished from Oulu; behind this is the front laboratory, with stencil-made wallpaper copying the original, which is dominated by a sand bath used for distilling with large retorts, and the distillation boiler connected to the sand bath with its wooden cooling vessel. The back laboratory has a fireplace for heating crucibles, and long-handled copper pots from the old town pharmacy of Turku. From the materials room you can visit the apothecary's atmospheric home, mainly as it was in Dr Pipping's time after 1785. The apothecary's room now so called was originally a kitchen, but Pipping changed it to a study/sitting-room and covered the walls with wall material painted in oils. The table is rococo, and the 'bathtub' sofa is signed by the Stockholm carpenter Holm.

The adjoining red chamber is feminine, with a mahogany sewing table made in 1789 in Stockholm by Gottlieb Iwersson, and a splendid inlaid Gustavian chest of drawers. The oak cabinet from Dalkarby Mansion dates from about 1750. The hall was also restored in Dr Pipping's time, but the present rococo landscapes (1750s) come from a mansion in Häme. The girl attendants are dressed in period costume.

Summer cruises are available from Auransilta bridge every day at 1.30 and Mondays to Thursdays also at 4 p.m., lasting two hours; around Hirvensalo at 4 p.m. each Saturday and Sunday, lasting three hours; one-way or return to Naantali (stopping near Hotel Ruissalo on the way) each day at noon; a two-hour cruise at 6 p.m. around the archipelago on Tuesdays, Wednesdays, Thursdays and Saturdays; and on Fridays a cruise to Naantali, leaving Turku at 5.30 and lasting 4 hours, including a tour to the President's summer palace gardens at Kultaranta or a 1½ hour's stop in Naantali.

Two-hour city bus tours are available. All-day bus cards allow unlimited riding on yellow inner-city buses and privately-run grey-blue suburban buses.

Though I have never been a journalist, I was invited to join a group of Finnish journalists accompanying the President of Finland and Mrs Koivisto

Turku. President and Mrs Koivisto outside Sibelius Museum

on an official visit to Turku. Their itinerary covered the round-the-world yacht *Fazer Finland*, a ride on a historic bus from Market Square to the museum ship *Sigyn* and the exhibition 'Sea Finland', a walkabout in and near the Market Hall to meet stallholders and customers, an inspection of a new trade school with a press conference, a visit to the Sibelius Museum with a recital by Finnish and Japanese artists, and an evening at *Rajaralli*, the play at Samppalinna Summer Theatre. H.E. Mauno Koivisto, tall and quietly spoken, might have been tailormade for the presidency of non-aligned Finland, with its unobtrusive defence policy. It does not do to tread on the Soviet Union's tail, and the socialist President is a master of the 'softly, softly' technique. A native of Turku, he was asked what should become of his apartment, now it has passed into official ownership. 'Anything but a museum!' he answered. How pleasant to be non-aligned! I was amused to see slightly puzzled Finns getting on the journalists' bus to 'Sea Finland', and permitted to remain on it and ride to the exhibition. Security exists, and plain-clothes detectives patently survey the scene in general, and each pedestrian in particular, but as long as American and NATO troops are kept out of the country, the Soviet Government has no need to intervene, and low-key espionage does not make Finnish cities (much less the countryside) a high risk area. There is no Olof Palme to threaten vested interests. President Koivisto comes from the working classes, but no one party dictates policy. Tellervo Koivisto, his delightful consort, equally attractive and intelligent, reminded me of the Icelandic Premier as a woman with tolerant convictions. The 67 seats on Turku City Council in 1986 were neatly balanced: 34 for the non-socialist parties, and 30 for the two socialist parties, that is the Social Democratic Party (16 seats) and the Democratic League of the People of Finland (14), with a further 3 seats held by the Green Party.

Evenings in Turku could be spent walking in Ruissalo or the parks or by the Aura where street dances are arranged on summer evenings. Organ recitals are held in the Cathedral, and concerts in the Church of Turku

Turku. Street dancing by the Aura on a summer evening

Castle, Concert Hall, Swedish Theatre, S. Henry's Church, Betel (Adventist) Church, Academy Hall, and Sibelius Museum. In August you might see a film of Mozart's *Marriage of Figaro* at the Casino or the Tallis Scholars performing early music in the Cathedral.

The oldest theatre in Finland is Turku Swedish Theatre (Åbo Svenska Teater) at Aurakatu 10. Designed by P.J. Gylich in 1839, it has a façade by Engel which has stayed remarkably homogeneous, even if the interior has undergone striking changes. Oddly enough, Turku did not form its own theatre company until 1894.

The Turku City Theatre could hardly present a more notable contrast, its straight rectilinearity dominating Aurajoki at Itäinen Rantakatu 14. Turku Workers' Theatre turned professional in 1916 and in 1946 united with Turku Theatre (1918) to form a single Finnish-language entity, but this modern building, by Risto-Veikko Luukkonen and Helmer Stenros, dates from 1962, with a larger auditorium to seat 668 and a smaller playhouse seating 120.

Samppalinna Mill (1860) is the sole survivor of the ten windmills which at one time whirred atop Turku's hills.

Close to Turku Theatre stands the Samppalinna Restaurant designed by C.J. von Heideken (1865) at Itäinen Rantakatu 10, and presented to the city in 1866 by P.C. Rettig. Rettig, the leading tobacco manufacturer in Finland in his time, created the most palatial residence in Turku behind high walls in the centre of town on the Left Bank. Opposite, at Hämeenkatu 28, stands the lovely Finnish Economic Society building restored by P.J. Gylich (1829–31) for the society founded in 1797 with the aim of promoting thrift, self-help, and the intellectual and material development of the Finnish people. The present-day façade was constructed in 1903.

There are two summer theatres: the Samppalinnan Kesäteatteri, at Samppalinnankatu 3 (mid-June to mid-August) at 3 on Sundays and 7 every evening, and the Turun Kesäteatteri, Vartiovuori (same period, at 3 on Sundays and 7 every evening except Sundays). At the latter, on a slope of the hill on which the Observatory and Maritime Museum stand, I saw one balmy summer evening a musical play called *Pirtu Kuningas* ('King of the Bootleggers') by Lars Huldén and Bengt Ahlfors, translated from the Swedish and directed by Stig Fransman. It doesn't matter if you can't understand a word of Finnish, for a blow-by-blow synopsis is presented with your ticket, and provided the weather is fine you will greatly enjoy the experience. The play, originally *Smugglarkungen*, set in the years 1919–32, when prohibition ruled Finland, features the bootlegger Wilho (played by Harri Laurikka), the seduced Saara (Päivi Sinkkonen), Judge Puska (Pertti Itkonen), and his lost first love Hilda Lähtenpohja (Riitta Elstelä). In a Brechtian conclusion, when Prohibition is repealed, Wilho dreams of travelling to Germany. New laws are being enacted there which will make it inevitable for certain wealthy people to want to leave the country: there is always a need for smugglers.

A few minutes away from the Vartiovuori Summer Theatre stands the former Observatory. Before entering, look for the markers outside showing the sea-level in 4000 B.C., then higher in 5000 B.C., indicating how far uplift has brought Guardian Hill ('Vartija' has the same root as Swedish 'Vård' and English 'Ward', a sentinel or watchman). The new Maritime Museum opened in 1986, hours being 10–3 in winter, and 10–6 from 2 May to 30 September. On the ground floor I enjoyed seeing models of the Hansa ships plying to Turku with wheat, skins, and wine from the 13th century to the 15th century. Here is a model of the Turku frigate *Pampa* built in 1891, and the *Nordia* of 1962, when cars were first loaded on to ferries at the end instead of the side.

The Observatory was built to designs by Engel in 1817–9: one of the very first designs the German architect made in Finland. After the Great Fire of 1827, the Observatory was saved but, when the University moved to Helsinki a year later a new observatory was founded there, and from 1836 to 1967 the Turku building housed Turku Naval School. The side rooms concentrate on the astronomical collections of Yrjö Väisälä, and the upper floor on navigation instruments.

I personally found the three-masted barque *Sigyn* (made in Gothenburg in 1887) much more interesting. This historic ship can be visited at Itäinen Rantakatu 48 between 10 May and 31 August (Tuesdays to Fridays, 10–3: Saturdays 10–5; Sundays 10–3). The barque was built to transport timber and its inaugural voyage was to Galveston, Texas, continuing with trips as far afield as Bangkok, Archangel, and Latin America. In 1913 the Swedish vessel ran aground in bad weather near Kristianstad and suffered terrible damage; but eventually it was decided to simplify her rigging, and a gaff sail replaced the square sails on the mainmast, the ship becoming a barquentine, plying coastal waters of the Baltic and the North Sea. The *Sigyn* came to Finland in 1927, when the port of registry changed to Vårdö (Åland). After cargo transport on small sailing vessels became unprofitable in the 1930s, the *Sigyn* was laid up. Restoration following damage during World War II allowed the museum ship to reopen in 1979 in Turku.

Beside the *Sigyn*, moored close to Martinsilta, you can find the frigate *Suomen Joutsen* ('Swan of Finland'), not open to visitors nowadays, as it is in permanent use as the Seamen's Training School. How intriguing are the destinies of ships! For *Suomen Joutsen* began life as the French cargo boat *Laennec* at St Nazaire in 1902, sailing until bought in 1923 by Norddeutscher Lloyd, who used the newly-christened *Oldenburg* as a training ship for German merchant-fleet officers until 1927. Two years later Finland

Turku. The Sigyn. (Courtesy of Turku City Tourist Office)

acquired it, refitting it at Uusikaupunki dockyard as a training ship for the Finnish Navy, making eight ocean voyages between 1931 and 1939 under the captaincy of Commander Kokkola. During World War II the frigate was used for supply and accommodation, but from 1949 to 1955 she continued to sail, on shorter hauls, reaching Turku from Porkkala in 1960.

The Environs of Turku

After a quick lunch of spaghetti and chicken salad in the Restaurant Foija (cellar of the Swedish Theatre, on Market Square), we drove out northwest, hoping to see some of the Seven Churches offered by a bus tour company, Louhisaari Manor, and Masku, for a banquet. The 'Seven Churches' dating from the 13th and 14th centuries are those of Nousiainen, Raisio, Masku, Lemu, Askainen, Naantali and Merimasku. Raisio is a pleasant little town, with fields of wheat and rape. Its church is open from 10 to 6. We crossed the Ukko Pekka bridge in Naantali to the isle of Luonnonmaa, then took the Merimasku ferry to Askainen, where the one-nave star-vaulted stone Church of S. Olaf was erected (1650-3) to replace the decaying wooden building by Herman Fleming, Governor-General of Finland and Admiral of the Swedish Fleet during the Thirty Years' War. In neo-classical style, the airy church has a ceiling of three octagonal star vaults. The porch and pulpit are reputed to have come as war booty from Germany. The Fleming family lived in Louhisaari Manor at the time, and the arms of Claes Fleming and his wife Kristina can be found on a plaque in front of the altar beneath which a passage leads to a burial chamber in which other members of the Fleming family lie. Claes Fleming can be seen portrayed on one of the stained-glass windows. The other major family connected with Askainen and Louhisaari is Mannerheim, whose yellow mausoleum in the cemetery was built in 1823 by Carl Erik Mannerheim. Jonas Bergman's *Christ on the Cross* dates from 1749, while August Tholander's *Christ in Gethsemane* dates from 1859. The detached bell-tower of 1779 is by Michael Piimänen. I have to remind myself that nobody comes to Finland for the parish churches, because I have for so long been devoted to England's parish churches (Greensted, Wing, Stewkley, Bradford-on-Avon and hundreds more) that I cannot imagine someone not savouring the intensity of the experience; this feeling of rural delight affected me not only in Varsinais Suomi but at Hattula near Hämeenlinna and Espoo near Helsinki. Take Lemu Church for instance, its walls two metres thick in places, with an original 13th-century vestry, and a stone font of roughly 1270. Nobody else interferes with the lazy tick-tock of a Lutheran Sunday afternoon in this vaulted nave, SS. Peter, Andrew, Jesus, James, John and Philip painted around the pulpit of 1644 in a never-ending motionless religious dance, a painting of Martin Luther looking on to see that no papal elements stray into the little church that was once Catholic. In every single church in Finland, and Lemu (between Askainen and Raisio) is no exception, hangs a letter sent by Mannerheim to all Finnish mothers on 10 May 1942. We have already seen Helsinki's Mannerheim Museum; now we can see his birthplace.

Louhisaari (Villnäs in Swedish) is an estate with a palatial building of 1655: one of only two Finnish noble houses of this period. The other, Sarvilahti, is owned by a foundation but privately occupied so closed to the public.

How late the Renaissance came to these wintry shores! It came modestly, symmetrically, and here at Louhisaari with unassuming small windows set in a plain whitewashed brick exterior, the grounds more impressive than the house. From 15 May to 31 August there are guided tours hourly from 11 to 5 on weekdays, and half-hourly on Sundays. Before the present manor house, a house on this site was occupied by one Nils Kurki, a Counsellor of the Realm, whose daughter married Magnus Fleming in the mid-15th century. We have met Herman Fleming (1619–73) as builder of the local church, Askainen, just across the main road, and it was he who built Louhisaari. In 1791 it was bought by Carl Eric Mannerheim, an outstanding leader who, becoming a Count in 1826, relinquished his many duties and took up scientific agriculture here. His eldest son Carl Gustaf, who inherited, earned international renown as an entomologist. Carl Gustaf's grandson, Carl Gustaf Emil, was to become the greatest military leader in Finland's history, Marshal of Finland, and for a short time also President. The house and grounds were acquired for the nation and opened to the public in 1967.

Of the three storeys, the highest was the festive floor and the lowest the service floor, and both retain their 17th-century style and furnishing. The middle floor formed the living quarters, and hence endured constant modernising up to the present time. The first and lowest storey, with 17th-century furnishings, has the great hall and women's workroom, a stone hall converted to a kitchen between 1792 and 1961, and a storeroom and pantry, all with low Renaissance vaults and stucco ribbing. The state rooms on the third or highest storey, with original beam ceilings, convey an immaculate picture of domestic life among the nobility during the Fenno-Swede period. Even the Late Renaissance painted decorations on the banqueting hall's ceiling and walls remain virtually unmolested by the passage of time. Only the fireplaces and doors were replaced in rococo style during the 18th century. Next to the banqueting hall is the 'Devil's Chamber', so-called from a tiny picture of a devil's head. The Great Chamber is Late Renaissance, apart from a rococo stove decorated with the Fleming coat-of-arms. The large bed-chamber in late baroque style has 17th-century paintings on ceiling and frieze, revealed during restoration. Marshal Mannerheim was born in the small blue bedchamber which has consequently been preserved in the style of the 1860s, with a painted Dutch rococo stove, and Biedermeier and neo-rococo furniture belonging to the Mannerheims. Next door is a servant's room with a step-ladder leading up to an attic where a young wife of Herman Fleming is reputed to have been kept captive during her husband's absence at the wars!

The middle storey shows where the nobility actually lived, beginning with the grandmother's bedroom, with Late Empire furniture and a vaulted ceiling repaired in 1792. The dining-room has been restored with furniture and a colour-scheme of the 18th century, though the stove is later. Rococo plaster decorations adorn the large salon, though the furniture is Late Gustavian. The grotto, a feature common in 17th-century manor houses, has paintings of the mid-19th century and Late Empire furniture. In the drawing-room note a charming genre painting by Alexander Lauréus (1783–1823) over the door; the room remains 1880s in style, but with Late Empire and rococo furniture. The green chamber has a rococo stamp on its gilt ornamentation, furnishings, cornice marbling and decorative painting. The Count's library, restored to its 19th-century form, seems much less inviting than the packed shelves of the Mannerheim Museum library in Helsinki. Beyond the Count's ante-chamber is the hall, with neo-classical furniture, like that in the billiards-room, opened in the south-east annexe. Here too is the women's working-room, as it would have looked about 1800, with original Louhisaari objects.

I headed for the Church of Nousiainen (on 'a little slope', as the name suggests), where pious legend tells us that Bishop Henry had his first episcopal seat. A wooden church on this site near the river Hirvi (Elk) is first noted in written records of 1232, but this early building was replaced by a stone church erected by Bishop Johannes I, who was elevated in 1286 and started on Nousiainen and Turku Cathedral simultaneously. The church is narrower and longer than other Finnish churches of the Middle Ages; another peculiarity is the brick motif: not only were bricks introduced following the fashion of mid-13th century Central Sweden (Lake Mälaren), but other wall surfaces have been painted to give the illusion of more bricks. When Maunu I became bishop in 1290, the body of the church stood some four metres high; he converted the two-aisle plan to three-aisle and added vaulting, expanding the triumphal arch to its present breadth, though its present condition dates from a restoration in 1370. With painted decorations and the sarcophagus of S. Henry, the mediaeval church was complete, and remained virtually untouched as a national shrine until the addition of a chapel south of the sanctuary in 1901 and the restoration of 1967–9.

The bell-tower by Matti Ledenius of Turku dates from 1760. But we have come here to celebrate the Middle Ages of Bishop Henry, and above all the survival of the dark limestone sarcophagus of 1415–20 with a fine brass, engraved with the bishop's figure surrounded by a splendid Gothic arch. The staring bishop stands on a wretched pint-sized imp, in legend his murderer Lalli of Köyliö. Equally small, denoting humility before the saint, kneels Bishop Maunu II, donor of the sarcophagus. The inscription is taken from Henry's Latin liturgy, the coats-of-arms interrupting it being those of Turku Cathedral and the Tavast family. Don't miss scenes from the life of Henry on the sides of the sarcophagus: such as the coming with King Erik in two ships to proselytize among the pagan southerners (Estonians and the Finns of Varsinais Suomi). A figure near top left suggests a pagan god holding a shield. Nousiainen's painted decorations may be primitive, even naive, but their boldness and vigour will endear them to any modern visitor. I picked out the Kirves family coat-of-arms on the second of the southern pillars from the sanctuary, and a very old image of a Viking ship on the third of the northern pillars, though there is a whole little gallery of geometric designs, tree-of-life patterns, and allegorical humans and animals. A wooden sculpture in the round of Bishop Henry is also mediaeval in age and spirit.

As our car sped towards Masku for the evening banquet, the evening light remained clear in July. Headlights were illuminated on every car on the road: it is compulsory to use them at all times when travelling, and traffic authorities report a reduction in accidents since they became mandatory. We stopped to pick some raspberries by the roadside; the rule is that you can pick fruit anywhere in the wild, though all land is privately owned, but not within sight of a house, or wherever clear signs of ownership, or against trespassing, are found. Raspberries, blueberries and lingonberries ripen shortly after wild strawberries. The arctic bramble has been so avidly picked that until recently its very existence was endangered, so now the hybrid arctic raspberry is gracing Finnish tables. I had time to explore Masku Church, built in 1232 and dedicated to S. John the Baptist and S. Ursula. Its single four-vaulted nave is decorated with 17th-century frescoes. A stained-glass window, representing the appearance of the angels to the shepherds (1916), was donated by Fredrik Aminoff in memory of his wife Ester. A fine mediaeval font in the porch has foot and stem of Estonian limestone. But the major feature is a great triumphal crucifix by a Finnish artist of the second half of the 15th century.

The evening's banquet (tickets at 200 FM from Stockmann's) is a regular Tuesday event in the summer, including in the price bus transportation to and from Turku Market Square, and singing and dancing by Fyyrkantti Folklore Club. Participants are encouraged to join in the festivities, for explanations are given in Finnish, Swedish, English and German as necessary. *Pitokarkelot*, as the evening is known, reconstructs a traditional southwestern Finnish banquet about a hundred years ago. In this richest part of Finland, each reveller has his own porcelain (not wooden!) fork, spoon and knife, instead of using common utensils to slop food out of a common pot. After being regaled with a song of welcome, we enjoyed cold dishes, such as home-made cheese, brawn, raw herrings and cucumber, followed by an unaccompanied mediaeval round dance based on *Kalevala* chant rhythms. The concert continued with a party of three *kanteles*, or Finnish zithers, played with the index finger, not a plectrum, and a wide, shallow drum, the drumstick touching the wooden frame, a girl leading the melody and being followed by three others. After a consommé and meat pasty, the dancers performed in couples a sung polka, that dance introduced by the Polish princess Catherina Jagellonica and her Turku court, then a lively minuet from the Turku archipelago, and ending with another energetic polka. A show of costumes included reconstructed patterns from the 18th and 19th centuries, especially from Karelia (dark blue and black, with a striped apron) and southwest Finland: vertically striped dress, red for festivals, and white aprons, the married women always wearing a white headdress.

Now followed hot dishes: various meats, liver, raisins, potatoes and turnips, concocted from a 19th-century recipe book. A girl played the accordion, introduced at that period into the country. As a last surprise barley porridge arrived, with raisin soup, then a quadrille team took the floor.

After the banquet I spoke to the vivacious young student Sari Haapamäki, who showed me her *kantele*. The Maskuntalo, or young people's hall in Masku, made a splendid barnlike setting for the folkdance, with ample room

Masku. Maskuntalo, with folkdancer Sari Haapamäki playing a kantele

102

for diners, dancers and musicians. Sari would be coming to dance again and to play the *kantele* next week, but in the meantime she was looking forward to a rock concert at Ruissalo.

Turku Archipelago

At 9.30 one bright, warm morning I stepped aboard the *Klara*, moored on the Aura beside *Suomen Joutsen*, on my way to Houtskari (*Sw.* Houtskär), returning by car with Rauni Schleutker across the archipelago, its bridges and ferries, via Korppoo, Nauvo and Parainen. The dear old *Klara* I discovered to be no less a heroine than the stalwart *Plymouth Trader* used in the Normandy landings of 1944.

While Sisko Hanttu was preparing coffee, her husband Captain Teuvo Hanttu supervised the loading of breeze-blocks for a new home in the islands, and dozens of beer crates and food boxes for holiday-makers in summer cottages.

Under way at last, we passed the water-bus quay and the brig *Sigyn*, named for the 'good wife' of Nordic myth, then the giant cranes of Wärtsilä shipyard to the left. You cannot go far downstream along the Aura without noting the presence of Oy Wärtsilä Ab, who made passenger ships, tankers, car-ferries and cargo boats not only for domestic use but also for many other countries, especially for the U.S.S.R. and Norway. An Englishman, Robert Fithie, established a shipyard at Turku as early as 1741. Another yard, called Ericsson and Cowie, appeared in 1842, and was acquired by its young Scottish manager, William Crichton, in 1863. The two yards merged in 1884 and acquired Oy Vulcan Ab Engineering Works in 1924. Crichton-Vulcan merged with Wärtsilä in 1938, and new yards were created in the 1970s at Perno, on the shore of Raisio Bay, north of Turku.

Then I picked out on the right the sloping green roof of the ice-breaker *Voima* ('Strength'), a green roof on Turunlinna, a tug pulling the ice-breaker *Dikson* from Murmansk (Finnish ice-breakers return to Finland for repairs), the cruise liner *Rosella* from Maarianhamina, a green frontier patrol-boat, and then into open waters, past a cruise liner making to Åland from Naantali. A gale warning is broadcast over the ship's radio in Finnish, Swedish and English, and we head for the Axe Narrows, south of Rymättylä and north of Airismaa.

Rauni and I chatted to some of the other passengers. Mikael, a tanned youth with the blond hair and blue eyes ever associated axiomatically with the Nordic peoples, is going on to Iniö, whereas we are to disembark at Mossala. The commonest names for boys of 18 or 20 in Finland now are Mikael and Janne: the best-loved girls' names are Johanna, Karoliina, Emilia and Susanna. Entry to the bridge is strictly prohibited by a printed notice, but Captain Hanttu welcomed me, and indeed all visitors, as the little *Klara* ploughed calm seas towards the first stop of Åvensor. Our wind was WNW, so the visibility was good, as only SE winds bring haze to the islands.

Low wooded mysteries, these inlets spring up like sudden mushrooms. Fishing is not permitted with trawl nets, but only with a fishing-rod, and by permission. You cannot light a fire on an island unless you own it. Could I guess why snakebites affect chiefly little boys and older women? No. Little boys run around barefoot, while girls tend to wear sandals or shoes. Older women generally pick berries and mushrooms while their menfolk are at work. There are only about three weeks when you can pick blueberries and lingonberries; a skilled woodswoman can pick a litre in an hour, and blueberries can fetch up to 19 or 20 FM a litre, the current rate being 7 FM to the £1 or $1.50. Berries may be sold on the open-air markets without tax being paid. The archipelago's industries include tourism (summer cottages), fish farming, fishing, and speciality farming, such as early potatoes, onions, and lettuce, for the summers are longer here than in the rest of the country.

The little jetty at Åvensor (in Finnish Ahvensaari) was crowded with holidaymakers awaiting the daily boat, which berthed at 12.10. Captain Hanttu operated a little crane which swung breeze-blocks and planks ashore, the cart arriving for the load being pulled by a Ford tractor. An inquisitive tern landed with a swoosh beside me. Ahvensaari ('Perch Island') boasts only ten year-round residents, but there may be three hundred at peak times during the summer. Nowadays you can't build summer cottages by the shore any more: they must be sited inland. Many vacations last six weeks, and summer cottages may be used throughout the rest of the summer at weekends from May to late September. A typical summer cottage on Houtskari (41 m^2) to sleep 4 in beds and 2 more on mattresses, would have cost 1,845 FM a week in 1988 between 30 June and 11 August, 1,620 FM a week from 9 to 30 June and 11 August to 1 September, 1,015 FM at other times of the year, and 585 at weekends. Converted into US currency, these costs would have been $395, $345, $215 and $125 respectively; in UK currency, about £265, £230, £145 and £85. Among Finns, the ideal summer cottage would be close to the shops, seashore or lake, and woods, but distant from the sound of motor traffic or sight of neighbours.

At 12.45 we reached Mossala village, on Houtskari. Houtskari and its surrounding 700 islands have 737 inhabitants the year round, 97% of them Swedish-speaking; of these, one is the poet Bernt Mårtensson, who celebrates his island in Swedish. His books are on sale at Mossala village shop, run by the genial Tore Mattsson for the last six years. He owns the shop but rents his house. Shop prices are roughly the same as in Turku, the best month for sales being July. Pagan custom decreed that houses should be aligned east-west. Pagan custom decreed that a decorated pole should be set up on Midsummer's Day, and there, billowing above the low hills of Mossala, bunting tossed in the wind atop a fine Midsummer Pole. It was strange to enter a Christian church on these islands so close to nature, so enveloped in the spirit of the pagan gods of wind, water, and woodland. Mary's Church, reddish-brown with white-painted rectangular windows, looks more like a house than a House of God from the exterior, but then these little insular communities could never have supported a large church: congregations remained stubbornly small. The interior is painted homely pastel blue below and white above; each little village has its own benches. The community here, I heard it whispered, remains inbred socially and devout. Churches were said not to have been built in a the form of a cross before 1750, but Mary's Church at Näsby is cruciform, though it dates from 1703. The little baptismal font is of wood. A votive ship hangs in the alien atmosphere of air, uneasily, like a gasping fish. I remembered the shopkeeper's name on encountering Anna Lovisa Mattsson (1863–1946) commemorated in the neatly tended little graveyard. S. Mary's can be visited between 9 and 8 on weekdays, and 10–8 on holidays.

On the map Korppoo looks like an island, but administratively it comprises over 2,000 islands; of its 1500 square km, only 162 square km are dry land. Of its 1200 inhabitants, 70% are Swedish-speaking. Michael's Church in Korppoo, open from 10–8, stands on the site of a wooden church, the first mention of a stone building being 1384. In 1952–3 archaeologists discovered foundation stones inside the north wall. Over the gallery, accessible by a spiral staircase, hangs an early 15th-century Crucifixion from Rostock, and ships have been painted just below the vaulting; many other paintings, red on white, survive, as does an early wooden altar carving from Sweden, probably of the 15th century. A wooden German carving of S. George and the Dragon (1510) preserves some of the original paint on the saint, but none on the dragon. The pulpit, unusually on the south side, dates from 1646. Here as elsewhere, anachronistic chandeliers spoil the overall effect; could not unobtrusive spotlighting or low-level pew-lighting create a more harmonious impact? As regards the exterior, the spire seems ridiculously thin and tiny compared with its squat tower.

On the drive-on-off ferry from Korppoo to Nauvo, operating back and forth throughout the day to minimise delays, I foolishly slipped the whole way down the observation-bridge steps, the sequel being that I visited Turku University Central Hospital later that evening, and was given emergency treatment, bandaging, and X-rays on a damaged hand, all for about US$6 or £4! Another Swedish-speaking archipelago, Nauvo (*Sw*. Nagu) is bridged by another ferry between its large and smaller islands, Storlandet and Lillandet in Swedish. Olof's Church is in Storlandet, as are a trucking concern and a

Turku Archipelago. The moving road from Korppoo to Nauvo

mink farm. The bell tower, on a hill overlooking the church, newly-repaired in 1964, has a green spire, black doors, and brown walls. A copy of the first Finnish printed Bible of 1642 is displayed next to a Carl XII Bible in Swedish (Stockholm, 1703), Though the vestry was locked, I managed to see the armoury, again painted white, with red paintings. The main body of the 14th-century stone church is vaulted with square brick columns. A humorous carved corbel, an open-mouthed man, can be seen on the pillar next to a local votive ship of 1971, near the south entrance. Seventeenth-century paintings of hope and strength on a northern pillar have regrettably not worn well, unlike a Solomon's knot and oval decoration on the northwest pillar.

Parainen (*Sw.* Pargas) is an archipelago town of 12,000 inhabitants (on 15 islands, 450 islets and skerries), of whom 60% have Swedish as their mother

106

tongue. Locally they say that the best thing about Turku is the bus to Pargas, which leaves every thirty minutes from the bus station or by the Porthan Statue stop near the Cathedral. The area is dominated by the cement works of Oy Partek Ab, but fascinating minor industries include gingerbread, ice-hockey games, and hydrocopters made by Nils Eriksson for use while the ice is thawing, making it impossible for cars, small ships or snow-scooters.

Though archaeologists have found Stone Age and Bronze Age remains on Parainen, no settled population has been identified before the 11th century. The rubblework church (open in summer from 10–8) dates from the 14th century as regards the walls, vaults, and pillars, though restoration has been frequent, the last taking place in the 1960s. The western part of the Agricola Chapel is the oldest sector of the fabric, dating from the 13th century; it was extended in 1690 to allow for the growth of the Finnish-speaking congregation who worshipped there, and is now a museum, with vestments, swords and keys. The door of the vestry is alleged to come from Naantali Convent, but no written evidence survives. The ticking clock was made by Jacob Sylvander of Åbo. Originally, there were small windows on the south and none at all on the north: now there are large windows to let in abundant sunshine. A painting by Petrus Henriksson of 1486 is one of the few works in Finland to depict God the Father.

Parainen's tourist office, Rese-Kaleva at Strandvägen 16, can arrange for you to hire boats or rent summer cottages. A bookseller, Walter Johansson, has energetically set about preserving and administering the Skyttala mansion, the church quarter cabin, the sailor's widow's cabin, and Björkfelt's small cottage on the 'Malm', helping to run a special arts and crafts day in July, when organ festivals are also held. The Old Homestead Museum stands open between Tuesday and Sunday each summer from 11 to 4. You can stay at the Airisto Tourist Hotel at Stormälö, in the far west of the main island. The public library (*Sw.* Bibliotek; *F.* Kirjasto) is the only pink library I have seen; once the town hall, it looks most inviting.

There are no more ferries now on the way back to Turku: just the bridges Kyrksundet, Hessund, Kirjala-Rävsundet and Kuusisto-Kustö. Kuusisto island, 15 km from Turku on the road out from Kaarina, has an old church, well worth seeing, and ruins of a bishop's castle. A castle at Kuusisto was first mentioned in a letter dated 1295; the present-day ruins are not however on that site but date from the 15th century, being demolished by Gustavus Vasa in 1528. Its stones were pillaged by local farmers, and to build parts of the external wall of Turku Castle and the church of Piikkiö, across the water. The eighteenth-century wooden church of Kuusisto is painted red and white like that in Houtskari. Pukkila Manor (1763) at Piikiö has become a museum, with a section for early vehicles in a large stone byre of 1901.

Naantali

To paraphrase Dr Samuel Johnson, 'Anyone who is tired of Naantali is tired of life.' I stepped aboard the cruise boat which sets off from the Aura bridge in Turku at 12 noon on summer days, calls at Ruissalo (12.45), and docks at the little jetty in Naantali harbour at 1.30. The boat returns at 3 (1.45 and 6 on Sundays), the trips running between 1 June and 31 August.

As your boat enters the harbour, you see rising on your left the headland of Ailostenniemi, with its Convent Church of S. Birgitta. It should never have been built here at all, for a conventual building had been finished at Stenberga, in the Valley of Grace at Masku. But the climate was found to be unhealthy, so the nuns and its very place-name 'Vallis Gratiae' (*Sw.* Nådendal; *F.* Naantali) transferred to this easily-protected hill. The date was 1443, and the dedication of the impressive monastery took place in 1462. With the coming of repressive Lutheranism, the monastery was destroyed; fire damaged the church interior in 1628 and again in 1756, the most recent of many attempts at restoration being that by Olli Kestilä (1965). With seats for 1,000, Naantali Convent Church has become a popular venue for concerts by such as Ashkenazy, Isaac Stern and the English Chamber Orchestra during the music festivals held at Naantali around midsummer. The most important work of art in the Convent Church (open from 12 to 6 in summer; otherwise from 12 to 3) is a mediaeval wooden roundel showing Christ Wearing the Crown of Thorns. Above it, behind the altar, is a fine 15th-century Swedish wooden triptych showing the Virgin crowned as Queen of Heaven flanked by S. Birgitta and her daughter Kaarina (Bridget and Catherine), surrounded by twelve apostles and four other saints. The Renaissance pulpit, inscribed in both Latin and German, was presented by Henrik Fleming in 1622 but its provenance is unrecorded. The piscina above the stone font comes from the original monastery. The church ship hanging from the roof of the south aisle dates from 1824. Robert Wilhelm Ekman's painting *The Woman Taken in Adultery* (1868) can be seen on the north wall, like the *Pietà* presented to the convent by the Polish princess Catherina Jagellonica, too optimistically attributed to El Greco or a pupil. Hanging from the roof of the north aisle is the nuns' 'dedication crown', below which they took their final vows in the presence of the bishop. A Gothic monstrance in the north aisle, used to display the Host in the pre-Reformation period, dates from 1369.

The church clock is painted with its hands at eleven thirty so that, according to the people of Naantali, when the clock strikes midnight, the world will come to an end. Life has always seemed slower-paced in Naantali than in Turku, or elsewhere, so a 'wise men of Gotham' tradition has sprung up in Turku, gently ridiculing their neighbours. A notice, the story goes, was

Naantali. Convent Church

pinned to the Town Hall when Naantali first acquired fire-pumps, that inhabitants should fill all their pumps and buckets with water three days before a fire.

Mediaeval Naantali was destroyed by fire in 1628, but the burghers stubbornly rebuilt their homes on exactly the same site, so the pattern of houses and courtyards remains resolutely mediaeval today, even if standards of hygiene have improved out of all recognition. I was shown round the two double rooms in Villa Waski, for example, at Mannerheiminkatu 10a: the rent in the most fabulously spotless accommodation I have ever seen anywhere was 280 FM for single occupancy (£40 or $60) and 350 FM for double occupancy, similar to prices at the Asunto Hotelli Gratiae, or the

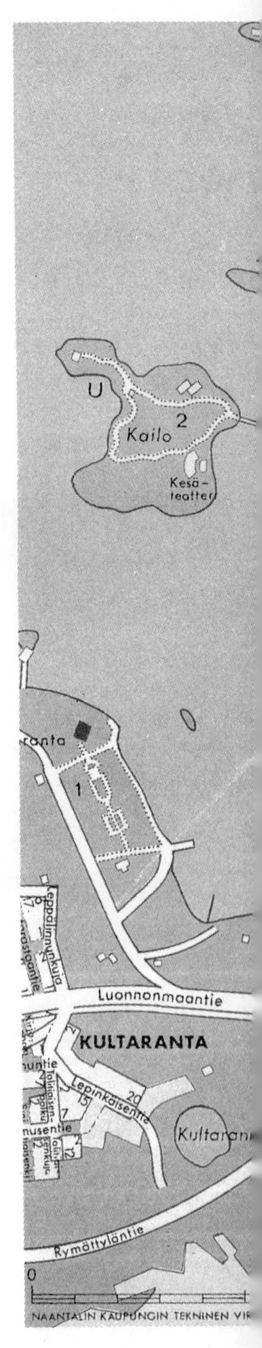

Naantali. Town Plan

KARVETTI
RUONA
Kalevanniemi
Lammasluoto
VÄINÖLÄ
MAIJAMÄKI
VILULUOTO
Luolalanjärvi
Järvelä
Suomen Sokeri Oy
Mobil Oil
Raumakari
Ruotsinsatama
Leirintäalue
Jäähalli
Urheilutalo
Posti
Rautatieasema

1. Kultaranta; the summer residence of the President
2. Kailo; recrention area, summertheather, picknick-area, beach, tennis courts
3. Convent Church; open 12–18 (15.4.–31.8.) 12–16 (1.9.–30.9.) at other times Sun 12–15
4. Kaivopuisto; park music, park chess, tennis courts
5. Boat Harbour; sightseeing boats to Turku
6. Tourist Office in summer; open 11–18; market place in summer
7. Room of Arts; open in summer 14–20
8. Fire Station, ambulance, alarm tel. 006
9. Museum; open Mon–Sun 12–18, (15.5.–31.8.)
10. Library; open 12–19, Sat 10–15
11. Art Gallery; open Tue–Fri 14–18, Sat–Sun 14–16
12. Medical Center, First Aid, tel. 752752, open 8–20, doctor on duty 20–08
13. Taxi, tel. 97041
14. Gasthaus Unikeko, tel. 751881
15. Bus station; busses to Turku every 15. min.
16. Tourist Office; open Mon–Fri 8–15.30
17. Town Hall; post office and telegraph, open 9–17, market place
18. Pharmacy; open Mon–Fri 8–21, Sat 8–15, Sun 11–15
19. Spa of Naantali, tel. 752300
20. Sports Hall
21. Telephone System; open 8–17
22. Police, alarm tel. 002; liquor store
23. Railway station
24. Camping; open 1.6.–19.8.
25. Sweden harbour; Viking Line terminal

U = beach
V = Yacht Harbour

© 1985
1 km

friendly little Café Antonius nearby. I took tea and chocolate cake at the Antonius, where the novelist Laila Hietemies ('Sandman') comes to stay for weeks at a time. The six rooms were all taken while I was there, but Mrs Ahtiainen showed me to the loft, occupied currently by her son, with a beautiful view over the town from this snug late 19th-century wooden building.

The home now occupied by the Café-Hotel Antonius once belonged to the saddler Johan Lindblom; his daughters Carolina, Charlotta and Josefina made ginger biscuits and hand-knitted dolls, and sold them in the harbour. Similar hand-knitted dolls can be ordered today, though they are very expensive, taking up to a month to create a pair: a boy and a girl in Naantali regional period costume.

If you don't want to pay a great deal for accommodation, the Kuparivuori Camping, 21100 Naantali (tel. 921–751 354) has 18 camping cabins @ 140 FM per day for four persons and 5 caravan places @ 49 FM per day between 23 May and 31 August, except for increases at midsummer (about 19–22 June) and Sleepyhead Day (about 25–27 July).

Naantali Health Spa, with 93 double rooms, charges 390 FM (single), 500 (double) during the low season, or 420 and 540 respectively from mid-June to mid-August to include breakfast, morning sauna, and weekday gymnastic exercises.

Houses in the old quarter ranging in date from the late 18th century to the middle of the 19th can best be admired in the district between the sea and Torikatu. Enthusiasts for Erik Bryggman's architecture should see Villa Haartman, at Luostarinkatu 3 (1926), but of course you have to come here for traces of old Finland, the flavour of the past: the Art Gallery by the Yacht Harbour, the Estate Museum at Luonnonmaa, the Farm Museum at Käkölä (4 km from the Kultaranta road, open 12–6 on Sundays), and the Naantali Town Museum. This last is situated in the house called Hiilola, many houses still preserving the names of the original owners: Hiilola, Lotila, Saksa, Hirvo. The windmills and cottages on the seashore may have disappeared but many survivals of the past can be seen in the Town Museum, in the 18th century burgher's house, open 12–6 during the summer. The bedroom has a late Gustavian chest of drawers and bed, with baroque chairs, table and long-case clock. The drawing-room has Biedermeier wallpaper (that is of the mid-19th century), but the furniture has been acquired from other local properties. An intermediate room displays an oak chest of 1762, a rococo cupboard and 18th-19th century silver. The first kitchen has been restored in 1850s style with peasant furniture of the epoch; the second kitchen shows 19th-century utensils. The early 19th-century chest in the hall belonged to the chief of Customs, Bredenberg, the last private owner of the house.

A less imposing house called Sau-Kallio has been added to the Hiilola complex, as has a windmill from Luonnonmaa.

Many other beautiful homes in Naantali are preserved as national monuments, a number having a loft above the decorated entrance doors, and living rooms separated by an entrance hall. The spa, informally begun under Professor Petter Elfving in the 18th century, was organised at Ailostenniemi from 1863, and reached its heyday during the Russian period, when Helsinki's Eira quarter, with its fine houses and parks, spread over its present area. The old spa, which claimed to cure coughs and headaches, gout, scurvy and paralytic strokes (oh gullible mortals!) finally closed down in 1962, and another took its place at Kalevanniemi in 1984. A footbridge takes you from Ailostenniemi to the islet of Kailo, with its picnic beach, tennis courts, and summer theatre.

I explored the marvellous public library, remarkably large for its population served, which does not exceed ten thousand. The little local yacht harbour near the town centre seems homely, but if you take Satamatie you will come to the Viking Line terminal for international cruises via Maarianhamina to Kapellskär in Sweden. And you might be staggered by the size of the unobtrusive industrial complex: a sugar refinery, Imatran Voima power station, Neste's oil refinery, and Mobil Oil's production plant.

But I was invited to tour the President of Finland's Summer Palace at Kultaranta ('Golden Beach'), an opportunity not to be missed at any cost. You can see Kultaranta park every summer Friday between late June and early August, taking a boat from Turku's Aura Bridge at 5.30 in the afternoon and leaving Naantali again at 8.15. The road leads across the Ukko Pekka bridge from Naantali, so called after 'Uncle Pete' Svinhufvud, the third President. The first, founder of the Constitution, was the lawyer Ståhlberg, the second Relander, the fourth the peasant Kyösti Kallio, the fifth Risto Ryti, an intellectual ultimately tried as a war criminal, the sixth the banker J.K. Paasikivi, General Mannerheim (twice, like Svinhufvud), and Urho Kekkonen, followed by the present incumbent, Mauno Koivisto. I write this sentence on Sunday 7 September 1986, as Urho Kekkonen is being buried in the Helsinki cemetery of Hietaniemi, where 3,000 war heroes and five former presidents are buried. While Paasikivi is recognised as the ideologue of Finland's neutrality, the shrewd implementation of this policy must be credited largely to Kekkonen, President from 1956 to 1982. Kowtowing neither to east nor west, like Albania in this one respect, Finland has sought (in a way entirely opposite to that of Albania) to maintain friendly relations with every country, and its sensitive understanding of Soviet politics, necessarily very profound and up to the minute, has led to more than four decades of peace and unparalleled prosperity. President Koivisto has taken his place in this direct line of accommodating divergent views

Naantali. Kultaranta. Rose-garden in the Presidential Palace grounds

while putting Finnish sovereignty before all else. The president traditionally handles Finnish foreign policy, leaving the Government to hew out internal policies by consensus within the framework of proportional representation.

Kultaranta exhibits informality and a relaxed attitude to security in total contrast to the attitudes in communist countries where photography of sensitive places can be a criminal offence punishable by death or imprisonment in labour camps. But the President's Palace, like so much else in Finland that seems straightforward at first glance, was not really designed for that at all. A 19-roomed granite palace with an idyllic view over Naantali Bay, Kultaranta was planned by the industrialist Alfred Kordelin to drawings by Lars Sonck (1916) with landscaping of the park carried out by Paul Olsson.

Kordelin was killed in 1917, during the War of Independence, and his palace passed to the state: since 1918 every President has stayed here, though in Mannerheim's case the duration of the stay was one afternoon, and in Kekkonen's every summer for 25 years. Cycling security guards waved cheerily to me, as I wandered through the Finland Garden (planted with white and blue flowers to reflect the colours of the national flag) and the magnificent 'Medallion', with more than 3500 fragrant rose bushes. I found Wäinö Aaltonen's sculpture of Kordelin, then felt my head sprayed with tingling cold water, from a fountain swayed by the swirling wind. Since the President was absent, a guard with a walkie-talkie encouraged me to climb up to the lovely belvedere, with its round table and art nouveau gallery; then up again ('Take as many pictures as you want!') to the aptly-named 'Paradise' Garden so remote from the delicate rustic sounds of Delius. Two pools with dark blue tiles reflect the moving branches: a white marble sculpture of *Adam and Eve* sculpted by Felix Nylund for Kordelin overlooks the pools, in the shade of leafy bushes.

The Track to Tampere

I could have chosen a flight from Turku to Tampere, Finland's second city, from the airport 7 km outside the city centre. Finnair also operates up to a dozen flights a day to Helsinki, up to ten to Maarianhamina for Ahvenanmaa, and up to six to Stockholm, with fewer at weekends.

But I preferred to bask in a train passing through gentle landscapes of fields, woods, beside lakes and hamlets or isolated farmhouses, The smooth modern train (costing one third of the air fare) takes two hours between Turku and Tampere: there is not much to slow down its even pace through Lieto (there may be no linguistic connection with the Italian word for 'happy' but the coincidence merited congratulation on that lovely summer afternoon), through Aura, and Kyrö. We stopped at Loimaa, and two attractive blondes entered the compartment, finding their reserved seats opposite mine. 'Hello,' said Marja, as the train slid effortlessly on its way to Humppila and Urjala, then to the important junction of Toijala, on the line from Helsinki to Tampere, Oulu and the north. She and her friend Riitta were on their way to Tampere to take part in the Flower Weeks, and the Theatre Summer, and hoped to see some of the rowing events on Tampere's Pyhäjärvi (Holy Lake). Marja and Riitta, speaking almost perfect English, without the trace of any accent that one might mimic, anatomised the morning's *Turun Sanomat*, so that I could appreciate the preoccupations of Finnish newspaper readers.

A typical issue of *Turun Sanomat* (itself characteristic of the Finnish daily press) devoted the first and last of its 24 pages to advertisements; page 2 to a

Turku. Rail Station. The train to Tampere

political leader and a feature (here a young student's project studying the morals of the older generation); and p.3 to a foreign leader (27 countries already boycotting the Edinburgh Commonwealth Games; the Naantali phones were out of order for two hours; the first crayfish of the season are very expensive). Page 4 printed obituaries, and advertised summer theatres and excursions; p.5 items of local interest; pp.6–7 local news, including an opinion that radiation from Chernobyl has not affected Lappish reindeer, but the effect on mushrooms is not yet known, and details on how to catch crayfish; page 8 previewed an art exhibition at Uusikaupunki; page 9 dealt with 'light' economics, noting that even more grain is to be grown by E.E.C. Countries; page 10 included gossip and an Andy Capp cartoon; page 11 numismatic notes, the weather and domestic news items; pp.12–13 printed foreign news, including the meeting of Bishop Tutu with Prime Minister Botha, and headlines in English; p.14 reviewed the production of Verdi's *Aida* at Savonlinna and a children's play at Naantali. With pages 15,16, 17 and 18 we come to the heart of the paper: a sixth of the whole issue devoted to sporting features, results and statistics, followed by four pages of small ads for jobs, summer cottages, apartments, houses, boats and cars, a 1974 VW offered at 7,500 FM. Radio and TV programmes from Finland, Sweden and Moscow filled p.23, while p.24 was devoted to ads and more cartoons.

Riitta asked me if I knew the story of the distinguished veteran Finnish politician, who was about to retire. A journalist interviewing him asked, 'What are you going to do when you retire, Sir?' 'Well,' came the answer, 'the first two weeks I'll just sit in my rocking chair.' 'And then?' 'Then I'll start to rock. . .'

At Urjala, I wondered if Väinö Linna would have recognised the little town he had left in 1937, at the age of seventeen, to seek work in a large textile factory in Tampere. The novelist's first, apprentice work, scribbled in spurts between his exhausting factory days and self-educating nights, was *Päämäärä* ('The Aim'). The novelist, whose most celebrated book, *The Unknown Soldier*, has sold more copies than any other book in Finland apart from the Bible and the A.B.C., expressed in his protagonist Valte the working-class aspiration to self-improvement for financial and intellectual gain. Valte moves from his rural home to a factory town and seizes every chance to understand the world about him, and the world of ideas too. He condemns extremes of polemical politics, while pondering ultimate questions of good and evil. He yearns for altruism in himself and others, but finds only greed and egotism. Valte strides to the bridge over Tammerkoski, the rapids on the canal dividing the two halves of the city, and impulsively starts to throw himself off the bridge to destruction. Then, like Saul on the road to Damascus, he experiences a blinding awareness of the beauty of existence, of life, and of his own potential. From a passionate yearning to die, he suddenly finds an equally passionate longing to accept all that life has to offer.

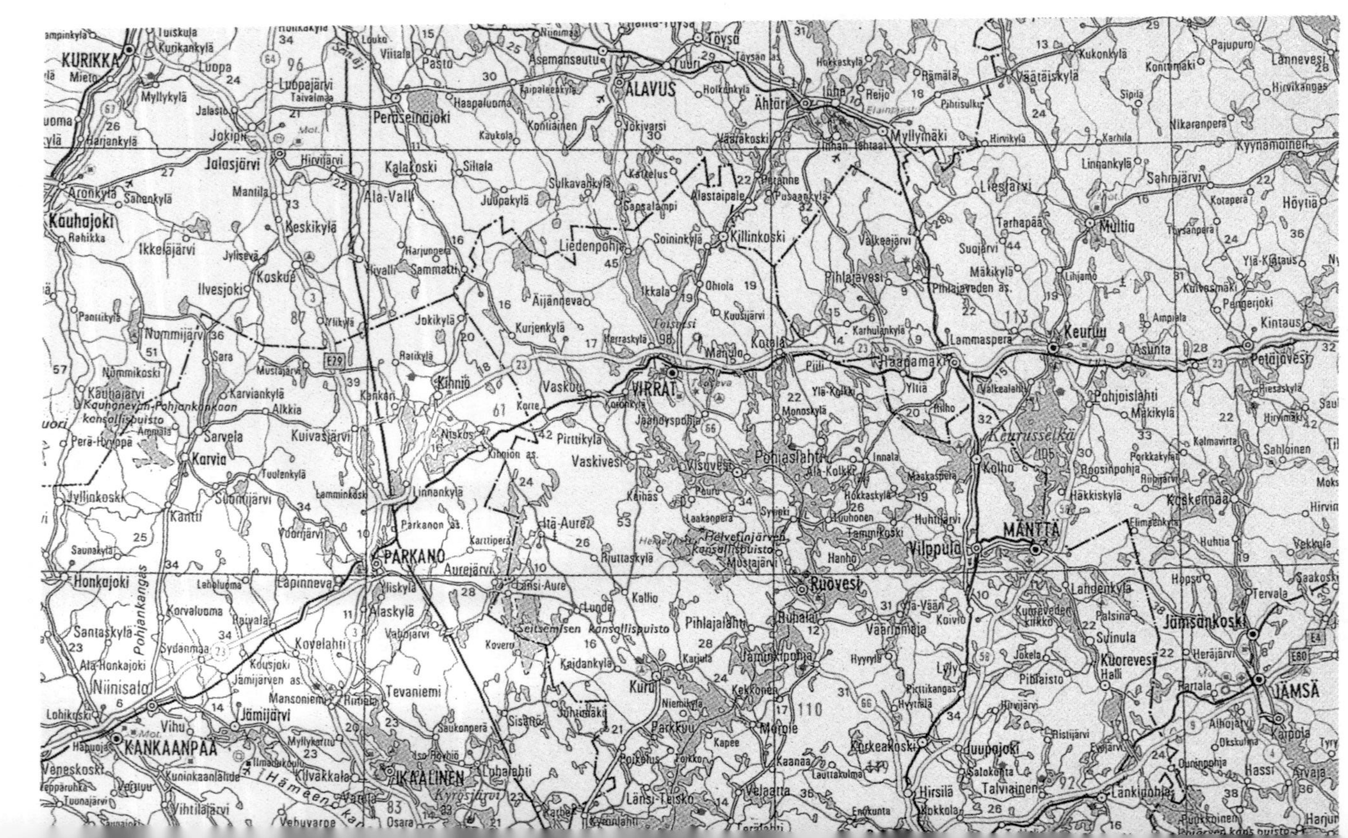

KURIKKA
ALAVUS
VIRRAT
PARKANO
MÄNTTÄ
JÄMSÄ
KANKAANPÄÄ
IKAALINEN
Kauhajoki
Niinisalo
Pohjankangas
Jämijärvi
Keuruu
Ruovesi
Vilppula
Mänttä
Petäjävesi
Multia

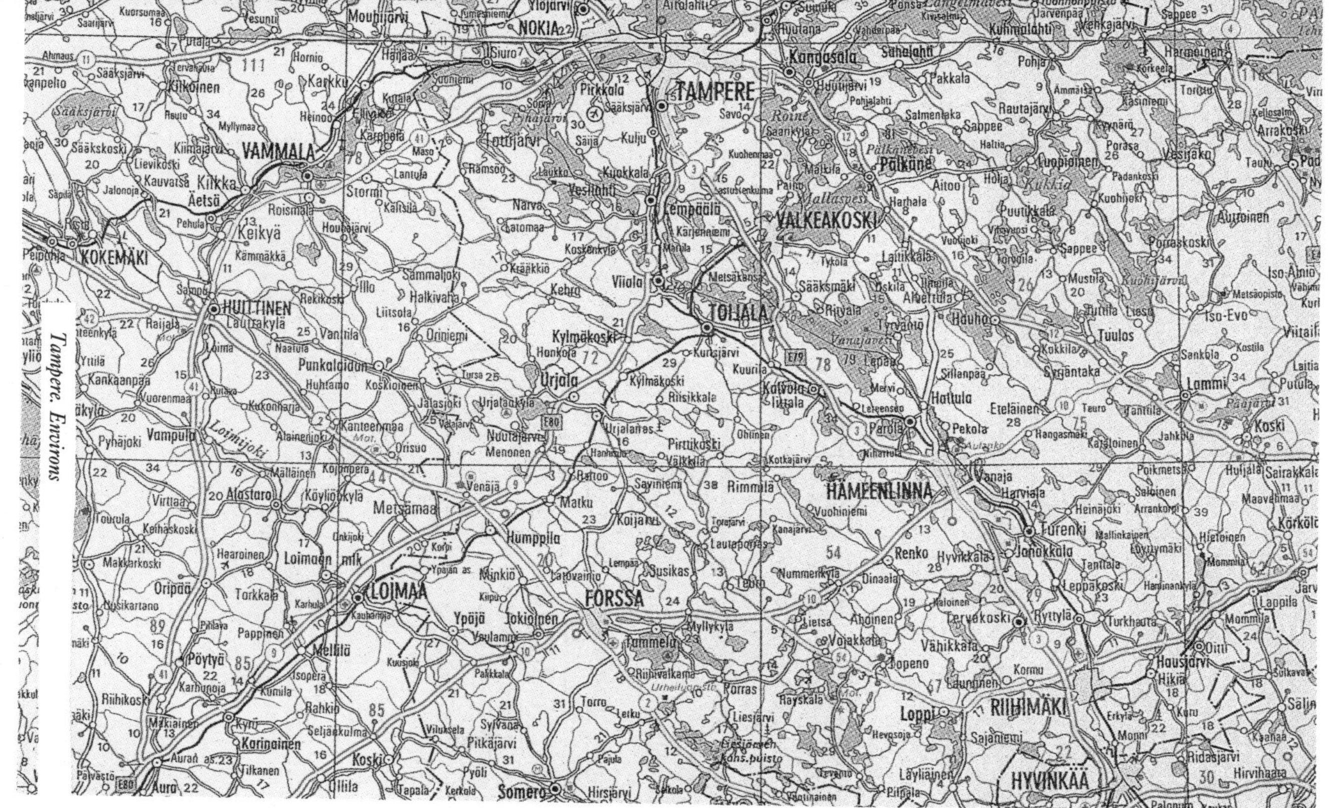

Tampere. Environs

TAMPERE

The rail station in Tampere is so close to the bridge over Tammerkoski that I wanted to visit that first, and Anja Saaristo, who accompanied me throughout my stay in Tampere, kindly offered to take me there immediately. On a warm summer evening, it needed an imaginative effort to empathise with a youth near to suicide. Girls in summer dresses, well-fed, well-educated, strolled past, and I saw how successive generations had risen from the ashes of hardship, the fear of alien domination, war, and poverty to achieve freedom, prosperity and confident independence. Finland has become a success story, not only economically and politically, but above all in that combination of common sense, sensitivity to beauty and good taste, and courtesy, that so many countries have never known or, if known, somehow lost. Väinö Linna, now a revered academician, walks in Hämeenpuisto, or Häme Park, every day, a living link with that past of deprivation and desperation. His town of the rapids has become the largest inland city in the Nordic countries and, extraordinary revelation, a city of Renaissance loveliness, with protected lakeland, parkland, woodland, and above all a new architectural blaze of glory that – only now coming to full fruition in the 1980s – is stamping Tampere as the most exciting twentieth century city in Europe, lacking the sleaze of London's East End, the poverty of Rome, the shabby nostalgia of Paris, and the drug-problem of Amsterdam.

The rapids created Tampere just as much as the glacial ridge of Pyynikki created Tampere. Five centuries ago, the rapids were used to power the first mills, then three centuries later industrialisation gradually spread, but water power and electricity are clean, so pollution by coal, coke and anthracite never soiled these Finnish skies, or damaged the lungs of its workers.

Gustav III, King of Sweden and then of Finland too, came in summer 1775 to see the rapids. They fall eighteen metres between the lakes called Näsijärvi and Pyhäjärvi: in a country as flat as a pancake, that is sensational. So Gustav, having factories in Sweden, immediately recognised the industrial potential of the site, and ordered the bemused handful of villagers to set up a factory here too. Then he drove back to Gripsholm. Four years later, Gustav granted a charter to Tampere as a free town, and provided a distillery. Then came a paper mill, run by Abraham Häggman from 1783, of which only the hexagonal chimney survives. The Russians seized Tampere in 1808, and when Tsar Alexander I visited the city in 1819, like the Swedish

Tampere. Bridges in the City Centre, looking north to Näsijärvi

king he rapidly divined the little town's potential as a hub of industry and commerce. A Scot, James Finlayson, came to establish a cotton mill in 1820, and started mechanical cotton spinning in 1828, attracting thousands of country-dwellers to settle and work in Tampere. In 1837 the factory area saw the construction of a six-storey factory designed by Carl Leszig of Viipuri, followed in 1877 by the so-called 'Plevna' workshop. Finlayson provided extraordinarily advanced facilities for his employees: a skating-rink, church, school, hospital, reading-room and kindergarten/crêche. Forty per cent of the city's five thousand inhabitants in 1860 depended for their livelihood on the mill. Finlayson's is still active, as is Tampella Osakeyhtiö, founded from a merger between Tampere Ironworks (1842) and a linen mill (1856). And don't think the British connection stopped with the name of Finlayson, who sold out to von Nottbeck. For in *Finland Today* (1911), George Renwick could say that in the years before World War I 'the prosperity of Tammerfors soon drew to it many people from Yorkshire and Lancashire, and in the streets a homely English accent is often to be heard'. Mrs Finlayson established the first school in Tampere and entered into a lively correspondence with Quakers whom Alexander I had invited to St. Petersburg.

121

Near Helsinki, in the suburb of Otaniemi, I had visited the modest one-room Paper Museum of the Finnish Pulp and Paper Research Institute, where I had learned that the earliest Finnish paper mill could be dated 1667, at Thomasböhle (between Helsinki and Turku), but this was on a cottage-industry scale, and following K.F. Idestam's establishment of a paper mill below Hämeensilta in 1865, and his expansion to nearby Nokia two years later, G.A. Serlachius transferred from Tampere to Mänttä. Tampere's paper mill attached to the cotton mill was so successful that others sprang up across Finland, notably at Valkeakoski, a little to the south. Other enterprises benefitting from Tammerkoski included a woollen mill set up by Tuomas Peterson (1847–1905) and – from 1856 – the knitwear factory Tampereen Verkatehdas, which shifted operation in the 1970s to Hankkio, between Messukylä and Kaukajärvi east of the city.

Helsinki is hemmed in by the sea on three sides, and Turku on two sides, Old Tampere was confined in its growth to the neck of land separating Pyhäjärvi to the south and Näsijärvi to the north, so expansion has been limited to east and west. The existence of the neck of land and its rapids is due to the termination here ten thousand years ago of a chain of glacial moraines running from Ylöjärvi in the west through Kangasala to Pälkäne in the east. The ridges of Pispala and Pyynikki, at their highest, rise 150 metres above sea level and eighty metres above the level of Pyhäjärvi: altitudes by no means remarkable in other parts of the world, but in the Finnish context quite outstanding.

So we started walking through the old quarters of Pispala, between houses climbing the hillside as in any Umbrian hill town, though the dates of these developments are mainly the 1890s and the 1920s. Prestigious new houses are now replacing some of the older homes and the atmosphere combines relaxation with prosperity, ubiquitous green trees, bushes and lawns filling every square inch between the two blue lakes. We strolled down Uramon-katu, then around the winding, precipitous streets, lanes and steps that reminded me of Coimbra or, nearer home, of Bath. Steps led down from Harjunpää to Portanpää where, at no.8, we arrived at the house-museum of Lauri Viita, open on Sunday afternoons between 1 and 4. Viita's *Moreeni* ('Moraine', 1950) is the epic of Tampere, narrating the rapid changes and sudden traumas of 1918, during the Finnish Civil War, Tampere being the last redoubt of the Reds against the Whites led by Mannerheim. Born in Pispala in 1916, Viita married the talented poet Aila Meriluoto, but became increasingly mentally ill and was killed in a car crash in Helsinki in 1965. Working first of all as a carpenter, like his father, Viita (it is pronounced unerringly like the Italian for 'life') found his true voice in two early works: *Betonimylläri* (1947) and *Kukunor* (1949), adapting *Kalevala's* four-foot trochaic metre *(Kootut Runot*, 1966) much as Mustapää had in the 1920s,

Tampere. Pispala. Lauri Viita's house and museum

Marja-Liisa Vartio (the wife of the poet Paavo Haavikko) in the 1950s, and Matti Rossi would do in the 1970s.

But it is the film version of Viita's epic novel *Moreeni* (televised again during my stay) for which he became best known and loved. His simple little wooden house, built in 1900–1, housed his own family, with a bachelor's room in the attic, and two of the other four rooms were let to other families. The house was sold in 1937, but acquired by Pispala Moreeni Society, then converted into a museum in 1977. From the window of the main room a lovely view extends across Pyhäjärvi. The table is laid with a tablecloth near a peasant sofa-bed; a sewing-machine by Clemens Mueller (1909) and an old stove in the wall: everything evokes a gradual evolution from peasantry to petit bourgeoisie, by a combination of hard work and fortitude (the Finnish word for it, *sisu*, is predictably untranslatable). We come back to Väinö Linna now, having left him transfigured from depression to exaltation at the Tammerkoski bridge. From Tampere he was conscripted into the Winter War against the Soviet Union (1939-40), which ended in stalemate. Then he fought in the Continuation War (1941–4), still against the Soviet threat, first in a machine-gun company at the front, and later behind the lines as an instructor. His great novel *The Unknown Soldier* (1954 in Finnish; 1957 in English translation) has been filmed, staged and made into an opera, all directed by Edvin Laine, the opera with music by Tauno Pylkkänen first performed by the Finnish National Opera in 1967. It hits out at state militarism, taking the viewpoint of the ordinary man, whose life and family and country are at stake in the interest of ideological abstractions such as patriotism, nationalism, capitalism or communism. The English translator David Barrett is currently working on Linna's massive trilogy *Here, Under the Northern Star* (1959–62 in Finnish), which describes the rise of a peasant farming family in Häme (the western plains) from poverty in 1880 to relative affluence after World War II. Linna traces their history in the larger history of Finland: Russian imperialism and the War of Independence, Civil War, the 'Thirties' depression and the unease accompanying the militarism of Hitler and Stalin. Linna's view of historical events resembles the sceptical position taken by Tolstoy, who suggests that events (especially in wartime, when more than one country is involved in decision-making) slide out of the hands of the helpless ministers and generals who are supposed to be directing operations. Linna's originality lies in the implication that the working classes were repressed and 'defeated' by the middle classes or 'Whites' in 1918, just as the opposite happened during the Russian Revolution across the border. Any neutral observer can see for himself which of the two systems has led to the greater prosperity, liberty, and harmony.

We can observe living conditions of workers from 1910 to 1970 in the Amuri Workers' Museum, between Satakunnankatu and Pirkankatu, at Makasiininkatu 12. Opening hours are 12–6 from Tuesdays to Sundays between mid-May and late August. We have already noted how industrial expansion caused housing shortages in Tampere, the population swelling from 3,200 in 1850 to 33,800 in 1900, 100,000 in 1950, to 170,000 in 1987. Amuri is in no sense a kind of handicrafts museum, like Luostarinmäki in Turku, but a vibrant restoration of twenty-five homes, two shops and a bakery. As in the Soviet Union at the same period, Amuri's one-storey buildings were long, with a shared kitchen, and many individual 'family' rooms where people lived in quite crowded conditions, so that one possessed only 'a room and a share in a kitchen'. The impression sought is that the

residents have just gone out. A co-operative store of 1934 reminds us that
Tampere Workers' Association opened the first such store in Finland in
1899 and Finlayson's opened the second in 1900; at the opposite end of the
building you can find a small store from 1946, a time when the nation was
still severely rationed after the War and people had to make clothes and
shoes out of paper in the absence of textiles.

The period 1911–39 is represented by a long house with a baker's oven
and shop in the basement, and thirteen flats above it. I was especially
touched by a student's rented room, with chairs, curtains, carpet, sheets,
briefcase, cap, shoes and wall-hangings: all made of paper.

Engel's town-planning grid, familiar from Helsinki and Turku, can be
found again in Tampere town centre, in the vicinity of Satakunnankatu and
Hämeenkatu. Here are the shops and department stores, often in highly
distinguished buildings, where you can find anything that can be found in
Helsinki or Turku. Try the Market Hall (Hämeenkatu 19/Hallituskatu 10)
for inviting displays of fresh meat, fish, fruit, vegetables, flowers, and dairy
produce, as well as such local specialities as flat loaves called *rieva* and blood
sausages. Hours are 8–5 Monday-Friday and 8–2 Saturday. The two
department stores, Stockmann and Sokos, are also on Hämeenkatu. Handicrafts can be bought in the shops of Pirkanmaan Kotityö Oy at Verkatehtaankatu 2, where the Tampere Tourist Office and the Finnish Silverline are
located. For ladies' fashions, gifts and handicrafts, try the Arctia Galleria in
Hotel Tampere, and Kehräsaari boutiques. The local Marimekko fabrics
specialist is Helvi Lehtonen, Tuomiokirkonkatu, the street where you can
also find the Academic Bookstore.

Across the main highway from Amuri is Särkänniemi recreation park,
including funfair and amusements, a children's zoo where youngsters are
encouraged to make friends with small tame animals, and a splendid
aquarium. A dolphinarium opened in 1985, and you can see seals from
below, in the enormous aquarium (open 10–8; seal-feeding times at 11 and
4). Pekka Ilveskoski, the architect responsible for these, also designed the
planetarium (year-round half-hour shows on the hour; earphones for
translations into Swedish and English) and the 'needle' of Näsinneula (1971)
at 560 feet the highest observation tower in Finland, open 10–5.30 in winter
and 10–8 from late April to late August. The fastest lift in the country (6
metres a second) zooms you silently heavenward towards the observation
levels and the restaurant, where a first-class meal can be enjoyed as you
circumnavigate the air above Tampere once every fifty minutes. The views
are stunning: two lakes, the peninsula of Lentävänniemi northward, the
cityscape eastward, glacial ridges westward.

After lunch, one of the best museums of modern art in Europe can be
visited in Särkänniemi. The Sara Hildén Art Museum (open daily 11–6) was

Tampere. Särkänniemi. Sara Hildén Art Museum

designed by Pekka Ilveskoski (1978), who subsequently created the Finnish Diabetes Course Centre (1980). While enjoying the permanent show and the various changing displays, remain constantly alert for the architectural brilliance of the ensemble and details: to ensure seeing both, I suggest you visit the whole area twice, once for the objects displayed, and again for their environment. On a day as sunny as Berwald's Fourth Symphony, I wandered through the different sculpture levels, from Rauni Liukko's witty *Rush Hour* (1970) to Harry Kivijärvi's hieratic *Great Gate* (1969) and Kimmo Pyykkö's *Balance*. The sculptures can be seen not only from all close angles, but also through the windows on the lower floor. The upper floor windows allow views of Särkänniemi Rock, Pispala Ridge, and Näsijärvi, the great lake extending as far north as Ruovesi, on the watery 'Poet's Way'. The exterior of the building has a light-coloured coarse aggregate on concrete;

126

the inner gallery walls are covered in white-painted textiles. Throughout, the emphasis is placed on air, space, light: I thought of the magnificent new museum at Paestum, and the new Sackler Wing at New York's Metropolitan Museum.

The art-collector Sara Hildén donated her collection to the foundation bearing her name in 1962, then the City of Tampere paid for the construction of a museum and its running costs. In its early years the collection concentrated on Finnish works, especially paintings by Erik Enroth between 1945 and 1963. Finland's graphic art has not achieved the international recognition accorded to its architecture, partly because political frontiers seem much less noticeable in painting and sculpture. It would be difficult to distinguish the geometric abstractions of Mondrian and Ben Nicholson from those of Göran Augustson (b.1936) or the whirling shapes of Hans Hartung from the *Person* of Juhana Blomstedt (b.1937). Juhani Harri's assemblages derive from the mental world of the American artist Joseph Cornell. But that is merely to say that restrictions applicable to language and literature, through quagmires of translation, are swept away in the plastic and graphic arts. Kain Tapper (b. 1930) comes from a smallholding family in Central Finland with an interest in crafts: his sculptures reveal a love and mastery of natural forms and natural woods, and to a lesser extent granite. Even more than Henry Moore, Tapper has dwelt on the magic of bone, in particular the skull, but his *Storm* (1973) and *Autumn* (1974) add painterly qualities of incision and patina that make him one of Finland's most outstanding artists. The same can be said of the Tampere painter and sculptor Kimmo Kaivanto (b. 1932), who is also a commercial artist. A figurative painter (except during the 'Sixties, when he turned to abstraction), he has used his growing reputation in ideological works designed to draw attention to world issues in peace, co-existence, and conservation. I asked to see, in store, the smaller 1969 and the larger 1973 versions of the ecological oil-painting *When the Sea Dies*: not all Kaivanto's works can be displayed at once. Kaivanto, who still lives in Tampere, has a clever satire on the fashionable von Wright brothers, *Fighting Wood Grouse* (1974). My eye was also caught by the Turku sculptor Mauno Hartman (b. 1930), whose *Horizontal Stoppage* (1966–8) makes profoundly playful Klee-like allusions to a workbench, a vertical xylophone, and a great pecking bird. *Taivaankanto* (wood, 1967) is translated in the catalogue as 'Pillar of Heaven' but *kanto* means 'tree-stump', and that is clearly what is intended by Hartman. Even more charming is his *Rose Song Tree* (1964), but then charm vibrates equally in a de Hooch-like *Interior* by Veikko Vionoja, a Schwitters-like *Composition* of found objects by Aarno Salosmaa, and a Tinguely-like *Screw Monument* by Kauko Lehtinen.

Tampere. City Plan

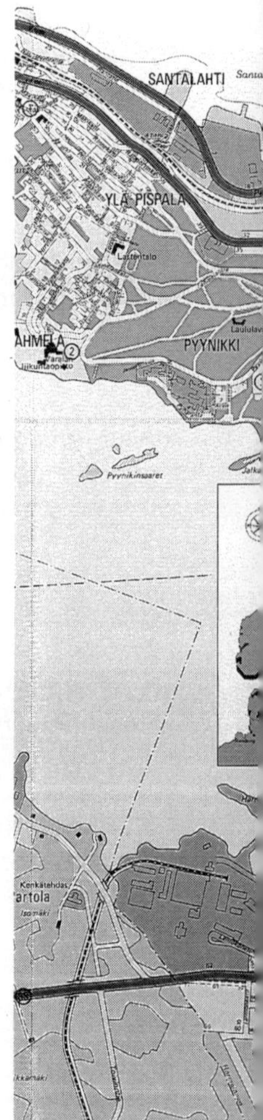

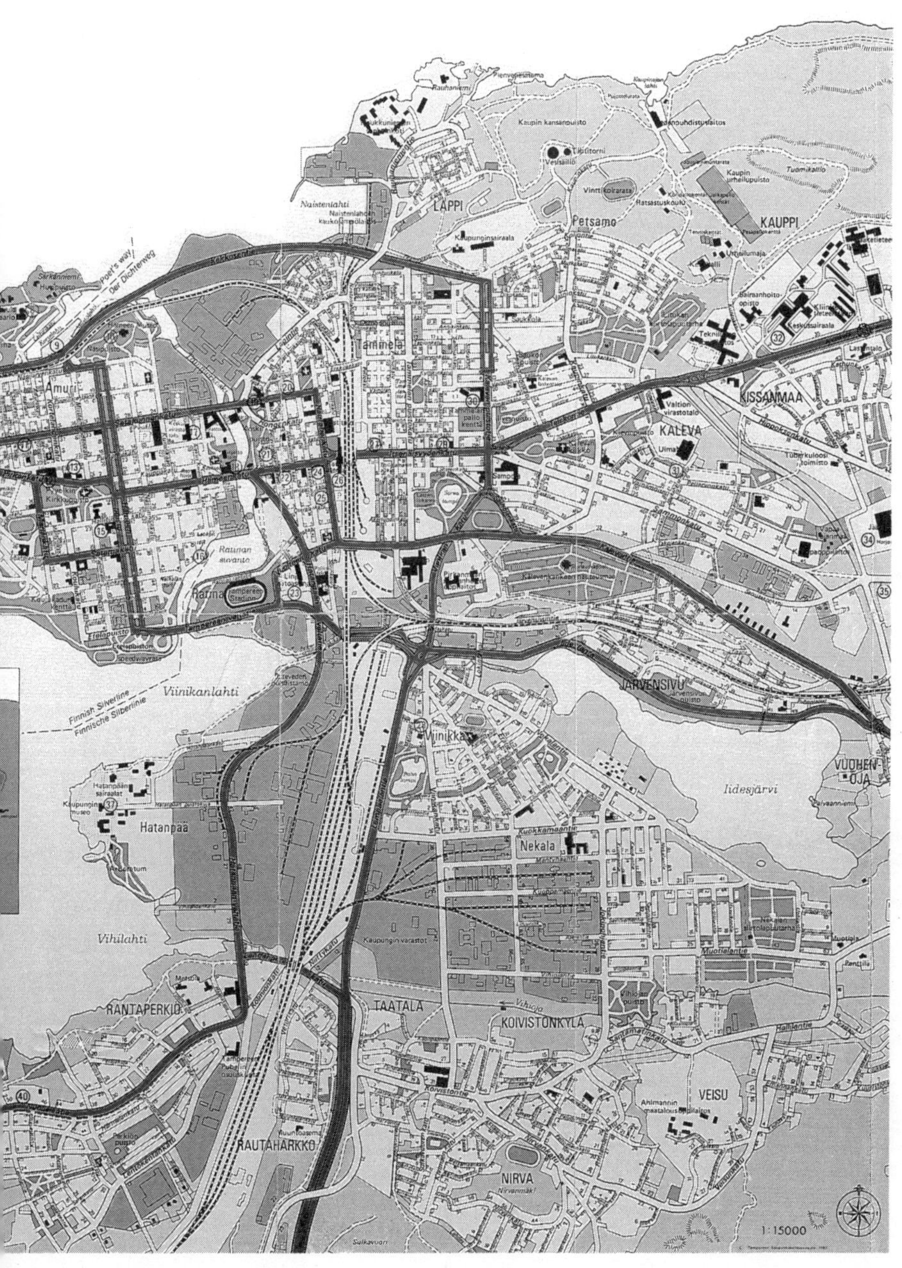

Rauhaniemi
Kaupin kansanpuisto
Vedenpuhdistuslaitos
Naistenlahti
Kaupin urheilupuisto
Tuomikallio
Tähtitorni
Vesisäiliö
Vintti koirarata
Ratsastuskoulu
LAPPI
Petsamo
KAUPPI
Kaupunginsairaala
Sairaanhoito-opisto
Keskussairaala
Teknillinen
Amuri
Tammela
KISSANMAA
Valtion virastotalo
KALEVA
Tuberkuloosi-toimisto
Uimala
Raunan suvanto
Kalevankankaan hautausmaa
Rauna
Tampereen Stadion
Finnish Silverline
Finnische Silberlinie
Viinikanlahti
JÄRVENSIVU
Järvensivun puisto
VUOHEN-OJA
Viinikka
Iidesjärvi
Hatanpään sairaalat
Kaupungin museo
Hatanpää
Kuokkamaantie
Nekala
Vihilahti
Kaupungin varastot
Muotialantie
RANTAPERKIÖ
TAATALA
KOIVISTONKYLÄ
VEISU
Ahlmannin maatalous-oppilaitos
Perkiön puisto
RAUTAHARKKO
NIRVA
Nirvanmäki
1 : 15000

An even greater service to gallery-goers in Finland is provided by the enterprising selection of international artists, dominated by Henry Moore's *Reclining Mother and Child* (1960–1), ideally placed to face the main door. Of its 2500 pieces, the Sara Hildén Art Museum can show only 10% at any one time, but you might well be lucky enough to see *Cogitation 1* (wood, 1964) by Tomonori Toyofuku (b. Kurume-shi, Japan, 1925), de Chirico's oil *Troubadour* (1940), and two brilliant oils by the underrated Belgian Paul Delvaux: *Summer* (1938) and the uncatalogued *Natural History Museum* (1942–3), its outer images three skeletons in a disturbing interior. There is the exhilarating shock of a Giacometti *Woman on a Chariot* (1943) seen against a lake landscape; and a *trompe l'oeil Portal* (1972) by the American Howard Kanovitz. An excellent optical-art gallery confronts the Finn Eino Ruutsalo with the Hungarian Nicolas Schöffer, the Argentinian Julio Le Parc, and the Italian Getulio Alviani. Add to these highlights masterpieces by Hans Bellmer, Hans Hartung, Paul Klee, Luciano Minguzzi, Picasso, George Segal, Tanguy, Vasarely, Wols and Zao Wou-Ki, in surroundings where every work of art can breathe in clear air and wide spaces, and you will realise why the Hildén Gallery has become a major element in the Finnish cultural scene.

Other major art museums are the Tampere Art Museum, originally a grain store designed by C.L. Engel (1838) at Puutarhakatu 34 (near Amuri Museum), and the Museum of Modern Art, originally a villa designed by Veikko Kallio (1928), modernised in 1966 by Reijo Ojanen, and situated roughly halfway between the old observation tower by Vilho Kolho (1929) built on the site of an 1888 tower made of wood, and Pyynikki Open-Air Theatre. Tampere Art Museum is open from 11 to 7, its conversion from granary to museum having been carried out in 1931 to designs by Hilja Gestrin. Changing exhibitions are held here: during my visit they celebrated the Moomin world created by Tove Jansson, and 'Finnish Art from 1800 to 1940', including works from Pyynikinlinna, the Ateneum in Helsinki, the Finnish Art Academy, and the Emil Aaltonen Collection. In chronological order, the most eye-catching *opere* included *Travellers by the Evening Fire in the Moonlight* (1817) by Alexander Lauréus; the *Kalevala* scene *Ilmarinen and Ukko* (1867) by R.W. Ekman; atmospheric landscapes by Hjalmar Munsterhjelm such as *Nightfishing by Torch* (1866) and *Autumn Evening* (1876); Turku archipelago landscapes by Fanny Churberg; the steady gaze of a *Young Woman* by Maria Wiik; the Parisian handling of cobbles and trees in *Lapland Street, Helsinki* (1882) by Aukusti Uotila; a sensitive *Italian Boy* (1880s) and contrasting *Little Girl Playing in the Sand* (1942) by Helene Schjerfbeck; *During the Directoire* (1881) and the *Portrait of Mrs Janckes* (1886) by Albert Edelfelt; Pekka Halonen's *Sunny Winter Landscape* (1911; it sounds more glittering in Finnish: 'Aurinkoinen talvimaisema') and his exact contemporary Gallen-Kallela's *Wilderness* (1914); Enckell's *Bird-hunters* (1919) and Simberg's *Red-paint Artists* (1911) together here as in S. John's Cathedral: a *Self-portrait*, introverted, staring at a mirror in anguish, by Einar Ilmoni (1880–1946), who lived in Kangasala, east of Tampere; a fine, vivaciously rhythmic *Studio Interior* by Alvar Cawén; the sombre melancholy of *At the Mirror* (1920) by William Lönnberg; an evocative *Work Party Dance, Teisko* (1920) by Kalle Löytänä; a de Hooch-style *Backyard, Porvoo* (1924) by Ragnar Ekelund; and two fine works by Reino Viirila: *Pispala* (1947), a Tampere view dominated by the old school with bright roofs and houses, like Patrick McElheron's County Wicklow scenes, and a serious, withdrawn *Self-Portrait* (1959), proving yet again that Finnish artists are never more at home than when analysing their own loneliness in the mirror.

Tampere's Museum of Modern Art is housed in a magnificent villa constructed for the pharmacist Oskar Severin Haapanen, and it is a tribute to the city of Tampere, its planners, and its 170,000 inhabitants, that it can mount exhibitions in two modern art galleries the year round. 'Temptations of Summer' ran the title of the temporary exhibition on Palomäentie, but you might look around you at the Italianate building and elaborate interiors as published in the Museum's notable illustrated history: *Tampereen Nykytaiteen Museo: 20 Years* (1986), since nothing could be farther removed from the purpose-built functionalism of the Sara Hildén Gallery than this solid bourgeois property for the well-heeled apothecary Haapanen and his wife Ingrid. Drawings by Edvard Munch in 1966, Sidney Nolan in 1971, Cuban artists in 1976, Salvador Dali and Günter Grass in 1981, Picasso and Reidar Särestöniemi in 1982: these are just a few of the hundreds of special exhibitions which have graced, bizarrely perhaps, these stout upper-middle-class walls, Seven hundred and more paintings and graphics in the museum's stock can be seen only selectively or by appointment. Of Finnish artists, I especially enjoyed works by Eino Ahonen, Simo Hannula, Mauno Hartman, Kimmo Kaivanto, Harry Kivijärvi, the brilliant op art six-stringed musical sculpture by Antti Maasalo, Otto Mäkilä, and Heikka Varja. Non-Finns who impressed here were the Scots Alan Cowie and Andy Dewar, the Frenchman Johnny Friedlaender, Ben Nicholson and Sidney Nolan, though the two Picassos are unremarkable.

Downhill, on the way to Pyynikintori, you can admire the new Conservatoire (unfortunately closed for the summer while I was there), with a splendid exterior credited to the City of Tampere Architect's Office, who completed it in 1975. Walking eastward along Pirkankatu you come to the Uimahallinmaja Tourist Hotel, the Hiekka Art Gallery, and on Pyynikki Church Park the Church of Alexander II, Tsar of Russia from 1855 to 1881. Not, as you might think from its name, an Orthodox Church, it was designed by Theodor Decker in 1880–1 as a Lutheran place of worship to celebrate twenty-five years of rule by the Tsar who won the hearts of many by his pro-Finnish stance. Red-brick neo-Gothic is no longer fashionable, and the interior was largely renewed to plans by Bertel Strömmer in the 1930s. But the noble pile has its own integrity, if one ignores the dreadful circular fountain with prancing infants mistakenly illuminated at night, a long way (mercifully) from the west door.

I stayed one night at the Hotel Rosendahl, in Pyynikki, where the people of Tampere come to dance the night away, and my room no. 472 had two distinct views: all that is necessary for 'the act of creation' as conceived by Arthur Koestler. Far off, above the gently waving treetops, gleamed the blue waters of Holy Lake, long and narrow like a stranded dolphin gasping for air. Close at hand, immediately below my window-ledge, stood a basketball net trawling for fish or ball in the late evening twilight. Two cars were parked in front of it, and two behind, as in the walk-through basketball game postulated by Hirohide Ogawa in *Enlightenment through the Art of Basketball*. Who is to say what is attack, and what defence? Why is a ball necessary, as long as we have an empty net?

Pyynikki is best known for the first-ever open-air revolving auditorium, based on a locomotive turntable, to a concept by Professor Olavi Veistäjä, inaugurated in summer 1959. The most popular production was a dramatisation of Väinö Linna's *The Unknown Soldier*, witnessed by nearly 350,000 spectators at 372 performances from 1961 to 1969. The theatre seats eight hundred and is invariably sold out, even on wet evenings, so make sure you book as far ahead as possible. A stage set is mounted for the whole season, from mid-June to mid-August, around the whole circumference of the revolving auditorium, so that the scene never actually changes: it is the viewpoint of the revolving audience that changes. Clearly, outdoor plays respond best to the combination of pools, rocks, grass, and wooden buildings that make up the natural wooded, lakeside setting of Pyynikki: Aleksis Kivi's *Seven Brothers* and Shakespeare's *Kesäyön Unelma*, or *A Midsummer Night's Dream*. In 1985 the summer play was Shakespeare's *Kuninka Äkäpussi Kesytetään*, or *The Taming of the Shrew*, but I had been forewarned that the 1986 Finnish-language production would be Ivan Sergeyevich Turgenev's *A Month in the Country*, so I made sure I was familiar with the lines beforehand, in English, so that I could savour the nostalgic satire together with the predominantly Finnish audience. It started at seven (3.30 at weekends) the leading characters arriving on horseback and in horse-drawn carriages to the delight of a full auditorium. We might have danced back in Tsarist time to summers lost a hundred years ago and more, with charming costumes and props reminding us that Finland too was Russian property then. The Polish director, Adam Hanuszkiewicz, had exploited every vista, every tree, and all the benign acoustics of this heavenly glade to produce an unforgettable performance.

Tampere. Pyynikki. Open-air Theatre

Next morning, after a sumptuous buffet breakfast at the Hotel Rosendahl, amid a hundred *Guten Tag*s of West German tourists, I headed for the nearby Pyynikinlinna, Mariankatu 40: the former mansion of Emil Aaltonen (1869–1949), an art collector whose home has been transformed into a venue for temporary exhibitions since 1984, open 11–6; 12–5 on Sundays in winter and 11–6 daily except Mondays from late May to late August. A disappointing show of *Finnish Women Painters* offered by way of real quality only works by Tuula Lehtinen, but a display describing *Women's Careers in Finland* gave an absorbing insight into the treatment of women. They were admitted into Finnish universities as early as 1901, and won the vote in 1906 (second in time to the women of New Zealand). The proportion of female

133

Members of Parliament, consistently around 15%, still exceeds the figure anywhere else in the world except possibly Cuba, and 90% of all Finnish pharmacists are women, 85% of bank staffs, and over 80% of dentists.

The rest of the day I devoted to the great churches of Tampere, from the glories of Messukylä (1434) to the 'Old Church' of 1824, Finlayson's factory church (1879), the loveliest Orthodox Church (1899) in the Nordic countries, the superb Cathedral (1902–7) which Siegfried Giedion has described as one of the most notable church creations anywhere in the world, then culminating in the magnificent new Kaleva Church (1966) and (at the other extreme) the disarming intimacy of the family-scale Hervanta Church (1979).

More than eighty per cent of Tampere's residents belong to the ten Finnish-speaking parishes, and one Swedish-speaking parish. The village of Messukylä, on the main road to Kangasala, has now become a suburb of Tampere, but during the Middle Ages the people met here on market days and attended mass ('messu' means both 'mass' and 'fair' in Finnish, 'kylä' denoting 'village') with travelling Catholic monks. The date 1434 was found on a plank of the Old Church, making it the oldest surviving building in Tampere: the vestry from that period adjoined the wooden church as was invariable practice during the Finnish Middle Ages, the nave aligned east-west, main door at the west, and an armoury in the form of a vestibule opposite the vestry. A stone church replaced most of the old wooden church in the early 16th century, including a new end wall and vault for the vestry. Messukylä church was repaired in 1636, decorated walls of that period having been uncovered in 1959. The pulpit dates to the 1660s, but the church as we see it today was remodelled and raised to a new height in 1796–7, when the armoury was altered and a new vestibule of vertical logs built at the west. A barrel vault replaced the old flat ceiling, and the pine pews and galleries took their present form, and the windows changed, except for the west window on the north wall, which retains its original 'Vaasa-style' shape characteristic of the 16th century. You may recall seeing the mediaeval wooden Virgin from Messukylä in Helsinki's National Museum, but the other carvings of the early 15th century remain *in situ*. The largest, in oak, represents the church's patron saint, Michael. The crowned figure is probably S. Olaf, of Norway, and the birch figure depicts S. John. You expect to see a separate belfry, as in most Finnish churches of the period, but in fact the belfry of 1795 was demolished in 1879, when the mediaeval church was deemed unsuitable for divine service and abandoned, being used for some time until its recent restoration as a granary. Its replacement, not far away, is Theodor Höijer's undistinguished neo-Gothic red-brick church built quickly to accommodate those who no longer felt it safe to worship in a tumbledown old church. Repaired to celebrate its centenary in 1979, the 'new' church removed acoustic boards placed there in the 1950s and the roof was restored to its original pastel blue.

The first church in Tampere city proper, also originally wooden, is in fact still made of wood. The 'Old Church', located on the former market square, now called Central Square (Keskustori) is the finest creation in Finland of the Italian architect Carlo Francesco Bassi (1772–1804), who emigrated to Sweden when young and became head of the Finnish State Building Commission, being succeeded in 1824 by the more celebrated German, Karl Ludwig (familiar in the Swedish form of Carl Ludvig) Engel. One could easily sacrifice the altarpiece, R.W. Ekman's sentimental *Christ in Gethsemane*, reminiscent of Murillo's quicker pieties, but the church itself, suffused with cream and white lights, has undeniable period charm. I particularly enjoyed the hemispherical altar rail, like the balustrade which Don Giovanni vaults to escape his pursuers, presaging that later descent at the invitation of the Commendatore.

While in Keskustori, admire the Town Hall on the west side (Georg Schreck, 1888–90) and the apartment block with shops next to it at Hämeenkatu 17 called 'Commerce House', by Andersin, Jung and Bomansson (1899). On the east side stands the harmonious neo-classical Tampere Theatre designed by K.S. Kallio (1913), with a main playhouse for 526 spectators and a smaller one for 131. Other important buildings on Keskustori include the former Central Public Library (1925) by Jussi and Toivo Paatela, with a monument before it depicting the national novelist Aleksis Kivi by Wäinö Aaltonen; the former office building of Tampere Paper Mill (1843); the Sumelius Building at Keskustori 1 (Grahn, Hedman and Wasastjerna, 1901); and the former Palander House at Keskustori 7 (Federley, 1900–5).

Finlayson's Factory Church was created by the Tampere architect Frans Ludvig Calonius in 1879 in the neo-Gothic red-brick style calculated to fit decently into a manufacturing environment, without a spire. Finlayson, a Quaker, decreed that no collection should be taken; instead, the factory paid fees to both preacher and organist. At first the church had no benches accommodating over 700 worshippers; it now seats 325, and is open from 3.30 to 5.30 between May and August. It is situated just south of the Häme Museum and Mältinranta Arts Centre, at Puuvillatehtaankatu 2. South again, at Satakunnankatu 16, stands the intriguing grey stone fire station (1908) designed by Wivi Lönn, the first woman professor of architecture in Finland.

The Orthodox Church (open 10–3 Mondays to Fridays, May-August), is situated between the railway line and the central bus station. It dates from 1896–8, and was consecrated and dedicated to S. Alexander Nevsky in 1899. Designed by Engineer Col. Y.U. Yassikov, the church was used by the

Russian garrison at Tampere as well as by local Orthodox believers. Today the congregation has 2200 members, 900 of them in Tampere district, and the rest scattered from the Gulf of Bothnia to Lake Päijänne. The design stems from 17th-century church architecture of the Muscovite tradition, and I recalled with a shock the almost identical cupolas of Kostroma's Church of the Resurrection-on-the-Debre of 1652. This pleasurable surprise, in a Lutheran land, led to a rueful check on the map. I was wrong again: Helsinki is, I had to remind myself for the twentieth time, only 443 km from Leningrad, but fully 900 km from Rovaniemi, so the invading Russian armies had so short a distance to travel (and such hugely superior forces) that the stalemate of the Winter War seems even now, with hindsight, to have been quite miraculous. S. Alexander Nevsky suffered terrible damage during the Civil War of 1918. After World War II many immigrants from lost Karelia came to Tampere and Pirkanmaa, the Orthodox Parish being founded in 1950 to cater for their spiritual needs, The church was restored in 1958–61, and reconsecrated, this time also to S. Nicholas. The highest of the seven cupolas symbolises Jesus as head of the church, the four smaller surrounding ones represent the apostles, and two others (above apse and belfry) together are taken to denote the seven sacraments. The iconostasis came from St. Petersburg. After the former Finnish Orthodox church of Valamo, on Lake Ladoga, was lost to the Soviet Union, some of Valamo's belongings came to Tampere, among them some of the icons, the brass church standards, the Gospels, and the monstrance.

While staying at the Grand Hotel Tammer, I overlooked the rapids stream and an ornamental fountain. Walking away from the rapids along Satakunnankatu, I would find at the corner of Rautatienkatu (literally 'Strada della Ferrovia') the park designed by Lars Sonck as a setting for his great Cathedral, built between 1902 and 1907. Art Nouveau at its zenith, S. John's Evangelical Church was created with a competition entry called 'Aeternitas', and became a Cathedral when the bishopric transferred from Porvoo in 1923.

The glory and the passion of S. John's cannot be appreciated out of their political context. The February Manifesto of 1899 had expanded Tsarist imperialism to spread Finnish legislation beneath the aegis of the Russian Government, virtually ending Finnish autonomy. Unconstitutional conscription was forced on Finns in 1901, and use of the Russian language was illegally extended to the upper reaches of Government, at the same time that Russian-language teaching increased in Finnish secondary schools. It was only in 1905, when the Tsarist Government had suffered a revolution caused largely by the Russo-Japanese War, that the illegal measures of the previous six years were repealed.

So the years of constructing S. John's in Tampere were years of repression and nationalistic fervour. A new Lutheran church would express Finnish religious aspirations, and the adoption of Fenno-Swedish architectural models would enhance patriotic emotions. Every detail of the Cathedral (as it now is) makes a dignified yet passionate statement about the honour of Man and the mercy of God. The vibrant use of a limited palette (white, brown lilac) adds to the shimmer and sheen of the presence of the Holy Spirit – glimpsed in Hugo Simberg's magnificent stained glass in the south gallery. You might think that the illuminated pulpit is the focus of the Cathedral, for it is so adroitly placed beside the broad altar in a broad church that it can be seen from almost every point. You might think that Magnus Enckell's beautiful *Resurrection* is the focus of the Cathedral, emphasising in its ethereal gauzy whites the victory of life over death, of hope over dread. But in fact there is no centre – not even the mysterious serpent encircled by angels' wings (*secco* and *fresco*) in the middle of the cupola. Each single element hovers towards its objective, and reaches it so that we are unconscious of any striving: only of the attainment. Paula Kivinen, authoress of the standard work on Tampere's art nouveau, has published a fine monograph on the Cathedral: *Tampereen Tuomio-Kirkko* (Söderström, Porvoo, 1961) but since it has appeared so far only in Finnish, I shall try to indicate some of the outstanding features of Lars Sonck's masterpiece, comparable in its success with the Florentine S. Lorenzo of Brunelleschi.

Magnus Enckell (1870–1925) was responsible for the choir window and the altarpiece, ready just before consecration in 1907. His fresco *Resurrection*, in muted flesh-colours, creams and shades of white, witnesses the rising from the dead of mankind, some naked and some still shrouded. The landscape could be a broad Finnish lakeland winterscape, but there are no trees: indeed no sign of nature risen, but only of mankind, emerging dazed from the left and entering their new lives towards the right. The faces of men, women and children are all recognisably Finnish.

Hugo Simberg (1873–1917) created the rest of the paintings and stained-glass windows. On entering, you will probably be struck first by the originality of the great fresco around the gallery, *Boys Bearing the Garland of Life*, showing the disciples as youths carrying a long rosebush, with its inevitable thorns, leading towards the two edges of the gallery, facing the Resurrection. Simberg noted on his sketches, that he painted the first boy on the northern gallery as S. Peter, 'a man with a great heart and imagination, solid as a rock'. Next, crouching to rescue a fallen rosebud, is the naked figure of S. John, in Simberg's words 'a dreamer, more poetical than practical, more of an idealist than a man of action.' His *Garden of Death*, based on a watercolour-gouache work painted in Paris in 1896, shows each human soul as a plant or flower to be tended after death before reaching the 'unknown land', again a reference to the Resurrection. I hope I am not alone in finding the crude workmanship of this fresco no obstacle to its religious function as a symbol: an icon. In the south gallery one can see a much more telling work, artistically speaking. Known as *The Wounded Angel*, the fresco, when originally produced as an oil at the Finnish Artists' Exhibition in 1903, was entitled by a long, enigmatic dash: no more. Two urchins in dark clothes bear a rough stretcher, on which sits a white angel, head bandaged and downcast. In the oil-painting (now in Helsinki's Ateneum), the other shore of the lake is flat and featureless. In the fresco for S. John's, the tell-tale turn-of-the-century factory chimneys show that the scene is the farther shore of Pyhäjärvi, roughly between Nikkilänniemi and Pereensaari.

Summer Sunday evenings at 7.30 resound to the majesty of S. John's 68-register organ, one of the great Romantic organs, and a recital given by the Italian Mario Duella also made use of the smaller organ, the concert including not only works by J.S., J.B., J.L. and C.P.E. Bach, but also a toccato by Alessandro Scarlatti, and a recently-discovered *Elevazione* and *Postcommunio* by the 18th-century composer Pellegrino Tomeoni, soon to be edited by Mario Duella himself. The acoustics for concerts, which can be attended by 2,300 participants, are predictably perfect.

Lars Sonck was assisted on details of the stonework, furniture and fittings by Walter Jung. Look for pine-motifs on the decoration of the granite pillars, Jung's brilliant vestry furniture, woodcarvings on the pew-ends and the outside door leading to the vestry. Examine Simberg's eloquent dove-motifs in carved stucco on the elegant pulpit. See how the rose-and-thorn motif of the long garland is picked out by *secco* roses and thorns curving eternally on the arches up to the roof. Ask to see the exquisite communion vessels by Ehrström. But again and again your eye will be lured back to the wondrous stained-glass windows, pinnacle of the art in modern times. 'The Cross and the Crown of Thorns' makes a circular softening above Enckell's rectangular alterpiece. In the organ gallery, another roundel depicts Sun, stars, and Earth. The south gallery, as we have seen, shows 'The Holy Spirit' in the traditional form of a white dove, within a starry brown foreground, within concentric starry circles of white, blue and mauve. The gentle arch of 'The Burning Bush' enshrines warm red flames within a lilac ground. The Greek letters *alpha* and *omega* denote the words of Jesus in the Bible: 'I am the beginning and the end'. In the north gallery stained-glass windows remind us of Christ and his followers by the emblem of a pelican feeding its young with its own blood; 'War and Peace' appear in the form of the white and red horses of the Book of Revelation (6: 2–4) and 'Death and Famine' in the form of horsemen of the Apocalypse, with the Latin letters INRI standing as always for 'Iesu Nazarenus Rex Iudaeorum'.

For antecedents to S. John's, one might do worse than visit the mediaeval stone churches of Ahvenanmaa (Åland) and for contemporary work of similar inspiration Lars Sonck's Tirkkonen Building in Tampere at Kauppakatu 6 (with Birger Federley, 1901, renovated and extended in 1985). The beautiful grey stone exterior extends most of the way up to the tower, which thins into a red spire, the total height being sixty-four metres.

Anywhere else on earth but in Venice or Florence, Rome or Istanbul, we might excusably leave such a building with a sense of frustration: what anti-climax can await us now? But not in Tampere. We are heading eastward, along Itsenäisyydenkatu to the fork where the choice is Teiskontie or Sammonkatu. Take the latter, with a sudden sharp left up to Liisanpuisto, in the shadow of Kaleva Church, erected in 1966 by Reima and Raili Pietilä. They have laconically stated their purpose as to make 'an experiment in a convex-concave morphology; a modern attempt to stay in the spirit and tradition of Gothic and Baroque, but without their stylistic limitations'. Unfamiliarity bred contempt among some observers twenty years ago, when Kaleva's parish church first emerged into the sky. Now, we can see more clearly: this is one of the boldest and most daring ecclesiastical conceptions ever brought to fruition. In its isolated position and its glorious internal amplitude it recalls Bramante's Tempio della Consolazione just outside Todi; in its breathtaking perfection of detail it recalls Borromini's intimate Baroque masterpiece Sant' Ivo alla Sapienza in Rome. But above all Kaleva

Tampere. Kaleva Church

is its own monument: it stands for the innovative capability of the human mind within the broad stream of tradition. The outer form, more clearly visible from above (like Nazca lines in Peru) resembles a fish, the early Christian communities' liturgical acrostic. The five letters of the Greek word for fish are also the initials of the Greek for 'Jesus Christ, God's Son and Saviour'. The walls are of slip-cast concrete; internally, the intention was to cover the concrete with acoustic tiles, but this view changed in the course of building, so that the interior walls remain untreated concrete, while the exterior walls have been faced in off-white tiles, providing a striking contrast to apartment blocks nearby. The untreated concrete showed traces of vertical movements from the slip mould, so fifty women were employed, sitting on scaffolding, to smooth the internal surface with leather, and so achieve a softer appearance. Acoustic surfaces were placed in the spaces between the parallel roof beams. Entirely contrasting effects are realised: from without, the walls are concave, inviting one within to safety like the Roman catacombs of the early Christians. From within, the window recesses are convex, with horizontal bars and ledges like the vision of Jacob's Ladder. An atmosphere of immense height – like Milan's Sant' Ambrogio – is created by a volume of 36,000 m^3 in the church proper. By night, you seem to breathe deeply, riskily, in the heart of a sleeping mountain. By day, you seem enclouded, wafting in aeons of space. It is an affirmation of Einstein's Age, echoing in its vertigo the high 16-metre 41-register organ locally made at Kangasala, the altar, Cross, and sculpture 'Broken Reed' – all by Reima Pietilä himself, and the dazzling white pulpit, seen from raked pine benches. The eighteen windows of thermoglass force their way ineluctably from floor to roof, without the interruption of a gallery, showing a park landscape. Take the door marked 'Kellotorniin', and a lift will carry you to the fourth floor, open white shutters allowing an awesome view of the great church below. Opening hours are 10–6 from May to August; otherwise 11–5.

In the sacristy I was invited to admire a lovely hanging rug, the traditional *ryijy* and the superb communion vessels designed by Reima Pietilä. Some of the church textiles were designed by Vuokko Nurmesniemi, but the textile 'The Gate of Life' is by Talvikki Forsström, white dominating both chapel and parish hall, on the third floor, where both children's day care and old people's facilities are located. The Kaleva parish, with over 40,000 inhabitants, has acquired for itself not only a glorious meeting-place, but a milestone in the evolution of Christian architecture.

Kaleva stands apart from its parishioners like a priest isolated from his congregation. Thirteen years later the Pietiläs brought to completion the very opposite: a church so intimately connected with its parishioners that it seems that, from the 'living-room' scale of its various parts, one is actually still at home. Southeastward from Tampere city centre, Hervanta is a new town in forest surroundings, with an indoor ice-rink and air-raid shelter, indoor swimming-pool and, beside the lake called Ahvenisjärvi, a breathtakingly beautiful leisure and congregational centre (1978–9), close to a shopping centre also designed by Raili and Reima Pietilä. The church remains open from 10–6 (May to August) or 11–1 (September to April) and must not be seen in isolation from its friendly red-brick surroundings. A narrow gate leads into an open semi-circular atrium where summer services can be held, below an openwork red-brick bell tower surmounted by a simple cross. The scale is dictated by the fact that Hervanta was created in the 1980s as an overflow town for overcrowded Tampere to take 40,000 inhabitants; in the event, the population has so far not exceeded 30,000, but it is very young in average age (a third of the population is below the age of confirmation), so that the apartment-blocks have play areas and safe walkways for young mothers with babies in prams and push-chairs. An all-weather building was sought, modestly low with only two storeys, to combine worship with leisure activities, and a shopping centre separate but very close.

The solution is unified, brilliantly simple, and aesthetically so pleasing that it might serve as a model for most planners. The congregational centre is about 3000 m^2, the leisure complex about 5,600 m^2, and the detached shopping area 9000 m^2. Brick in various shades of red has been laid horizontally in the church-leisure complex, and vertically as tiles in the shopping centre. Outdoor metal surfaces are painted blue and red, enlivening an already stimulating environment.

Hervanta Church is low-ceilinged and broad, with warm, soft lighting, a beautiful cross behind the altar making its own quiet brick effect. The windows of the long low building give on to the lake and park, and the playful turret and of the leisure centre, the 'mediaeval city wall' encircling the whole, and the factory-brick together produce a magical effect of a mediaeval Tampere that never was, brand-new like a fairy-tale just published. The sliding partitions between church and halls are of green wood, mimicking the forest all around. I felt as comfortable and safe as a baby in the womb. Since there is a growth away from the church towards secular activities such as arts and sports, the leisure centre provides a vast range of daytime, evening, and weekend hobbies at very low cost. The sports room can be hired for about $1 equivalent; experts from Häme-Satakunta Handicraft Association teach pottery, weaving, knitting and sewing for $2 an hour plus the cost of materials; for the same price one can use the whole billiards room, one of the tables, from St. Petersburg, being more than a century old. There's a carpentry room, a photography darkroom, gymnastics room, ballet hall, and graphic arts studio.

The shopping centre takes us back to covered eastern bazaars, like

Damascus or Baghdad, but with indigenous characteristics such as warmth, neatness, and style. From the mezzanine, I looked down on both sides of the shopping plaza: colourful awnings, little boutiques, and varied shops mingling with green gardens cooled by a fountain and basin, and with an aviary. But Hervanta is growing, organically, like plants in a flourishing garden. The future elsewhere in the world may not become anything like this, but how wonderful if it could!

North of Hervanta, near the lake called Kaukajärvi, the Kaukajärvi estate (1965) was built to house about 8,000 within easy reach of the city centre but still in semi-rural lakeside surroundings. The land formerly belonged to Haihara Manor House (1878) which has been preserved as an open-air museum, with a farmyard implements museum like that at Ruovesi, a windmill from Pälkäne (to the east), an old wagon-shed from Finlayson's

Tampere. Haihara Manor, with guide interpreter Anja Saaristo

142

factory, and a small cottage where the national poet J.L. Runeberg spent the summer of 1834, as a guest of the Tampere family Lundahl. You can reach Haihara by blue city bus no. 24 to Kaukajärvi terminus. The Doll Museum and Costume Museum remain open from 12 to 6 between May and October; otherwise from 12–4, every day but Fridays. The Doll Museum, founded in 1966 by the cat-lover Gunvor Ekroos, comprises more than 2400 dolls, including a Peruvian rag doll from the 12th century and superb specimens from the 20th century. Mrs Ekroos' Costume Museum, founded in 1974, offers changing exhibitions of clothes set against period furniture and *objets d'art*. And between June and August do not miss the handicrafts show from 12–7. Outstanding paintings include Berndt Lindholm's *Sea Landscape* (1880) and Elin Danielson-Gambogi's *Forest Landscape* (1890).

Three other museums should be seen if you have the chance. If you stay at the Härmälä camping site on the south shore of Pyhäjärvi (open June-August), your way into the city centre passes Hatanpää peninsula, with its heavenly rose garden on the lakeside, its arboretum, and the Tampere City Museum in Hatanpää Manor House. Open 12–6 Tuesday-Sunday, the Museum shows the evolution of Tampere in interiors ranging from Neo-classical to Functionalist. Since captions are exclusively in Finnish, it is worth noting that the present building, by no means the first on the site, was built in 1883–5 to designs by Odert Sebastian Gripenberg for the Idman family who owned the property and the whole estate from 1825 to 1913, when Tampere City acquired the entire property, renovating the manor house as a hospital. The byre and villa in the grounds are still used by the hospital. The upper floor of the Hatanpää Manor House is devoted to the early history of the city, its industrial development, paintings, plans and models of old Tampere. See the chaotic, semi-feudal town plan of 1822 Tampere drawn by J.G. Wallenius, then the neat restructuring into a grid pattern by Engel in 1830, the slow change to 1868 and the speeding up of the process in the plan of 1889. The ground floor has a corner room furnished in a style typical of a 19th-century Finnish manor house. The basement shows crafts, local industry, sport, medicine, the fire brigade, communications, the workers' movement, the Civil War of 1918, city administration, and theatre life. My most vivid memories of the City Museum are the ornate two-storey entrance hall, repainted in its original colours in 1970, and two paintings by a Finnish painter I had come to love: Elin Danielson-Gambogi (1861–1919). *In the Lamplight* and the *Potato Harvest* (1893) show her at her delicate best. If you find the flamboyance of Hatanpää Manor overpowering, try a walk through the arboretum to the lakeside, rose gardens bathed in sunlight, breeze wafting into your face from Pyhäjärvi's warm waters.

Häme Museum provides a fascinating comparison, in an equally aristocratic edifice, called Näsilinna, near Näsijärvi, built in 1893–9 for the von Nottbeck family (of Germanic origin, from Russia) by K.A. Wrede. Brought by Tampere City in 1905, it opened as a regional museum in 1908, and can currently be viewed daily except Mondays from 12–6. The first floor has a library divided into two rooms furnished in renaissance style (1550–1660, in Finnish terms), baroque (1660-1720), and an original salon, 1720–70, in rococo style. Room 13 is a drawing-room for special displays, while Room 14 is a bedroom rebuilt from Viljakkala. Rooms 15–16 contain ecclesiastical objects, in the old dining-room. The hall is original, except for an organ from Kuorevesi (1854). Upstairs you can find a farm cabin rebuilt from Kylmäkoski (not far from Toijala) and early sculptures: a 14th-century Virgin and Child, and a 15th-century Bishop Henry. Näsilinna proves as unsatisfactory a museum building as Sara Hildén's is excellent, the latter being purpose-built.

The third museum which you might consider adding to your itinerary is the Technical Museum at Itsenäisyydenkatu 21, near Kaleva Church. Open from 12–6 daily except Mondays, it will interest all those keen on technology, from cars to planes, and textiles to telephones. For motoring enthusiasts, the Vehoniemi Car Museum will make a trip east to Kangasala mandatory. Opening hours here are 10–8 from mid-April to mid-August, then 12–6 until late September, and 12–8 at weekends only from October to mid-April.

We have already seen the Conservatoire in Pyynikki, but there is another Conservatoire which is even more interesting, because it was built as a home for the aged ('De Gamlas Hem') by Birger Federley in 1903, in the ample exuberance of Jugendstil. It can be found by asking for Pirkanmaan Musiikkiopisto, overlooking the southern park or Eteläpuisto, at Eteläpuisto 4. The surrounding streets are still cobbled, and the turn-of-the-century atmosphere has been sensitively retained by loving restoration. The roof has probably the largest single stained glass in the Nordic countries. A wooden balustrade whirls up from the latticed ground-floor door, and a painted sea-wave pattern adds life and movement to open arches. I was amused by cats painted on the staircase and the Jugend tables and chairs. The basement was converted from a laundry to a library in 1984.

The following morning, I opened my Tampere newspaper, *Aamulehti*, amid a chatter of blond Swedish families at the scatter of breakfast tables in the Grand Hotel Tammer, to find that the temperatures the day before had been 24°C in Agadir, Morocco; 25°C in Istanbul, and 26°C in Tampere. I read the scores again, and they were right. It was no fluke either: Tampere recorded a temperature higher than Agadir's again the day after. Though no architect, I had recognised by the shivers running down my spine that Tampere Lake City had become the architectural avant-garde city of the age, and I was anxious to improve my acquaintance with her latest marvels. First to the UKK Institute for Health (designed by Pekka Helin and Tuomo Siitonen and opened in 1984), then to the new Tampere Workers' Theatre (1985), lunch at the Hotel Ilves (1986), and in the afternoon to the Tampere Central Public Library (1986). The national anthem contains the lines 'Finland has always been poor and will always be poor', sounding oddly in the context of vigorous new multi-million Finnmark construction, but a comparison with Medicean Florence shows that artistic excellence need not rely on vast state subsidies if income is spent wisely, using the best materials and taking advantage of innovative planners, architects, artists and craftsmen. I quite seriously press the analogy. Let us start with the Urho Kaleva Kekkonen-Instituutti, overlooking Näsijärvi's blue waters, in a wooded park much enjoyed by ramblers and cyclists: the Kaupin kan-sanpuisto. The district, on the northeast boundary of Tampere City, lies close to the old residential area called Petsamo, mostly dating to the 1920s. Bus 8 comes to the door, and no. 3 has a stop ten minutes away. The UKK Institute, a gift from the Finnish people to their President on his 80th birthday, is devoted to research into preventative medicine, offering advice on healthy activity such as the correct amount of physical exercise for each individual, a balanced diet, and basic health care. The effects of the sauna, especially possible dangers to those suffering from cardio-vascular prob-lems, are studied together with such questions as the necessary amount of sleep, problems of the spine and back, and how to slim without ill-effects. Families can try testing their fitness on machines available for public use during working hours. A video presentation in Finnish, Swedish and English sets the scene, within the overall W.H.O. programme 'Health for All by the Year 2000', a world target terrifyingly ambitious. The building, benefitting from a policy of large windows and many of them, above as well as to the side, has reinforced concrete construction, the frame cast mainly *in situ*. The concrete elevations are faced in blue and white ceramic tiles and thin plastering.

Ten Finnish research workers and fifteen auxiliaries staff the Institute. The entrance lobby looks particularly attractive, with welcoming exhibition space. The ground floor has workshops, research sauna, keep-fit rooms, and changing-rooms. Exercise facilities are surrounded by a first-floor gallery with a research indoor running-track, with direct access from there to laboratories. Accommodation for up to twenty persons has been provided on the third floor. It cost 120 FM (US$23) to stay there in 1986. A separate unit within the complex comprises conference, training and restaurant facilities. Throughout, the atmosphere is one common in Finland: light, space, good taste, optimism. I appreciated the use of slender white columns throughout, and small circular white lights in the restaurant.

Much more exciting than Amsterdam's flawed new Muziektheater is the opulent new Tampere Workers' Theatre, Hämeenpuisto 30–32, designed by Marjatta and Martti Jaatinen and opened in 1985, with a reinforced concrete frame behind a façade chiefly of red brick laid *in situ*. The enterprise, initiated and financed by a foundation set up jointly by the State and Tampere City, cost 107 million FM. If the term 'workers' theatre' reminds you of the eastern bloc rather than of non-aligned Finland, the implication is intended, for as early as 1901 the Tampere Workers' Association was presenting its own dramatic productions in its assembly room, with its own theatre leased from the Workers' Association between 1905 and 1985. It was only in the 1920s that professional actors were engaged, though facilities proved decreasingly adequate as productions grew more sophisticated. The glorious new theatre, a blaze of windows along Hämeenpuisto Avenue, consists of three and four storeys, with a tower of 32 metres, roughly the height of a ten-storey apartment-block. The Jaatinens have created three definite units: stage performances; refreshment areas and administration; technical, staff and storage areas. Main doors allow access from Satamakatu and Hämeenpuisto to a computerized box office, while stage door and trade entrance are located on Papinkatu. Inside the theatre, 750 raked seats are on one floor, in a semi-circle; the first five of the seventeen rows (mounted on air cushions) can be moved to the stage or to another part of the auditorium. Additional seating capacity can bring the audience total up to 922. The colourful curtain, designed by Katariina Metsovaara (her name means 'Woodgrouse Hill') has been woven locally by Oy Finlayson Ab, and can be either raised or drawn to the side. I was kindly shown backstage by staff for whom the prestigious new theatre is a long-planned dream executed beyond their wildest expectations. Dressing-rooms for 45 actors, frequently for two or three each, resemble five-star hotel rooms. A rehearsal room, duplicating stage conditions, is separated by a sound-proof door so that two full-scale rehearsals can proceed simultaneously. The wardrobe department has areas for costume designers, dressmakers, leatherworkers, and shoemakers, with a costume store below it. Furniture and scenery stores are on the first floor. Other facilities include laundries, dyeing-room, silkscreen printing, hairdressing, costume repair room, producer's office, musical director's room, stagecraft office and a staff canteen roughly equidistant from all various functions. The props room contains areas for metalwork and carpentry, plastics workshop and electrician's workshop, with a workshop to create scale models of sets. Lorries transferring sets can be driven from Papinkatu right up to the stage. The stage, on the second floor, revolves on an air cushion and is twelve metres in diameter. Almost infinitely adjustable, the traditional proscenium stage can be lowered sixty cm to form a Greek theatre. If the first few rows of seats are moved to the sides a Shakespearean-style stage appears. For an arena-style theatre, seating is moved to the back of the stage.

As to the theatre's policy, it is now the only professional workers' theatre in Finland, and as such remains committed to the spirit of the labour movement and rejection of the star system. The former director Taisto-Bertil Orsmaa, who took over in 1986, required his productions to give rise to debate (presumably not like the debate which arose when an Oulu audience was pelted recently with eggs and excrement?) and to 'shake people out of their present state of mental passivity to experience life and ponder over things'. One is puzzled to work out how the current production of Lerner & Löwe's *My Fair Lady* or indeed a dramatisation of Tolstoy's *Anna Karenina* fit Orsmaa's purpose. In the Basement Theatre (TTT-Kellariteatteri), small productions take place, such as Dante's *Divine Comedy*, with the strikingly beautiful Soili Markkanen and the thoughtful Harri Rantanen. Other works in repertory during my stay in Tampere included Erkki Mäkinen's *Last Waltz in Viipuri*, and a farce by Dario Fo produced by Arturo Corso, performed in Finnish. I should dearly like to have seen the TTT's production of Aleksis Kivi's *Kullervo* (1922) and Brecht's *Resistible Rise of Arturo Ui* (1970). But whatever the play, any evening spent in this magnificent new Theatre must become an event.

Just next door to the Basement Theatre you can enjoy a marvellous Russian meal at the Restaurant Natalie (Hallituskatu 19): a special menu at 43 FM includes borshch (beetroot soup with sour cream), zrazy (stuffed escalope of veal), and coffee. The service charge is 14% on weekdays and 15% at weekends. Before or after lunch at Natalie's you might enjoy a visit to the Lenin Museum (at the same address, open 11–3 Tuesday-Saturday and 11–4 on Sundays). Reverent, hushed Soviet visitors tiptoed around the shrine-museum, respectful of the part that Tampere played in shielding Lenin during his escape from Russia. He met Stalin in Tampere in 1905, and used Finland as a place to meet and plot with revolutionaries both Finnish and Russian. On 6 December 1917, Finnish Independence from Russia was recognised on behalf of the Bolshevik Government by Lenin whose plan, obviously, was to promote the cause of a Marxist Finland. The Lenin Museum in Tampere stands therefore as a footnote to a history of Finland that never was. Wallpaper and furniture, clocks and carpets: everything has dated. The Tampere that Lenin knew is fixed here like a fly in amber.

Lunch at Hotel Ilves seems even more memorable in retrospect because the hotel had only just opened, claiming to be 'Scandinavia's most glamorous hotel', the main architect being Maunu Kitunen. Arnold Lerber designed the 'After Eight' night-club, Gestranius the 'Le Gourmet' restaurant, main lobby and ballroom, and Leif Frelander the informal café-restaurant and pub-style restaurant and terrace. Chef-de-cuisine Raimo Huhtamäki and elegant public relations manageress Inger Franzen entertained us to a gourmet experience, mingling nouvelle cuisine with Finnish flair and international ingredients. Le Gourmet might offer among its hors d'oeuvres raw salmon spiced with melissa and ruff roe on toast or paprika pudding, Roquefort sauce and pearl slices marinated in white wine; as a soup, clear perch with vegetable pearls and perch croquettes; among its fish dishes bream quenelles, birch-sap butter sauce and spinach mould; for the meat course, possibly Chateaubriand marinated in cognac, tarragon butter and potatoes duchesse; as dessert, either a chocolate basket and wild strawberry mousse, or homemade ice-cream on almond, flavoured with chocolate flakes, rum and candied ginger, with apricot sauce.

When the hotel opened, the presidential suite at Hotel Ilves cost about US$300 per night, eight standard suites $180, and 336 rooms (mostly double) ranging from 560 FM ($180) for a lower-situated single, to 580 FM ($110) for a higher-situated double. Forty-eight rooms are suitable for guests suffering from allergies and two are designed for handicapped guests. The hotel's position near the banks of the Tammer resembles that of the attractive Cumulus or the more traditional Grand Hotel Tammer. But Hotel Ilves is Finland's hotel of the future – even if a spruce London double-decker omnibus marked 'Southall Garage' adds a homely touch of the past, when it takes visitors to Särkänniemi at noon, 2 and 4 every day, returning at 3, 5, 6 and 7.

The afternoon was to be devoted to examining a wood grouse ruffling her feathers. Tampere's old central public library, a conventional building on four floors built in 1925, is being converted into a cultural centre. A former paper-making factory building, next to a tall chimney, has been adapted as a newspaper and magazine reading-room. Dozens of Finnish journals are supplemented by a wide range of foreign subscriptions: two copies of *The Guardian* are available, *Le Monde, Pravda,* and *The Times* of London. Storage facilities enable hard copies to be filed for one year after receipt: then they are converted to microfilm. The reading-room opens during the summer from 9–7 on weekdays and 9–3 on Saturdays; in the winter also on Sundays from 9–9. Tampere's new central library, possibly the most beautiful library ever created (with the Biblioteca Nazionale Marciana in Venice, the Biblioteca Malatestiana in Cesena, and the Benedictine Monastery Library in Admont, Austria), has been designed in the shape of a wood grouse. Yes, ruffling her feathers. The Leon Battista Alberti of our age, Pietilä has said, 'When it comes to nature, we Finns are linked to one another by a distinctive and deeply-felt consensus. "Finnish nature" is a concept that we all understand. We transform that feeling of ours into an element of design. Like a shaman? Is Finnish nature really a mere fiction, an oddity? No, nature

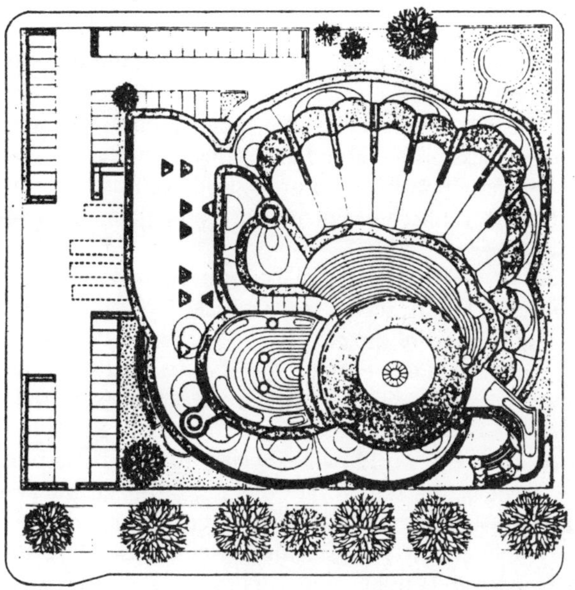

Tampere. Central Library Plan (1986) by Raili and Reima Pietilä (Courtesy of Raili and Reima Pietilä)

Tampere. Central Library

is more.' Pietilä affirms that modern buildings can be coherent entities associated with nature in the same way that musical compositions can be. As articulate in words as in design, Pietilä has said, 'I am against abstract perfection but I am for its concrete counterpart. I am against the kind of architecture that confines reality to consensus, because in so doing it makes nonsense of the whole of our existence. I am against encapsulation, quantification and restrictive mass production. I am against rootlessness and placelessness.' Again, 'Man cannot return to nature in Rousseau's sense, but if man so permits, nature can return to man. Architecture is one way in which this can be done.'

Completed in 1986 (apart from an integral Natural History Museum which opened later), the new library forms the pinnacle of Scandinavian secular style. It is located at the axis of the city, where Kirkkopuisto adjoins Hämeenpuisto (Church Park and Häme Park), fixing the city's future firmly in a cultural context. Stone, copper and glass comprise the leading materials, on three main floors, to a total budget of 70 million FM, of the 83 million allocated. This new wonder of the world, with its soft, rounded contours welcoming one to every facet of the sculptural building, forms an integral part of the park, like pecking sparrows at their own microcosmic level. All the building materials are deliberately Finnish, with basement cladding and steps of Viipuri granite, façades and curving eaves of copper, and windows of green pine. Pietilä notes: 'The window sections possess the roundness of a branch, thereby giving the impression that the external space continues into the large main hall. The interior space forms a winding and changing series of segmental vaults, thus conjuring up the image of wind-filled spinnaker sails. Seen directly from above, the plan is truly bird-shaped.'

The day the new library opened, eleven thousand residents joined, that is six per cent of the city's entire population, and they borrowed sixteen thousand books. Tampere also has thirteen branch libraries, six hospital libraries, and three mobiles. Of the hundred staff, ninety per cent are women and eighty work in the branches. About 50% of the inhabitants of Tampere belong to one library or more. The library's finance derives equally from city and state. Opening hours are 9–9 in winter and 9–7 from June to August on weekdays, with 9–3 opening on Saturdays throughout the year, and reference library winter Sunday opening from noon to 6. The forty parking spaces are divided equally between staff and readership. A café on the premises is leased out.

But bare facts and figures offer no inkling of the heady pleasure to be gained by walking up gently spiralling stairs, by reading below special non-glare lights on comfortable chairs, by glancing through random columns placed like freely-growing trees.

Reima and Raili Pietilä would stand with Leon Battista Alberti for Kaleva alone, but with the creation of the central community complex of Hervanta and the Central Public Library in Tampere they have presented Tampere, Finland, and the world with some of the most enthralling, exciting and beautiful buildings ever brought to fruition. Attractive designs have been carried out by the husband-and-wife Pietilä team at Dipoli congress and Students' Centre and the Institute of Technology Campus near Helsinki; at Tapiola; in Kuwait; a church at Lieksa, East Finland; an Old People's Home at Pori, West Finland, and in the 1980s also the Finnish Embassy in New Delhi.

Reima Pietilä was born in Turku in 1923; his wife Raili in Pieksämäki in 1926; their studio is in Helsinki, at whose Institute of Technology they both trained.

The floors and doors of their office are of untreated wood, as in old Finnish farmhouses for centuries. Reima champions regional architecture against the faceless internationalism rampant throughout the modernist movement. 'The classical way of thought is a duality, with order on the one hand, chaos on the other hand, and nothing in between. But in my view *everything* with human value lies in between. We are not aiming for perfect order; what we want to avoid is too much chaos. We want to expand the temperate zone of well-being, in architectrue as much as in any other field.' The visitor to Tampere's library, known affectionately as *Metso*, the wood-grouse, or capercaillie, feels just this sense of wellbeing in the highest possible degree.

The next phase of Tampere's architectural adventure will be a new Congress- and Concert-Hall, between Mallard Pond (Sorsa Lampi in Finnish) and Yliopistonkatu (University Street), just opposite the main University complex east of the railway track. The great hall will accommodate up to 2000 persons, the small hall about 500, and a rehearsal hall up to 300. The horizontal thrust of the façade is interrupted by the great hall's elegant polygon. Sakari Aartelo and Esa Piironen, the architects, have clearly chosen to take another leap forward from Alvar Aalto's Finlandia Hall concept for Helsinki, combining a congress hall with a concert hall in ambitious ambivalence, the raked auditoria providing a perfect sightline for everyone, with acoustics to match.

Nearby stands the University of Tampere, renamed in 1966 from the Faculty of Social Sciences, in Helsinki from 1949 and from 1960 in Tampere. Its four other faculties are Economics and Administration, Education, Humanities (especially strong in Finnish and foreign languages), and Medicine. Vocational sections teach Social Studies, Public Administration and Social Security. Some seventy professorships cater for 1000 students. Emblematic of the city's transition from industry to culture is the fact that the University Library is now housed in an old shoe factory. I also visited the modern Technical University (1965), where all instruction is in Finnish. Three thousand students attend courses in the four departments: Architecture, Civil, Electrical and Mechanical Engineering.

The Environs of Tampere

Reima Pietilä's confident association of Finnish art and architecture to nature led me along the motorway from Tampere northeast towards Jyväskylä. At Orivesi I turned south towards Längelmävesi, on whose shores stands the home and sculpture-park of Professor Aimo Tukiainen, with an open-air art exhibition from early June to mid-August, between 11 and 6. Buses and taxis are available from Orivesi rail and bus stations: the lakeside situation is superb, brilliant sunshine dappling the ground through a natural treescape. At any other time you can see Professor Tukiainen's property by appointment (1 January to 15 May, tel. 90–495818; elsewhen 935—54323). The organiser of Purnu's biennale is the Helsinki art-dealer Kalevi Heinänen, who also welcomes visitors to his Naive Artists' Foundation in Helsinki (3–6 every Thursday, tel. 90–6980636) and here in Purnu you can see selected naive artists, such as Juha Tammenpää of Vaasa and Olli-Pekka Riihikoski of Harjavalta. Probably Finland's best naive artist, however is Håkon Bromberg. The linear abstraction of Göran Augustson recalls Mondrian; Einari Levo's pop art resembles Roy Lichtenstein's; Kokoschka reincarnates as Teemu Saukkonen. But I found a number of artists with distinctive images: Arvo Siikamäki's 'Unknown Victim'; Lea Ignatius's cool landscape, and works by the questing spirits of Kain Tapper and Kimmo Kaivanto. Interplay between birdsong and gouache, pine-shade and bronze, squirrels and murals, makes these seven exhibition halls (and inevitable café) an unforgettable afternoon out. Twelve thousand visitors made their way to Purnu in its first year, and with the completion of the outdoor relief *Tree of Life* by Aimo Tukiainen in 1985, Purnu now stands fulfilled, from the dream he had when he bought the site as a summer cottage in 1962. On rainy days the halls are weatherproof; on hot summer afternoons a rowing boat lolls invitingly at its mooring beside the sandy beach. Herra Heinänen invited me to spend some time in his traditional wood smoke sauna down by the lake.

The sauna, of the 'smoke' or chimneyless variety, possesses a mystique for the Finns, as it does for Scandinavians generally, similar to the hygienic purity of the Japanese, for whom ritual bathing and cleanliness early became a religious requirement within the State system of Shinto. Babies first saw the light of day in the Finnish sauna, sick were tended there, and the sauna was also used for preparing malt and crushing flax. Like the Turkish bath, the sauna cleanses by perspiration, but whereas a Turkish bath produces damp air, the sauna produces dry air. Your modern Finnish hotel will have a

Lake at Purnu, near Orivesi

sparkling, hygienic new sauna, but the traditional kind is a simple one-room log cabin blackened with smoke, with a furnace covered by stones in one corner. Bathers sit on a wooden platform fitted with slats to allow the hot air to circulate. The stones become red hot, when water is cast on to the stones, sizzling and evaporating immediately, all moisture being absorbed by the wooden walls and platform. Steam creates an almost stifling dry heat, which made me gasp when I first enjoyed a sauna, but then clears the nose and throat, inducing a feeling of wellbeing that is indescribably close to the harmony of the spheres, to the serenity and vision achieved by deep meditation. Traditionally, one then beats the bodies of one's companions with leafy birch branches, then plunges into the nearby sea or lake (there is almost always a sea or lake nearby in Finland) or if that is frozen one can roll in the snow outside the sauna.

It is important to realise that sauna is by no means a quick bath, but a healing and refreshing treatment, reducing stress and altering one's attitude from one mode, such as the working day, to another, such as an evening with the family, or in my case winding-down from mental stimulation to sleep. After sauna, nothing could be more wonderful than lying on the shore of a lake, and gazing at the watery red rays of the setting sun. A warning: sauna is not for those with cardio-vascular weaknesses.

International languages: sauna, music, nature, painting, sculpture, and architecture can be understood by any visitor of sensibility; but Finland has its unique language and literature, repaying tenfold the study given to them. Listen to the sounds made by Arvo Turtiainen (1904–1980) in a poem on the 'Winter War' with the U.S.S.R. (1939–40), *Fifty Below Zero*.

Tammiöinä
purivat tähtien hampaat
rauskuen
pakkasen leipää

In those January nights
the teeth of the stars
gnawed
the bread of cold

Tammiöinä
purjehti kuu
kuin ruumisarkku
taivaanlaen siniseen helvettiin.

In those January nights
the moon glided
like a coffin
in the blue hell of the sky.

Mustat metsät
vavahtivat
ja revontulen patsaat
pysähtyivät.

The black forests
shivered
to a standstill, remote
the columns of the aurora borealis.

Välähti
pakkasen tikari
Kuoleman kädessä
tammiöinä.

The dagger of cold
flashed in the hands of death
in those January nights.

That traumatic year of 1939 saw the Nobel Prize for Literature awarded to a Finn, Frans Eemil Sillanpää, to whom the following homage was paid by Per Hallström of the Swedish Academy: 'None of us knows your Finnish language; we have been able to appreciate your works only in translations, but no doubt exists about your mastery as a writer. Simple, brief, objective, without the least affectation, your language flows with the clarity of a spring and reflects what your artist's eye has seized'.

Sillanpää, unlike the Norwegian novelist Knut Hamsun, has fallen out of favour in recent decades, but I was determined to follow the 'Sillanpää trail' from Tampere northwest to Hämeenkyrö, hoping to discover a key to the personality of this provincial peasant awarded the world's greatest literary prize. The way to Nokia leads past the intriguing Gadd Family Mausoleum, commemorating the family of Professor Pietari Adrian Gadd (1727–97), a botanist, chemist and local historian born across the road in Kaarila. The date on the picturesque weathervane is 1785. Nokia's wooden church, designed by Engel in 1837, stands far above the road on the left at the top of a hill, with a lake on the right. Shortly thereafter we drove through the wild scenery of Melo, with its hydro-electric power station on the river Nokianvirta, then over the beautiful bridge at Siuro, taking a minor road north to Jumesniemi. In the district of Laitila we headed for the birthplace of Sillanpää, called Myllykolu ('Mill Rapids') in the local dialect. Myllykolu opens from 1 June to 17 August between noon and 5 on Tuesdays to Saturdays and noon to 6 on Sundays. Two of his parents' three children died in infancy, so Frans Eemil grew up as the only child of peasants whose ancestors had once owned land but lost it when they fell into debt. Sillanpää's best fiction deals with the poverty of rural families, and their pride: *Hurskas kurjuus* (1919; translated by Alex Matson as 'Meek Heritage', 1938), and *Nuorena nukkunut* (1931; translated by Alex Matson at 'The Maid Silja', 1933). Compulsory education lay far in the future during his boyhood, so it was a matter of luck and determination that enabled him to progress from a village primary school to Hankijärvi grammar school, and then to Tampere (autumn 1896) at the age of eight, when he found accommodation in a poor carpenter's home with a crowd of other tenants; he had to supplement what his father could afford by earning for himself, and luckily a rich industrialist hired him as a private tutor for his own son until Sillanpää left to study at the Imperial Alexander University in Helsinki, though he never graduated. Through the son of the painter Eero Järnefelt, the young provincial student met at Tuusula, just outside Helsinki, not only Järnefelt, but the composer Sibelius, the painter Pekka Halonen, and other intellectual leaders, but mental instability showed itself early in agoraphobia and a sense of insecurity.

Myllykolu stands in wide fields. The old wooden house has three rooms: the central room displays photographs, autograph letters and copies of his books; another has a stove, two single beds and a spinning-wheel, cradle, and a Bible on a table. I sat on the wooden step, gazing out on the sunny fields. 'I wondered where you were', said Anja, using the same words that a young nurse had addressed gently to an old man at the psychiatric hospital near the Arboretum the day before. 'I wondered where you were, dreaming all alone out here.' Below the cabin, entirely hidden in a glade over a rivulet, a summer theatre lay abandoned. Several evening performances are given, usually adapting Sillanpää for the stage, in the three summer months, but silence lapped over the wooden benches now, a silence interrupted only by the flapping and calling of birds, and the low ripple of a stream wandering past our feet.

Near the hamlet of Heinijärvi, Sillanpää's parents had bought a little log cabin in 1905, and the young man returned to it at the age of 25, on Christmas Eve, 1913, staying there to affirm his solidarity with the peasant class he had temporarily – and in his view mistakenly – deserted. A few months later, he met a 17-year-old servant girl, daughter of a poor tenant farmer, and two years later married Sigrid, confirming his allegiance to the peasantry. A director of the Söderström publishing house at Porvoo took the trouble to penetrate the pseudonym 'E. Syväri' and Sillanpää, disciple of Hamsun and the great Russian novelists, found himself famous in autumn 1916 with the publication of his first novel *Elämä ja aurinko* ('Life and Sun'), celebrating not only the love of young people, but also the splendour of Finnish nature.

It is this happy period, and the black early years of World War I up to 1916, that Sillanpää spent at Töllinmäki ('Shanty Hill') now open at the same times as Myllykolu. His parents lived in the two front rooms: they built a third at the back as Frans Eemil's bedsit study. An ante-room, a hall and store, held logs and food, and kept out draughts from the main room, with its double bed and two windowlets. The little bed and desk and store in the writer's room are perhaps not as evocative of his precious, formative years here as are the books still on the shelves: Hamsun and Lagerlöf, Juhani Aho and Turgenev. A separate sauna can be found at the back of the cottage. After the Civil War between Reds and Whites ended with the victory of General Mannerheim and the Whites, Sillanpää entered a period of creative depression, leading to his gloomy but poetic masterpiece *Meek Heritage*, in which destiny deals capriciously with the life of an orphan boy whose very name changes symbolically with each change of task, felling trees to helping on a farm. Repulsive as a lad, he became an objectionable old man: Sillanpää asks us whether he was ever really treated like a human being once throughout his long and weary life.

Sillanpää's tales and sketches of life and people in Hämeenkyrö have bestowed a loving nostalgia for the small town among all Finnish readers. So do go to see his grave in the cemetery and the Hämeenkyrö Local History Museum (a former granary) opposite the church, open from 11 to 5 between 1 June and mid-August. But more than anything else bask in the atmosphere of hayfields and woods, the friendly welcome on village streets on the 5 km of country roads between Töllinmäki and Hämeenkyrö.

What happened to Sillanpää? By 1926 he had six children and found it increasingly difficult to pay bills, so took up Söderström's offer to edit a new journal in Porvoo. But after three years of desk life he found such routine intolerable and appealed to the rival firm of Otava for relief. Sillanpää consequently found himself again in Helsinki in 1930, and spent six years writing intensely and brilliantly, still on the Hämeenkyrö region and its characters. Overwork, alcoholic indulgence, and depression ended his creative life in 1963, and when his wife died in 1939, even a Nobel Prize could not rouse him from the depths. His family tended him after his release from psychiatric hospital until his death at 75 in 1964.

Sillanpää's Töllinmäki, near Hämeenkyrö

Sailing to Visavuori

I suppose there could be a more pleasant way of spending a day than cruising the lakes between Virrat and Tampere or Tampere and Hämeenlinna, but offhand I can't imagine how. At 9.45 a.m., after a leisurely buffet breakfast at the Cumulus Hotel (which boasts a complete leatherbound set of Strindberg's works on a shelf high between two lifts), I boarded at Laukontori the m/s *Silver Star* of the Finnish Silverline. I met the vivacious Virva Joensuu, accompanying a party of Germans from Tampere to Hämeenlinna, where she would meet and escort back a group of Americans to Tampere. The sun was already warming the deck as we berthed alongside the Hotel Rosendahl jetty at 10 a.m. before the leisurely 2½-hour cruise to Lempäälä. I chatted to a smiling Japanese born in Nara, the former Japanese capital from which I had set out to write my book *Japanese Capitals* the year before. Maeda Kazuo had spent the last 5½ years as an oil engineer at Ras Lanuf in Libya, where I had spent nearly nine years as a Librarian. Kazuo expressed astonished amusement at the news that Libya had stopped all teaching of English as an anti-American gesture. All textbooks, grammars, and manuals have to be translated into Arabic before they may be admitted into schools, colleges or universities, a system that can only damage further education for generations to come in Libya: a fanaticism reminiscent of China's Maoist 'Cultural Revolution', which became the opposite of cultural. Virva suggested that I had something to eat: she herself would take nothing more than a grapefruit in deference to her figure. She hinted at Tampere's alleged disadvantages for the younger generation, who wanted more of a London life, or say that of West Berlin. She taught me as much Finnish as she could compress into a couple of hours, while the lake landscapes, woods and summer cottages slid past the smooth, whooshing *Silver Star*. The longest Finnish palindrome she managed was *saippuakauppias*, 'soap-seller'. She explained the Finnish passion for dancing. Rather like the Irish 'Ballroom of Romance' immortalised by William Trevor, Finnish ballrooms and open-air dance floors provide the easiest method for conventional and diffident people to meet. The chances are that the husband and wife you meet in the train or at the theatre first got to know each other while dancing, and the romantic frisson attaching to these encounters still lures them back to the dance floor at every available opportunity. I mentioned that the band at the Rosendahl looked distinctly grizzled. Virva chuckled: yes, they play for the older generation, with tunes from the '30s to '50s.

The speed of the *Silver Star* created a fresh gust of wind in our faces as she made swift progress after the Sound of Sotkanvirta towards the historic estate of Laukko and the Iron Age cemeteries of Vesilahti. The mixed deciduous-coniferous woods on both shores offer a constantly-changing panorama, behind a myriad summer cottages, with motor-boats or rowingboats tied up to their private jetties. Flat as a sparkling canvas, the lake is veiled at distant edges in a drift of white mist that breathes and sighs, breathes, sighs, and breathes. The shores would be lost, if land indeed exists there, but the lake is so immortally long that men have to rev up motorboats to deceive themselves: by speeding they try to reduce real distance to apparent distance, so rendering themselves more potent, more significant, if in the event more comic, more pathetic. The wide lake resembles waterfalls of literature, that cascade long after men are dead and their daily lives forgotten, their graves demolished to make way for new houses, which decay in their turn, making way for new tenements, new graveyards.

On board the *Silver Star*, a monochrome framed portrait of President Koivisto smiles enigmatically at the sunlit passenger lounge

Exactly on time we drew into Lempäälä jetty, its name like the bleating of a lamb. On the left we caught a glimpse of the church of 1440. I lunched on the boat, then after eighty minutes we arrived at the 2-km long canal of Toijala, passing under the railway bridge near the junction of the Tampere-Turku and Tampere-Helsinki lines. At Toijala jetty dozens of Finns watched us moor, and exuberant kids leapt off a short pier into the lake. A swift kayak sped past. On the twenty-minute cruise to Visavuori we saw cows grazing as on Aelbert Cuyp's Netherlandish meadows, sharp-eyed gulls enjoying excellent fishing, and rocks jutting out of the water like missiles left over from the epic battles of *Kalevala*. The trip of over 4½ hours had cost only $19; the return fare is much lower than double the single fare.

The *Silver Star* continued to Viidennumero (at 205 metres, the second longest suspension bridge in Finland), Hattula, and Aulanko, reaching Hämeenlinna at 4.50. But I was keen to alight at Visavuori, to see the home and studio of Emil Wikström (1896–1942), situated just above the jetty, extravagantly lovely lake views to one side, and woods to the other.

Of the generation before Wäinö Aaltonen, Emil Erik Wikström was born in Turku, worked in Paris, and won a bronze medal there at the Universal Exhibition of 1900, and a Grand Prix at the Universal Exhibition of 1937. If you find him a sculptor of the second rank, then the surroundings will make up for any initial disappointment. Of the naturalist school, Wikström shows all the handicaps of an artist who never allows fantasy to intrude on that solemn monumentality which made him an ideal candidate to execute such portraits as *The Young Axel Gallen* (bronze-relief, 1884) and the Lönnrot Monument (Helsinki, 1900). Minor artists are often badly served when their studios reveal the domestic bungling of designs that should have been destroyed: contrast the Rodin Museum in Paris, or Henry Moore's studio at Much Hadham. No, Wikström seems never to have achieved in his work the sublimity of his beautiful studio home, with its astronomical tower, from which the starstruck sculptor would view the heavens at night by telescope. Anja's car was waiting to take me to Hämeenlinna through the juniper-scented countryside, wild strawberries hiding in the shadowing woods.

I stopped to admire a field of ripening wheat, typical of the new farming abundance in Finland, a country which has known terrible shortages of food at frequent intervals throughout its history.

Hämeenlinna (Tavastehus in Swedish) has a population of 43,000, but a historical significance out of all proportion to its size. We stopped first at the Local History Museum, near the public library, on Lukiokatu, open 12–4 on weekdays and 12–6 on Sundays. Built as a private house in 1882, it became the Historiallinen Museo in 1910. Sections cover the Stone Age (8000-3000 B.C.), the Bronze Age, and the Iron Age. Roman coins found at Lempäälä are followed by seven church sculptures from Urjala. You can see typical farm tools, cowbells, a late 18th-century clock by Fredrik Blomqvist of Turku, 19th-century glass, silver and porcelain and penny-farthing bicycles of the 1880s. I liked best the town views, Häme Castle doggedly claiming most of the attention, as in the charming wintry watercolour painted by J. Starck in 1833.

Hämeenlinna Art Gallery can be found, across the bridge where the lake called Vanajavesi narrows, in an old granary designed by Engel in 1838. Its mainly Finnish collection includes important works by Gallen-Kallela, Albert Edelfelt, Järnefelt, Halonen and Simberg. My favourite is Hjalmar Munsterhjelm's oil of Häme Castle. Opening hours are 10–7 on weekdays, and noon to 6 at weekends, with an evening extension to 8 on Thursdays.

Sibelius, the writer and critic Cygnaeus, and the poet Paavo Cajander (1846–1913) were all sons of Hämeenlinna, terminus of the first railway line from Helsinki, completed in 1862. The Sibelius Museum opens daily in summer from 10 to 3 on weekdays, and 12 to 4 on Sundays. A sleepy town of art, culture, parks and lakes, Hämeenlinna grew up, very gradually, north of the 13th-century fortress, receiving its town charter as late as 1639. But it was moved south of the castle in 1779, and given a town plan grid like those of Helsinki, Turku and Tampere.

Häme Castle became the provincial stronghold of the Swedish Government from the 1260s, with a garrison capable of defending Swedish administrators bent on taxing the industrious people of fertile Häme. The earliest fortified camp included a squareish grey stone wall with defensive towers at three corners, with (it is believed) wooden shelters for the garrison, and a well twelve metres deep, now dry. Within the next thirty years vaulted brick rooms made life more comfortable for the conscripts, the main hall being Finland's earliest surviving banqueting hall. During the 14th and 15th centuries, the new 'brick castle' arose, and from this period dates the King's

Hämeenlinna. Castle in a drawing of 1833

Hall vault, a high-water mark in mediaeval craftsmanship. During the time of Gustavus Vasa two strong gun-towers were added, but the old south tower was destroyed, before a rebuilding phase which included a new Lutheran chapel. The so-called King's Hall and Queen's Chamber were named for the visit of Gustavus II Adolf and his queen in 1614. After the war between Sweden and Russia the castle underwent a new epoch of restoration, the old main fort became a granary, and a new crown bakery was erected for the army's use: this has become a café. When Gustav III decreed a new site for the town, the castle walls and ramparts came under restoration. The two-storey main guard-house dates from this time, but the garrison rooms in the northern wall building had not been completed when the castle surrendered to the Russians on 8 March 1808. Shortly thereafter the Russians demolished the 16th-century western gun tower, completed the ramparts, and enlarged the prison; in 1837 the whole complex was converted to a prison following designs by the ubiquitous Engel. In 1953 the castle and its outbuildings were handed over to the authorities in charge of historic monuments and, after energetic excavations and restoration, Häme Castle now looks much as it did before conversion into a prison in the 19th century, the aim being to provide banqueting facilities and a museum with

Tuiskula
Kirstula
Savikko
Aulangon Heikkilän Lomakylä
Hälvälänselkä
Leirintäalue
Aulangon ulkoilumaja
Aulangon-järvi
Levonhaka
Kariniemi
Aronkulu
AULANKO
Luonnonsuojelualue
Hatunniemi
Hotelli Rantasipi Aulanko
Aulangon vuori
Kärmeskalliot
Hakalanniemi
1.0 km
Kihtersuo
SAIRIO
Mummunmäki
Kilometrimäki
Paroplankatu
PUISTONMÄKI
Kellumäentie
Kaupungin puisto
Salomaankatu
Papinh
OJOINEN
Härkätie
Hämeen-Tampereen valtatie
PULLERIN-MÄKI
Parolantie
Tiirönmäki
Härkätie
Djoisten kno
Linnan kasarmit
HÄTIL
Moottorirata
Pullerin kentät
Linna
Huhtamäki
KEINU-SAARI
Hyppyrimäki
Ampumarata
Rinkelinmäki
2.7 km
Brahen katu
KAURIALA
Parolantie
Luonnonsuojelualue
Ahveniston järvi
Ahveniston ulkoilupuisto
0.8 km
Soraharjunkatu
Turuntie
Suomen kasarmi
Urheilukeskus
AHVENISTO
Kanta-Hämeen keskussairaala
Poltinahon kasarmit
Ahveniston hautausmaa
MYLLYMÄKI
Vanaja-vesi
KANTOLA
Punaportti
Rapamäki
Raakonkatu
Siirtolapuutarha
Jukola
Virveli
Visamäki
Nuppola
Lucilajanvuori
Kankaantaustantie
KANKAAN-TAUSTA
Ristivuori
Vanajan asevelikylä
Lauria
Alaspää
Hattelmalan sairaala
Mattinen
Hiero
Raakkula
Kolkka
Hovila
Luolajan koulu
Suvikas
Seppälä
Lassila
Hakovuori
LUOLAJA
Hattelmajärvi

permanent and temporary exhibitions. It opened to the public in 1979, daily between 10 and 6 from May to August, and between 10 to 4 for the rest of the year. Guided tours, available in Finnish, Swedish, English and German, can be thoroughly recommended. Like Turku Castle, Häme Castle stands on high ground overlooking the lake and the plain. The heart of the castle is the old square Inner Ward, cobbled stones connecting all four sides of the castle at ground level, and a wooden passageway (with stone steps up to it) at first-floor level. Look carefully at the sophisticated brick ornamentation: especially the recesses with background panels (originally whitewashed), pointed arches, and North German 'Windberge' patterning topped by fleur-de-lis. Many of the ground-floor rooms and doors have been replaced. The bakery could accommodate six hundred kg of bread in each of six ovens. The late 13th-century great hall, also known as the Constable's Chamber, is now used as a restaurant. A mediaeval chapel has been restored to its original function.

You reach the first floor by a new staircase instead of the two narrow flights within the wall that provided access in the Middle Ages. Out of the window, undulating cumulus clouds floated below tufts of smoky cirrus. A ladies' outing from Lappeenranta was clearly overcome by at last setting foot inside the legendary Häme Castle, from which a province was – albeit uneasily – long administered. On this first floor one can readily piece together enough facets of mediaeval life to roll back the centuries. Here is a scurry of scullery-maids disappearing round a corner, there a lonely Swedish

Hämeenlinna. City Plan

1. Ahvenisto sports center
2. Alko — Liqueur shop
3. Vocational schools
4. Vocational training schools
5. Aulanko, Hotel Rantasipi Aulanko
6. Häme provincial administration
7. Hätila church
8. Jehovah's wittnesses convention hall
9. Ice hall
10. Kauriala school and open college
11. Kanta-Häme central hospital
12. Commercial college
13. Market place
14. Town theatre, provincial archives and youth center
15. Town offices
16. Kauriala senior secondary school
17. Kauriala sports field
18. Central school and local museum
19. Central congregational center
20. Library
21. Church
22. Kyyrölä clay industry
23. Meat industry college
24. Bus station
25. Castle
26. Senior secondary school
27. Tourist information
28. Dairy school
29. Minitheatre
30. Motor-racing circuit and automobile museum
31. College of music
32. Ojoinen school
33. Orthodox church
34. Fire station
35. Police station
36. Poltinaho secondary school
37. Poltinaho congregational center
38. Post office and telecommunication
39. Town hall
40. Riding stables
41. Railway station
42. College of nursing
43. Harbour
44. Clay industry Kirstula
45. Sibeliuspark
46. Birthplace of Sibelius
47. Poultry farming school
48. Art gallery
49. Tampere university/ Hämeenlinna teacher's trainig school
50. Technical school
51. Tennis center
52. Health center
53. Tuomela school
54. Swimming baths
55. Hämeenkaari sports center
56. Vanaja church and museum
57. Wetterhoff
58. Co-educational school

soldier humming a ballad to his far-off sweetheart to console him through a dark winter's night in a land where his language is totally unknown to the sullen peasantry, dour tillers of a flat and alien land. The rooms are barrel-vaulted here, groin-vaulted there; the windows stronghold-small, the walls whitewashed, the floors of brick or board. Heating was by hot-air stoves or open fireplaces. No furniture but hard benches, hard beds, plain tables, and simple chests. The Queen's Chamber, so-called in 1614, in fact dates back to the 14th century, and the adjacent King's Chamber has been restored in shape by following the rib endings and pointed arch shapes found in the walls. The six-groin vaulting is similar to that in the contemporary Turku Castle.

On ascending to the second floor, you come to a sequence of exhibitions laid out partly in three store-rooms (numbered 302, 307 and 311) added in the 1720s, when the castle turned into a granary, and partly in the existing rooms (such as 303). Room 303 shows the Vaaraslahti treasure of 6,000 17th-century copper coins, impractically weighing over 100 kg, worth about 18 months of a slaughterer's pay in 1653. Sweden was Europe's chief copper producer at the time, having started to mint copper coins, as well as the traditional silver, in the 1620s. In Finland, copper coins were the principal coins of exchange, though gold and silver were brought in by men who had fought in the Thirty Years' War and became the main raw material for gold rings and silver cups and spoons, if not retained as heirlooms.

Room 302 offers a fascinating overview of the development of brickbuilding, from Lombardy in the tenth century, arriving (with Mecklenburg craftsmen) in the 13th century first at Turku and then at Hämeenlinna. Drawings and superstitious signs have been found on bricks, shown here.

Room 307 should be studied for the display of *ryijy* rugs from all over Häme. *Ryijy* were known in Denmark as early as the Bronze Age (1000–800 B.C.) and probably spread to the other Nordic countries and then to Finland, but since East Prussian textiles of this type are known, it is not impossible that the technique came simultaneously from the south, as well as the west. *Ryijy* are known in Norway, Öland, Åland, and the archipelago of Turku (in Finnish Turunmaa Saaristo). They are known in Finland from the mid-15th century, when they were used as blankets by courtiers and servants too, woollen pile downward. The 'best period' for the *ryijy* extended from the mid-18th century to the early 19th, when increasing foreign contacts increased the range and quantity of dyes available, especially the favoured indigo blue. Woven for dowries, they passed from generation to generation, counting as 'parts of the widow's bed.'

Aulanko Park, nearby, has a hotel, a youth hostel, and one could camp here or hire a cottage. Hiking, jogging, a children's outdoor theatre, horseriding, a picnic beneath the pines: there is something for everyone at

Hattula. Church interior.

Aulanko. but I was headed for the Holy Cross Church of Hattula, on the main road back to Pälkäne and Tampere. The 14th-century masterpiece can be seen from 1 – 15 May (9–4), 16–31 May (9–6), 1 June-15 August (10–6) and 16 August-7 September (12–4), an ample reason for visiting Finland before autumn sets in. Outwardly, Hattula looks like any other mediaeval Finnish church: a walled churchyard with gatehouses on opposing walls and a separate belfry in a third wall, the church itself in a simple rectangular shape having a connected porch on the south and vestry on the north. But, as you would expect from its proximity to Häme Castle, it is made of brick rather than the grey stone usual elsewhere in Finland. And astonishment spreads like an eagle's wings, one step inside. For a hundred and eighty *al secco* frescoes festoon the walls, and have done so since 1510 when they were painted, though they were covered with lime after the Reformation. It is argued by Olof af Hallström that a Crucified Christ with Mary and John, in a niche above the choir window, was painted in the 14th century, the date of a wooden sculpture of the Triumph Crucifix, to which cult the church was dedicated. But generally the church represents the northernmost flowering of South Baltic decoration, in particular the sequence portraying for the illiterate the life and works of Jesus. Framing the sequence is a vision of the

165

Creation and the Last Judgment. The creation of Eve shows Adam sleeping in Paradise, characteristically in Finland shown as a meadow beside a lake! The vault paintings in the south aisle depict legends of the Virgin Mary, while the western vaults show the public life of Christ, including miracles and the Woman of Samaria. Paintings near the western doorway portray the Transfiguration of Christ above S. Martin and S. Hedvig, the Stigmata of S. Francis and two married women and devil. The west and north walls are covered with scenes of suffering, death and Resurrection of Christ; paintings north of the altar concern S. Christopher and the Last Judgement. The vaults near the east wall show scenes from the life of Moses and the legend of the Holy Cross. While most of the many mediaeval sculptures are Finnish in origin, a S. Olaf must be a North German import. One pulpit dates from 1550; more ornate is the other, a fine Late Renaissance example of the 17th century. The overwhelming impression remains that of vigour, almost Italianate colour (though with inevitable provincialisms in composition, figure-drawing, and perspective), and a burst of invention and bubbling high spirits altogether out of keeping with such plain pomp as Helsinki's Lutheran Cathedral. Hattula is frankly irresistible.

So too is Iittala Glassworks, on the Toijala road from Hämeenlinna to Tampere. You could easily spend a whole day in the Glass Centre, as fascinating in its way as Murano, in the Venetian Lagoon. We started with an excellent fish soup in the restaurant, then enjoyed the Museum just as much. Iittala Glassworks was founded by the Swedish master Petter Magnus Abrahamsson in 1881, exactly two centuries after the first Finnish glass factory was set up at Uusikaupunki, on the west coast. The Finnish Glass Museum at Riihimäki may present a more comprehensive view, and Nuutajärvi Glassworks too makes a pleasant excursion, but if you are near Iittala, this museum offers a splendid survey of one aspect of Finnish glassmaking. Eight glassworks in Finland produce domestic and 'art' glassware, but Iittala and Nuutajärvi comprise whole village communities: together, these two employ almost a thousand people, and the reputation of Finnish glass ensures that the industry will stay strong. Aalto's 'Savoy' or 'Aalto' vase – which has now sold over 150,000 copies – was designed in 1936 as an upright vase with fluid curves in the body wall. At the end of the 1930s, functionalism combined with aesthetic beauty in form, decoration and colour to create a new movement, in which individual masterpieces ranked even higher than mass-produced wares of great refinement. One thinks of Tapio Wirkkala's *Chanterelle* (1946), Helena Tynell's *Rialto* (1960s), or *Lancet* (1952) and *Winds* (1983) by Timo Sarpaneva. You will revel in the creative power of Göran Hongell, Jorma Vennola, Valto Kokko, and Mikko Karppanen. Roughly half the Iittala production is exported, and you can buy wares from the entire range (including bargains slightly

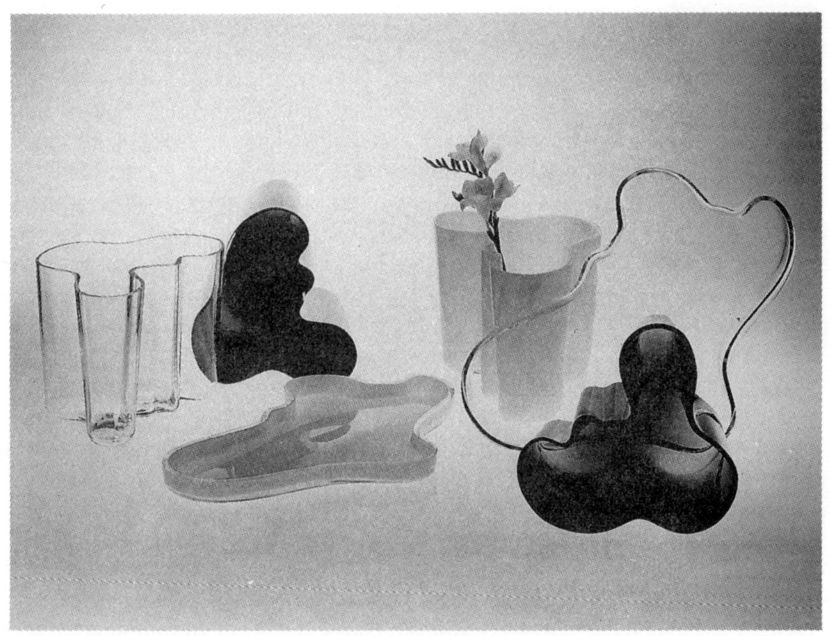

Iittala. Alvar Aalto's glass design of 1936 (Courtesy of Iittala Glassworks)

defective) from the factory shop, whose staff will ship products home. Children have access to a park with sheep, games, swings and climbing frames. A textile shop is run by Arja Toiva, a pewter shop by Arttina, and a general gift shop by Aarikka. Guided factory tours the year round start at 11, 1 and 3 from Monday to Friday. Glassmaking is visible in a small workshop adjoining the restaurant, daily from May to September and daily except Mondays and Tuesdays throughout the rest of the year, and you are invited to try your skill at glassblowing.

On the way back to Tampere, I stopped at Voipaala Art Centre (open 11–6 daily between 17 May and 17 August), the studio of the sculptor Elias Ilkka, and took pleasure in an art exhibition in the old manor house with works by Raimo Heino, Eero Hiironen, Marjo Lahtinen, Viljo Mäkinen, Tuula Pyykkö-Tuisku, Kari Tuisku, and Pirkko Valo, among others. It stands close to the old stone church, as does Sääksmäki Local History Museum.

The Poet's Way

The greatest contrast imaginable with the breathtaking switchback rail journey from Lima's plain to cloud-capped Huancayo – the highest rail journey in the world – must be the leisurely, quiet, serene cruise on Näsijärvi north from Tampere to Ruovesi and Virrat. S/s *Tarjanne* leaves the jetty at Tampere's Mustalahti at 10.45 a.m. every Tuesday, Thursday and Saturday during the season (running from mid-June to mid-August). It reaches Murole at 1.15, Hirsisaari at 1.32, Ruovesi at 3.10, Visuvesi at 4.45, and Virrat at 6.30, returning the following morning at 10.45.

The sparse sound commentary is solely in Finnish, for we are starting to fall off the foreign tourist's map of Finland northward along Näsijärvi. The only foreigner on board, I again noticed the joviality of the summer Finn, expansive in open-necked shirt, with a ready smile that I am assured vanishes with the onset of seemingly endless wintry nights. Captain Jussi Mäenpää, from Turku, sagely approved my choice of Thursday: 'Saturdays are always too crowded,' he added, hooting to alert speedboats and swimmers to his proximity. My questing spirit relaxed perceptibly, as the horizon on each side fluctuated gently nearer or farther, tall trees advancing and receding on the banks of great Näsijärvi, ribbons of green below the endless azure of a cloudless sky and the placid waters of an unpolluted lake. Birds appeared rarely, and far off. Captain Mäenpää had sailed the world, but he brought me up short with his laconic statement that you can work on boats all your life in Finland without ever seeing the sea. Restrained, dignified, the Finns on board chatted quietly, even infrequently. Tending to portliness in middle age, they could perhaps be considered the Austrians of Scandinavia as the more aggressive Swedes are the Germans of Scandinavia. An elderly lady was reading the new novel by Kalle Päätalo (guaranteed to sell 100,000 copies every autumn), and two middle-aged men, their eyes gnawing remorselessly at a chessboard between them, seemed equally oblivious to the day – again, according to *Aamulehti*, warmer in Tampere than in Morocco. In conversation with a young man from Pori, I was asked why there was so much violence in Northern Ireland, and recommended that he read a history of the Plantations. 'It cannot condone the violence, of course,' I hastened to add, 'merely explain it. If the British were to leave Northern Ireland now, the latent civil war would burst its present barriers in a tide of blood like that in Lebanon.' Most of the passengers had by now tired of the lakeland landscape so entirely different from the mountained enclaves of England's miniature Lake District, and were drawn inwards to themselves, like their habitual winter selves, eyes glazed towards a stoic nothingness, or a comfort of stoves and sauna. Then Captain Mäenpää hooted repeatedly, and we drew up at Murole jetty, boisterous with excited children. As *Tarjanne* eased away again, I was offered lunch of salmon, veal, beefsteak or reindeer cutlets, followed by strawberries and ice-cream and coffee. Summer cottages seemed more numerous hereabouts, trying to resolve the equation that you try to get as far away from towns and neighbours as possible, but the farther you travel, the more likely you are to find those with a similar inclination, and. most Finns have the same inclination. . . *Tarjanne* passed an enormous raft of floating logs, making the heart leap suddenly towards a vision of Lapland. Mosquitoes are supposed to abound in June, July and August, but I have to confess that I never heard or saw one from Helsinki to Ivalo, far beyond the Arctic Circle, and all the warnings about taking a mosquito coil to Ruovesi and environs seemed needless.

As I alighted from the delightful eighty-year-old *Tarjanne*, exchanging farewells with Captain Mäenpää and Hjalmar from Pori, a few tentative cirrus clouds were tasting the sky, but found themselves overcome with blue and disappeared, like flies. The boat pursued its relaxed course towards Virrat (the name means 'streams'), nexus of the Lake Route and north-ernmost town of the region called Pirkanmàa, the town's population just below 10,000.

I was met by car, and taken first to the Poet's Spring, named for Johan Ludvig Runeberg, who became Finland's national poet, despite writing in Swedish. Runeberg may have been intimately connected with the southern coast (studying in Turku and spending the last forty years of his life in Porvoo), but his 'Finnish' consciousness, so crucial to the development of the nation's literature and burgeoning nationalism, developed hereabouts, while a tutor on the Ritoniemi estate from 1825 to 1826. While there, he probably met the soldier who inspired *Fänrik Ståls sägner* (1848, 1860; translated by C.W. Stork as *Tales of Ensign Stål*). These are not tales at all, but ballads extolling the courage of ordinary Finnish soldiers in the course of duty. By that time, his narrative poem *Elgskyttarne* had surprised his contemporaries by its unfashionable theme: the ordinary Finnish people. This at a time when literary fashion decreed, following Byron and Pushkin, that Childe Harold and Evgeny Onegin should exemplify aristocratic romanticism in narrative poetry. I found Runeberg's spring, with its plain wooden bridge a rustic version of Japanese artifice at Ohara near Kyoto, as romantic as any lines from Keats or Lermontov. Young lovers had tossed *penni* coins from pockets and purses into the pellucid waters, shallow like any Roman fountain yet in air as clear and pure as that of Mont Blanc.

Nearby stands the church of 1778, six years younger than its baroque bell-tower. With seats for a congregation of 1500, the church has an octagonal central dome and steep roof. In 1905 it was panelled and painted to proposals by Akseli Gallen-Kallela. Its dome is white; brown and cream are the colours below, including the gallery, while the benches are in subdued green and blue, like the pulpit. The undistinguished *Transfiguration of Christ* by B. Reinhold (1876) bears above it the inscription 'Tämä on rakas poikäni, häntä kuulkaat' ('This is my beloved Son: you must listen to Him'). In the graveyard I found a church-boat called *Eeva*, with fifteen sets of rowlocks to show that it was intended to be sculled by thirty men and youths and to carry about sixty to a hundred people from their village to the nearest church: this church. Look for the gravestone inscribed IMPI MARJATTA (1891–1895), 'The Maiden Marjatta', commemorating a little daughter of Akseli Gallen-Kallela. When the grave was fresh, the artist could see it from his hilltop home across the water, but the remorseless passing of time has seen to it that trees now impede that view, have done for several decades past, and always will do, despite the intermittent memory of men.

A lakeside museum, beside the quay, presents some historic rural buildings, but on no account should you miss the Open-Air Museum, near the exit from Runeberg's Spring to the main road. A six-sailed 18th-century windmill proclaims the entrance to the museum open in May and from mid-August to mid-September between 11 and 4 every day but Sunday; except 12–6 daily between 1 June and mid-August. The complex is divided into two enclosures, representing a small farming community between a hundred and two hundred years back. Both buildings and equipment come from Ruovesi parish, but not from this actual place. The cottage living-room and workroom from Hanho is 18th-century in age, and shows how children were kept out of harm's way in a hanging high-chair, with an early 'hole-chair', and a huge open fireplace. Contemporary granaries have ridge-pole and birchbark roofs. In summertime, the women would sleep in the clothing store and balconied barn. Look for the 17th-century outdoor larder, cowshed, cattle-yard and swing-arm well with a water-trough leading to the cowshed; sleighs, bellows and forge; an 18th-century sauna with a peat-roof used also for preparing flax and beermaking, and a fish-shed with hanging fish-nets.

At one time the Gallen-Kallela home and wilderness studio remained open for visitors at set times, but in recent years, due to the understandable strain of entertaining so many visitors, it is opened by appointment only (tel. 934–2623, or write to Kalela, Ruhala (Ruovesi), addressing your request to Mrs Aivi Gallen-Kallela during the summer there, and in winter at Snellmaninkatu 15 A 7, 00170, Helsinki 17, tel. 90–179589).

Kalela resounds silently to the gong of artistic history, not only to painting, sculpture and architecture, but also the singing of Pirkko Gallen-Kallela, Akseli's daughter-in-law, and the interior design of Pirkko's daughter Aivi, both of whom still reside there in the summer. You can reach Kalela by boat, for it perches like a capercaillie poised for flight amid pines; or by car to a

Ruovesi. Open Air Museum. Windmill

Kalela. Akseli's painting Marjatta and Dog (1892) (Courtesy of Kalela Museum)

glade in the woods, then by a short walk through sweet-scented pines to the boatshed, sandy beach, grey outbuildings, to the warm redpainted log walls of the studio-home atop a headland commanding grand lake views. A superb expression of Finnish wooden architecture, Kalela was started in 1894 and completed the following year when the foremost Finnish artist of the age heard – in Berlin – that his beloved little daughter Marjatta had fallen ill and died at Ruovesi. At Christmas 1895 he drew his first woodcuts from a new press: *Defence of the Sampo* and – commemorating Marjatta's passing – *The Flower of Death*. Gallen-Kallela now entered his most prodigious period as a graphic artist, creating for instance *Lemminkäinen's Mother* and *Joukahainen's Revenge*. His daughter Kirsti was born in 1896 and his son Jorma (later to marry the singer Pirkko) in 1898. From 1905 he visited Kalela less and less frequently, returning to live there in 1915, and repairing the home before he finally abandoned it in 1921. Jorma restored the derelict home when it came into his ownership in 1936, but he was killed in action during the early part of the Winter War, after which Pirkko and Aivi have lived here, in recent years only during the summer, holding concerts, art exhibitions, and courses in pure and applied art. There are more than a hundred important works by Akseli and Jorma, as well as two bronzes of Akseli by Emil Wikström of Visavuori. Nobody can fail to be touched by Akseli's portrait of *Marjatta and Dog* (1892), and by the stubborn, selfless devotion to their wilderness studio shown by the ladies of the family. The underrated Jorma is represented by a vivid painting of a *Coffee Service* (done when he was only 16), and several other works of distinction, including a portrait of *Pirkko* (1933), *A Cardinal's Funeral* (Paris, 1920), and *Heating the Smoke-Sauna* (1936).

Among Akseli's portraits, look for those of his wife, the refined society girl Mary Helena Slöör, whom he had met in childhood and adored in passionate paintings and letters. They married in 1890, after separation while Akseli worked in Paris, producing his greatest work there: the *Demasquée* of 1888. The atmosphere nowadays remains redolent of those heady days of his rise to fame in the 1890s before his international fame resulting from the 'Iris' room at the Paris Universal Exhibition. Aivi stressed that the fireplace became the heart of Kalela. In winter, logs blazed day and night and the fireside became the family's focus; the artist himself asserted that 'a fire in the hearth has its place deep in the soul as a symbol of our common Finnish spirit, even though the worship of fire may arise. . . from the same primitive instincts in all peoples of the world.' A music mezzanine allows a pianist or singer to be seen from the staircase, ground floor or first floor. My own favourite room, comfortably screened from the studio by red woollen curtains, is the excellent little library, the main library having gone to Tarvaspää. Aivi showed me splendid new editions of the *Kalevala* and

Kalela. Jorma's painting Heating the Smoke Sauna (1936) (Courtesy of Kalela Museum)

Kanteletar and Kivi's *Seven Brothers* with Gallen-Kallela's illustrations, published between 1983 and 1986 in de luxe and standard editions.

You might be particularly attracted to a tiny meditation room attained from a bedroom above the library: an ivory tower in which an artist might think and dream, like Wikström's astronomical tower at Visavuori. Look carefully at every detail, for you will find that most of the furniture was designed by the artist himself, down to the cushions, rugs, hinges, ashtrays and doorhandles. A loom for weaving, awls for cobbling, and hammers and chisels: this is a workshop not only of an artist, but of an artist-craftsman-designer, as prolific in poster design (the famous lithograph BIL-BOL of 1907) as in oils (*The Charred Tree* painted on a lynx hunt in 1906). His wilderness-studio is made memorable by the charming presence of the two ladies, witty and thoughtful, international by inclination yet Finnish by instinctive response. Kalela was a visit I shall never be tempted to forget, sunshine glinting through the pine tops down to moss and bracken.

On the way back to Tampere I called in at the holiday resort of Maisansalo, a complex with hotel, restaurant, self-catering apartments, a sports centre including tennis, volleyball and badminton, camping area, and safe playgrounds and pools for young children. The m/s *Pyynikki* sails for

Maisansalo from Särkänniemi in Tampere every Wednesday, Thursday and Friday at 10 a.m., giving you two hours for lunch and returning at 2.

Much more exciting, oddly enough, is nearby Murikka, a course-centre for the 150,000 members of Finland's Metalworkers' Union set on the bank of Näsijärvi 40 km from Tampere, in the sprawling community of Teisko. Designed by Pekka Helin and Tuomo Siitonen, Murikka was completed in 1977, except for the sauna building on the south side of Taipaleenniemi, completed in 1978, destroyed by fire the same year, and subsequently rebuilt to much the same design by Katras/Kari Raimoranta and Tuomo Siitonen. Murikka exhilarates by its profound sensitivity to the natural environment of Näsijärvi's rocky shoreline, its just scale, appropriate use of materials, and thoughtful deference to the leisure and training needs of its users and staff: much the same virtues shown by the Pietiläs in Tampere's new public library. If we exclude the lakeside sauna, Murikka has five buildings. Around a garden stand three: the main building, with auditorium and lobby; the accommodation, with windows opening on to nature; and the sports complex incorporating a full-size basketball court and a swimming pool, together with its own sauna and gymnasium.

Apart from this complex, for users, is a fourth area for maintenance, and a fifth for staff housing. The idea was to celebrate the skills of Finland's largest union by incorporating metal into as much as the building as was tactful, given the nation's natural predilection for wood. So, for example, the columns and beams of the main building and sports complex are of steel, and the swimming baths have hot-dipped galvanized steel structures with an epoxy coating. Metal frame structures are made of Finnish steel profiles and edged copper moulding. The building was by and large unit-built, showing that units of differing frame materials may be combined to great advantage, avoiding the tedious uniformity of a single frame material or unit type. The comfortable reception area resembles that of a five-star hotel, and the picture windows of the green restaurant relax the eye while one sips freshly-brewed coffee. Green carpets and settees distinguish the quiet library; the sports building gleams a cheerful russet-red.

But we had an appointment with the lady who opens the new Teisko Church for visitors at unusual times, usual times being 11–3 in summer and 11–1 in winter. It was designed by Matti Åkerblom in 1788, that is ten years after the church at Ruovesi. The pulpit, of 1650, was rescued from Teisko's first wooden church. The prevailing colours within are blue and grey, with a white dome, but brownish red without. I wandered down to Näsijärvi, gazing through the trees in the churchyard across to the other bank. Everything here is so quiet and peaceful that it comes as no surprise that the 2,000 winter residents are swollen by a flood of 12,000 more to summer cottages.

A hare sped with hardly a sound through deep undergrowth. The excited churchwarden told us that a bear had been sighted in Teisko only yesterday: a rare event indeed nowadays. Teisko's local museum opens daily except Monday from noon to three between June and August.

Our perennial headlights (required at all times by Finnish law) shone ahead in the full light of early evening: dark would not spread its wings until after ten o'clock. By the roadside I stopped to pick little blueberries, then followed an elk's clumsy trail between high undergrowth until a flattened glade showed where it had rested several hours before. It had then made off in one of any three directions, so I abandoned that chase in favour of hunting berries.

The wooded countryside, flat as the chessboard in *Through the Looking-Glass*, occasionally expands into chequered fields, then contracts again as trees fall in soldierlike at each side of the road. You come here as a delighted townsman, glorying in the hidden glut of raspberries, tiny wild strawberries, blackberries succulent and tangy, never thinking of the farmers to whom this land was once a weary challenge, until they tamed it, and slowly became its prisoners, chained to the slow flux of seasons. Their forefathers wrested the

Museosilta, between Teisko and Tampere

176

terrain from the wilderness, jealously guarding their new lands as the Gods and Nibelungen in turn guarded the ring they had snatched from the Rhine. Writers like Aleksis Kivi and Sillanpää understood the lure of the land, of the forests with their sombre, ancient chants echoing from their distant, noble, primaeval memories. Like Don Quixote, the *Seven Brothers* of Kivi's classic novel returned to their abandoned home after discovering the necessity to leave home in the first place: the Biblical overtones of the tale of the prodigal son are not lost on any Finnish reader.

An extraordinarily beautiful bridge, called 'Museo-Silta' because it is no longer used as such, cast its echoing shadow in a creek between dense woods. And then to Tampere: lights and music.

A CASE OF LAPPISH MADNESS

You may be able to appreciate Finland's art and culture in its cities and their surroundings, but to experience Finland itself in its natural setting one must remember Tacitus' footnote: 'the Finns are extremely wild', and make tracks for the wilderness whence the true Finns came, and whither they return, not only to summer cottages, but for winter sports, hunting, fishing, and the inexhaustible solitude of lakes and forests.

Above a line drawn roughly eastward from the head of the Gulf of Bothnia, to all intents and purposes from Kemi to Kuusamo, solitudes intensify, for this is the Finnish province of Lapland, the northern third of Finland. Great Lapland includes parts of Norway, Sweden and the U.S.S.R., for in former times, before they became the largely sedentary people they are today, the Lapps migrated seasonally over a huge area with their reindeer herds, recognising no national boundaries.

The capital of their Finnish province, where they form a minority, is Rovaniemi, a city they regard as 'the south', though it lies on the Arctic Circle. Many Finns seem drawn ineluctably northward, towards the fulfilment of their inmost heart's desire: the wealth of unspoilt nature. Many foreigners, notably Swedes and Germans, accept the lure of Lapland once, and many of them thereafter succumb to a recognised phenomenon: a kind of still, open-eyed nostalgia for fells and lakes, for forests and endless skies. This is Lappish madness, and the farther north I explored – to Rovaniemi, to Sodankylä, to Tankavaara, to Kaunispää -the more deeply the cadences of this madness gnawed into my bones. I sang with the unnerving joy of returning boyhood. I sprang and leapt like a scruffy urchin fresh out of school. I lay, luxuriating in bracken, pine-scent wafting around me, summer sun dazzling so that I had to protect my eyes with my arm, lulled by calm yet alert like a beast to every strange call, whether a wolf's distant howl or the uncanny clip-clop of a jack-snipe.

I had arrived by air from Helsinki to Rovaniemi, via Oulu (*Sw.* Uleåborg), where a victorious Rovaniemi football team had just secured a seven-nil away victory, celebrating in great style on the flight back. The flight to Oulu had been spectacular enough, woodlands and lakes interspersing with so few signs of habitation throughout that I had to pinch myself to make sure I was waking in a world suffering from overpopulation. But the flight from Oulu, with the Gulf of Bothnia on our left, seemed an endless study in forests, as

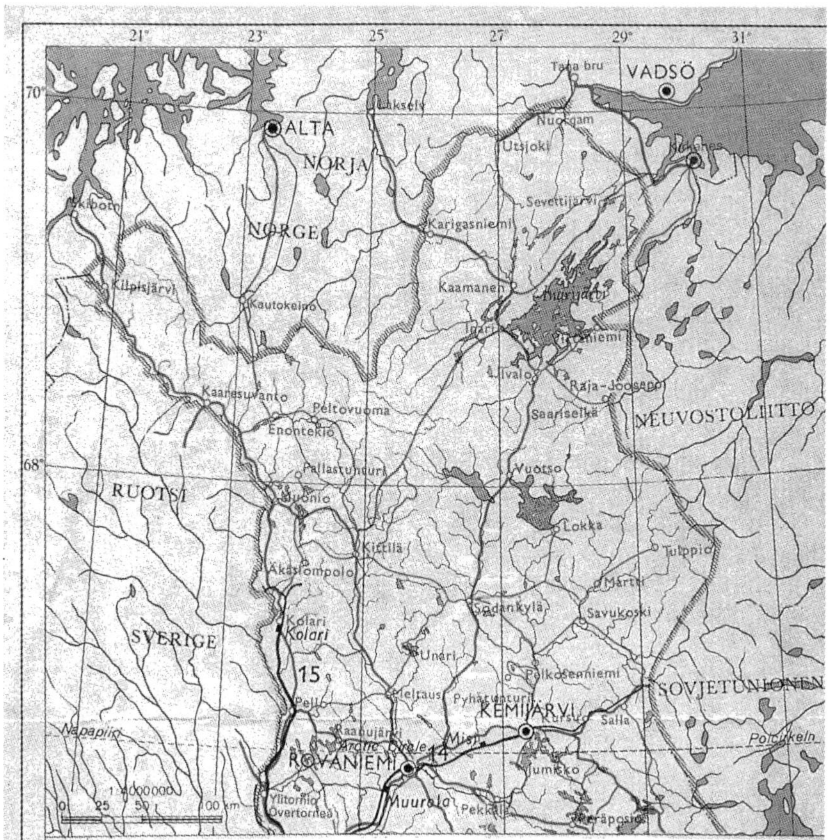

Lapland. Map

though trees had suddenly, inexplicably, taken over the earth. The glitter of
Kemijoki below us pointed us in the direction of Rovaniemi; we circled; we
landed. I remembered a saying of Eeva Kilpi's: 'I need my annual
four-month escape into nature. After that time in the Finnish woods I can
tolerate my fellow beings better.'

For some reason never explained, buses do not meet the first and last of
the five aircraft reaching Rovaniemi daily in summer months, and you are
charged by taxis a flat rate of 10 FM anywhere to town ($2), a distance of
eight km. I was surprised to find the Hotel Pohjanhovi not only crowded, but
also cacophonous with *two* live bands playing simultaneously, so that if
dancers rocked out of one half of the room, they would find themselves

Korkalovaara
Sahanperä
Erkkilän-
saari
VI
Kivelönne
Hillapolku
Koulukuja
Korkalovaaranne
Mäntyvaaranne
KAUPUNGIN
KESKUSVARIKKO
SANTAMÄKI
RAJAVARTIOSTO
24
21
18
20
36
ETELÄ-
RINNE
14
KAUPPATORI
19
10
VETURITALLI
JÄÄSKELÄINEN
1
3
5
9
8
7
Veitikanoja
TAVARA-ASEMA
13
TEOLLISUUSKYLÄ
Hallitie
POSTIAUTOVARIKKO
IX
Teollisuustie
KATSASTUS-
KONTTORI
PALOASEMA
Harjulampi
Kirkonj
Valtatie N:o 4
Keminne
IV
KAPPELI
AHKIOMAA
V
Kotisaari
NIEMELÄN-
KANGAS
III
23
2
RANTAVITIKKA
KORVANNIEMI
Pappilantie
VIIRIN-
KANGAS
17
ROVANIEMI   Kemijoki
0   200   400   600   800   1000m
MAATALOUS-
OPPILAITOS
KOT

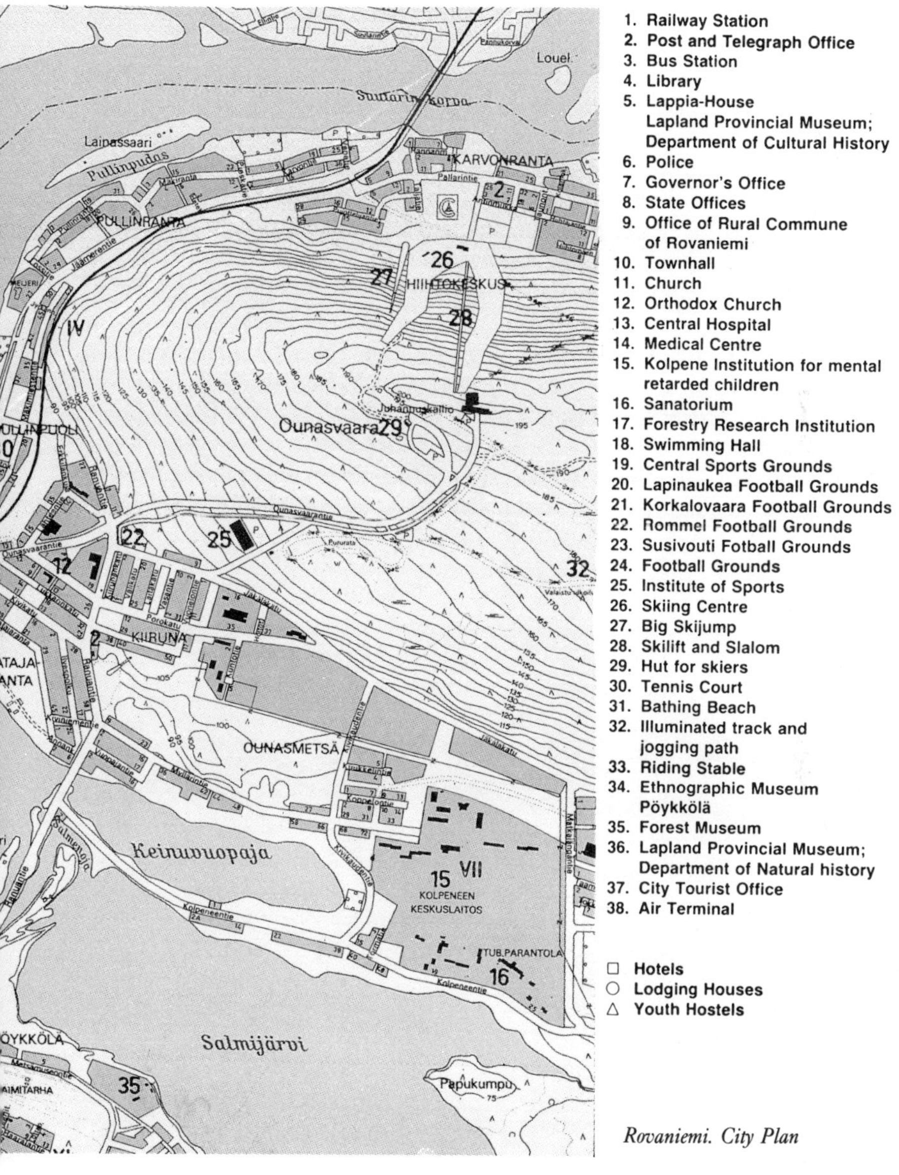

1. Railway Station
2. Post and Telegraph Office
3. Bus Station
4. Library
5. Lappia-House
   Lapland Provincial Museum;
   Department of Cultural History
6. Police
7. Governor's Office
8. State Offices
9. Office of Rural Commune
   of Rovaniemi
10. Townhall
11. Church
12. Orthodox Church
13. Central Hospital
14. Medical Centre
15. Kolpene Institution for mental
    retarded children
16. Sanatorium
17. Forestry Research Institution
18. Swimming Hall
19. Central Sports Grounds
20. Lapinaukea Football Grounds
21. Korkalovaara Football Grounds
22. Rommel Football Grounds
23. Susivouti Fotball Grounds
24. Football Grounds
25. Institute of Sports
26. Skiing Centre
27. Big Skijump
28. Skilift and Slalom
29. Hut for skiers
30. Tennis Court
31. Bathing Beach
32. Illuminated track and
    jogging path
33. Riding Stable
34. Ethnographic Museum
    Pöykkölä
35. Forest Museum
36. Lapland Provincial Museum;
    Department of Natural history
37. City Tourist Office
38. Air Terminal

☐ Hotels
○ Lodging Houses
△ Youth Hostels

Rovaniemi. City Plan

suddenly expected to waltz in the other. The kind of hotel you visit because other people come, the Pohjanhovi provides service at dinner so slow that my reindeer-farmer acquaintances at the same table fretted visibly – even in Lapland, where time is said to be infinite.

'I can't hear what you're saying!', I yelled at Risto Saukkoriipi, from Ranua. 'I said, we have a Finnish proverb, "The path is long and is strewn with many rocks".' My meal, consisting of fish soup, reindeer steak and Arctic cloudberries with ice-cream, proved very tasty when it did arrive. Rowdy laughter amid plentiful beer gave the impression of Mahagonny, that frontier boomtown, rather than forested Lapland, and I slid silently past a banquet toastmaster taking a few minutes off for a drag at a cigarette, beyond two heavies at the door employed to restrain the eager youth of Rovaniemi from dancing the night away within, and shot into the lift with my copy of Walter Bacon's *Highway to the Wilderness* (1961), about an Englishman's three years at Ivalo in the 1950s, with his Finnish wife Arja.

Rovaniemi's bedrock may be two thousand million years old, but mankind did not emerge until well after the Ice Age, which ended ten thousand years ago: you can see post-glacial marks on Ounasvaara, on the opposite bank of Ounaskoski. The first settlement here has been found at Ylikylä, north of the

Rovaniemi. Ounasvaara, showing glacial action (Courtesy of Rovaniemi City Tourist Office)

present town. 'Rova' is the Finnish equivalent of the Sami 'roaivvi', a forest clearing with birch saplings; 'niemi' means a cape or promontory. The modern town dates back to the 15th century, became an independent parish in 1632, divided into town and county in 1929, and earned city rights in 1960. Of the thirty-two thousand residents, a quarter are below fifteen years of age. Trade and service industries dominate employment in Rovaniemi, more than 10,000 of the 15,000 employees being engaged in business, transport, civil service, banks and insurance. Only three thousand work in building and industry, and fewer than 350 in agriculture and forestry, indicating the enormous changes in lifestyle since Rovaniemi was a backward provincial town in the early years of the century, or a smoking ruin at the end of the War in 1944. Twelve thousand of the 200,000 German troops in North Finland were stationed in Rovaniemi. The nine thousand inhabitants were evacuated in the autumn of 1944 to Sweden and East Bothnia, and the German troops retreating northward destroyed the town in October.

Alvar Aalto provided a vision of new Rovaniemi in 1945, outlining proposals for renewal based on an antlered reindeer shape, the head jutting into Ounaskoski, and the antlers piercing the districts of Aronperä, Lapin-rinne, and Karinrakka. The multi-storey and terraced houses of the Korkalovaara housing scheme were built in 1957–61, and Aalto's Aho Commercial Building on Koskikatu the following year.

The town centre of Rovaniemi might seem pretentious for a population of around 32,000 but, taken in the context of its regional significance in the vast Lebensraum of Lapland, and the 7,500 sq km of Rovaniemi County, the plan falls into place as a futuristic concept which will take a long time to date, if indeed it ever does. The project was designed by Alvar Aalto in 1963, and begun two years later. Hallituskatu ('Government Street') forms a kind of Italianate piazza (much like that of Boston, Mass.), where the future Town Hall tower block will overlook a fan-shaped library (in the centre) and face Lappia House, a cultural complex for congresses, theatre, and concert-hall.

Rovaniemi Public Library (1965–8) has a major room lit from the north, with the Adult Lending, Children's, Lapp, and Reading Room departments. Other rooms on the main floor include workrooms, study-rooms, reading-rooms, discussion-rooms, administration, conference hall and exhibition hall. A lower floor contains a music library. Opening hours are 11–7 (to 8 in winter) and 10–4 on Saturdays, the exhibition hall and newspaper-room being opened from noon to 4 on Sundays. Having identified myself as a librarian, I was allowed to enter the library on a Sunday afternoon, when it was closed to visitors, and browsed among the richly-stocked shelves of Finnish and foreign books, silently applauding Aalto's lighting and expert use of space.

Rovaniemi. Lappia House, designed by Alvar Aalto (Courtesy of Rovaniemi City Tourist Office)

Lappia House (1st phase, 1970–2; 2nd phase, 1972–5) made a great impression on me even before I entered, the roof of the façade resembling gentle Lappish fells. The basement is currently devoted to three exhibitions, but when the impressive Arctic Centre is complete, these indoor museums will be centralised there. The ground floor, with offices and a lobby, has a floor of marble sawn from quarries at Tervola; buffet and foyer have furnishings designed by the Alvar Aalto Bureau. The Main Hall (427 seats) and Congress Hall (130 seats) may be combined if necessary. The second floor has a rehearsal room and the Music college with changing-rooms for actors; actresses change on the third floor. Contours are repeated from Aalto's glass vases, to the Finnish Pavilion for the 1939 New York World Fair, from his M.I.T. Dormitory of 1947–9, to the undulating ceiling of Viipuri Library's lecture-hall (1927–34). Guided tours of Lappia House are conducted at 10, 1 and 4 from Mondays to Fridays between 1 June and mid-August. To a certain extent, Aalto's buildings look back to the age of the receding glaciers, when Finland's smooth, low contours first took shape, without a single mountain of any size. One cannot imagine a Finn inhabiting (or even designing in Finland) those tall skyscrapers routine in aggressive Manhattan. This may be why the winning Danish design for the new Arctic Museum of Rovaniemi (1980s) northwest of Highway 4 astonishes by its

184

horizontality, and the unassuming icicle-shaped glass arcade is intended to complement the surrounding landscape instead of dominating it.

Pride and joy of Lapland Provincial Museum during my visit was a wooden carving of an elk's head dated by pollen analysis and radio-carbon to 5800 B.C. Found in Lehtojärvi, it may have decorated a cult-staff or a boat-prow. A small curved knife from Rahkokangas (Sodankylä) comes from a Stone Age cremation burial between 2800 and 2000 B.C., but the earliest Lapland settlement so far excavated is that of Törmävaara (Tervola), with characteristic Comb-Pottery of about 3000 B.C., as well as slate axes, chisels, arrowheads, flint tools, quartz tools, and an amber pendant. Foundations of fifteen huts have been located on a bank dating to the mid-third millennium B.C., and the site has yielded a fine red-slate knife with a miniature elk's head carving.

The earliest pottery excavated so far in Finland comes from shore settlements on the left bank of Kemijoki near Valajaskoski. Dating to about 4,000 B.C., finds include slate tools, axes, chisels, picks. The Niskala settlement on the west bank of Valajaskoski was occupied from 3500 to 1500 B.C.: up to twenty Stone Age settlements were found to have an elk-headed slate knife, the usual range of slate and stone tools, and also articles imported from Eastern Russia, Northern Sweden, and even Denmark.

Rovaniemi itself goes back to the Stone Age as an inhabited site, for good strategic reasons, being on a headland commanding the confluence of Ounasjoki and Kemijoki. Korkalonniemi was inhabited by Stone Age settlers, who left tools, and became a seasonal fishing ground of the Lapps and the so-called Kemiläiset, or 'dwellers at the Kemi river'. Excavations from 1959 have so far yielded a fine stone bear-head hole mace, quartz tools, burned bone, flint and stone tools. The visitor is brought abruptly up to relatively modern times with finds from the 1961–5 digs at Juikenttä (Sodankylä). The first phase of occupation there extended from 500 B.C. to 100 A.D., but the second phase, from 1200 to 1600, appears to have been settled by semi-nomadic Forest Lapps only in spring and late summer, and to have incorporated a place of religious sacrifice as well as homes. Bronze and copper objects have turned up, with bone and iron tools. This prehistoric exhibition has now been transferred away from Rovaniemi, whose Tourist Office will give current information on where it can be seen.

The Lapp Exhibition proves that the romanticizing of the West towards the Sami people of the northern countries is terribly superficial. Luckily the Chernobyl disaster in Ukraine caused hardly any distress and hardship to the Lapps, or Sami as they call themselves, because it seemed not to contaminate to any significant level the ecosystem on which both reindeer and Sami depend. Some 30,000 Sami live in Norway today, 15,000 in Sweden, nearly 4,000 in Finland, and about 3,000 in the Soviet Union. The four northern regions of Finland counted 3,798 Sami in the 1970 census: 403 in the northwestern region of Enontekiö, 1,043 in the northeastern region of Utsjoki, 2,094 in the central Inari region, and 258 in the southern Sodankylä region nearest to Rovaniemi. Only in Utsjoki region do Sami constitute a majority over the Finns, and everywhere the northward urge to buy land for summer cottages is placing a great strain on traditional Sami lands and rights. Especial hardships trouble the Koltta, or Eastern Sami, who left Petsamo when the area became Soviet after 1945. Their economy, based on a winter village and related summer pastures with ancestral waters, collapsed when they were moved to poorer waters at Sevettijärvi, north of Inarijärvi. In 1964, a sixth of the population of Inari depended wholly or partly on fishing for their income, but water regulation (such as the Paatsjoki power station, operant since 1948) has reduced fish levels significantly. Reindeer-breeding is even more significant in terms of people employed in the industry, and revenue, To run a snowmobile, you must have a minimum herd of 300 reindeer, thus ruling out the smaller Sami herd-owner. The nomadism of the 1960s and before has given way to scientific farming: most reindeer are sold through commercial outlets run by Finns, who process and market the meat. This sale deprives the Sami of traditional deer products such as meat, blood, milk, skins used with natural thread to make adequate clothing, horn, bones, oil, glue and so on. Hunting for caribou played a great part in Sami life before commercial reindeer breeding gave them assured income; after the caribou became extinct the Sami's favourite game became ptarmigan, in a season lasting from October to March.

In 1973, a Sami Institute was founded to promote Sami interests; it is sited in Kautokeino, Norway, very close to the Finnish border north of Enontekiö. Protection must be freely given by all nations in which the Sami live as small minorities, for their rights are often, if not always, ignored on the questionably 'democratic' assumption that a national majority should determine national policy at the expense of each of its minorities. Look what happens to the Gypsies throughout Europe, for instance. Tourism plays havoc with the Sami, as does indiscriminate industrialisation, and the further dilution of Sami population in the spread of majority population both seasonally and permanently. The nine Sami languages, belonging to Finnish's Finno-Ugrian group rather than to the Indo-European group of Russia and Scandinavia, are constantly in danger of extinction. Finnicization in politics tends toward decay in Sami language and Sami literature; even literacy becomes a problem where there are few outlets for writing and no good commercial reason for learning Sami properly as a tool of artistic or literary communication. I tried to find books published in Sami at the Lapin Kansan Kirjakauppa in central Rovaniemi, the biggest bookshop in Finnish Lapland's biggest town, but found nothing at all: no grammar, no dictionary, and not even a simple school reader. The bookshop in Ivalo does have some Sami books, including Kirsti Paltto's *Voijaa, minun poroni!*, which has sold tens of thousands of copies. Finland appoints provincial artists to promote Sami culture, among them the music performer and recording artist Nils-Aslak Valkeapää and his successor Jaakko Gauriloff. Utsjoki district uses Sami within its municipal services, operating a bilingual kindergarten, and its schools have Sami-language textbooks and teaching manuals up to the leaving age of 18. Enontekiö district also offers Sami-language instruction to Sami children, the rest of the curriculum being in Finnish. Broadcasts offer news and schools programmes in Sami.

Those who have no time to visit the vastnesses of Lapland should try at least to spend a couple of hours in Lapland Forestry Museum and adjacent Ethnographic Museum in the suburb of Pöykkölä, by the shore of Salmijärvi, off Ranuantie.

Age-old felling techniques vanished in the 1960s with the mechanisation of the lumber industry, and the Lapin Metsämuseo shows a way of life already bewilderingly remote. Opening hours are noon to 6 daily (except Mondays) between mid-June and mid-September. The first wooden building you come to, 4 km from the city centre, is the ticket-office, originally an office-home belonging to a forester in Rovaniemi, and dating to 1937. The museum proper begins with a reconstructed horse-driver's log cabin of the early 20th century, with furnishings of the same epoch. The major building is the forest headquarters, accommodating the overseers, storekeeper, accountant and any other white-collar staff: this example, of 1939, came to Rovaniemi in 1970 from the upper Luiro. Soviet prisoners-of-war lived in it during the Winter War of 1939–40. Then you see a trading store of the 1920s from Savukoski, a stable of the 1940s from Jumiskojoki, a tool-shed with implements from the time when horses were used in lumbering, a smoke sauna, a log-floaters' cabin of 1904 used until 1961 at Koivu in Tervola, a steam tugboat built at Oulu in 1898 and reassembled on Kemijärvi, working there till 1962, and finally the Sandberg Locomotive. Mechanised felling using steam locomotives began with two engines at Nuortti in 1913–14. One locomotive is still there, and the other has been donated to the museum. The idea of moving these monsters from the railhead at Rovaniemi reminded me of Werner Herzog's movie *Fitzcarraldo*, in which the Peruvian rubber baron Carlos Fitzcarraldo is shown organising the trans-shipment of a river boat through the Amazon jungle. The seven-ton tender, heaviest part of all, was dragged along Finnish forest ways by six pairs of horses. The locomotives, once in place, could pull up to nine pairs of sledges each, and each sledge carried up to eighty logs. Since the locomotive itself weighed twenty tons, you can readily imagine the difficulty of descending slopes! Mechanical problems incessantly plagued the

Sandberg Locomotive (Photographed in the late 1930s) (Courtesy of Rovaniemi Forestry Museum).

enterprise, which failed because World War I interfered with the supply of spare parts, and they stopped production in spring 1916, after transporting more than 150,000 logs.

Nearby stands the Ethnographic Museum run by a local society called Rovaniemen Totto since 1957. Admission in summer is 12–4 daily (June through August) and elsewhen by appointment (tel. 181 095). I was astonished to find records of settled agriculture in Rovaniemi in their Middle Ages, that is roughly five centuries back, long before the first roads connected Lapland with the south. But this prosperous North Bothnian farmstead is hardly typical of local landholdings, for in 1850 Pöykkölä became the largest in the parish, with 5400 acres, or about 2200 hectares. The farmers there were still in fact the Pöykkö family registered as owners in 1640, and it did not pass out of their hands until 1910. Most of the seventeen buildings on the site date to the 19th century, though not all stood here originally. The main complex consists of three buildings: the manor house itself, a great storehouse, and the winter cow-barn, the last parallel with a much smaller summer cow-barn. The grounds also display two granaries, a shed and blacksmith's shop then, clockwise, a hay-shed, fish-barn, threshing-house, smoke sauna, boathouse, boat-shed, two-storey barn and

188

clothes shed. From the southern window of the manor house I gazed out to the boathouse above Kemijoki, across the green lawns, at my side a spinning-wheel that could have come straight out of Wagner's *Flying Dutchman*. The living-room, roughly eight metres square, acted as a workroom for all the family during the long summer days, with windows on three sides. Women worked between the oven and the southern wall, whereas men occupied the rest of the space, the two sexes meeting for meals at a communal table at the far end. An oblong ante-chamber leads to the kitchen and dairy. The drawing-room has the daughter's original bridal bed; the formal drawing-room is seen next, then the mistress's chamber and the master's chamber.

Rovaniemi. Pöykkölä. Manor House

The large two-storey storehouse has a fascinating collection of photographs from before Independence and after, including buses in 1923. The lower floor displays carts, sleighs, prehistoric finds, and tools used in everyday occupations. The upper floor has a splendid model of Muurola's great salmon dam, and another of the 1857 seed-grain storehouse ordered by Rovaniemi Parish Council. Other exhibits demonstrate the significance of reindeer husbandry, agriculture, fishing and hunting in Lapland. If you spend the third Sunday of July in Rovaniemi, don't miss the Marjetta Day festival at Pöykkölä's courtyard, with singing, dancing, barbecued salmon and other seasonal delicacies.

Rovaniemi Parish Church, the fourth on the site at Kirkkotie 1, was designed by B. Liljeqvist and completed in 1950, with seating for a congregation of nine hundred. Its altarpiece, a fresco on the theme of 'The Fountain of Life', is an academic work by Lennart Segerstråhle, less inspiring than the splendid curved archway framing it. The scene is Ounasvaara, above the confluence of Kemijoki and Ounasjoki. Depicting the struggle between good and evil, Segerstråhle makes a Sistine Chapel-like divide between the good, accepting the waters of eternal life, for whom angels blow exultant trumpets; and the evil, who turn their back on Christ, below angels trumpeting doom. Antti Salmenlinna's stained-glass *Atonement* ('Sovitus' does not mean 'adaptation' in a religious sense despite what the local leaflet asserts) sadly exemplifies the rule that Finnish artists have never managed to overcome the aesthetic-technical problems of stained glass as a medium of expression since the apogee of S. John's in Tampere. Opening hours are 9–8 between 1 June and mid-September.

On the other side of the river stands the new Orthodox Church, at Ounasvaarantie 16, designed in 1957 by Ilmari Ahonen and Toivo Paatela. When the Orthodox monks fled from Valamo, or Valaam Island in Lake Ladoga or Laatokka to Heinävesi, halfway between Kuopio and Savonlinna, they brought their treasures with them, and some of these treasures have found their way to Rovaniemi Orthodox Church, which may be seen by appointment (tel. 312 361).

Near the pleasant Ounasvaara camping site, we ascended Ounasvaara on a chair-lift to Hotelli Ounasvaara, for the best view in miles: across Ounasjoki to the town. Marked ski and hiking tracks run for 25 km, and illuminated ski tracks for 14 km. At the Sports Institute of Lapland, courses are held throughout the year in a variety of disciplines, from shooting to tennis, from swimming to slalom. Ounasvaara boasts a holiday village (cabins to sleep six) and cottage accommodation, as well as the unique Ounasvaara Hotel, with a sauna in each of its 48 double rooms and seven large suites. As it was summer, I whirled down Ounasvaara on the German-made sledge-slope, not used on rainy days; the whole metal course is dismantled for the winter, and rebuilt at the beginning of the following summer.

Rovaniemi. Spire of Lutheran Cathedral

Rovaniemi's other hotels include the Rantasipi Pohjanhovi, Pohjanpuistikko 2; Hotel Gasthof, Koskikatu 41, opened in 1986; City-Hotelli, Pekankatu 9, one of the Point Hotels Group; the Oppipoika, Korkalonkatu 33, run in conjunction with the local Hotel and Restaurant School; Polar Hotel, Valtakatu 23, where I enjoyed a memorable luncheon of mushroom soup, salmon and salad, and cranberry pie; and Lapinportti, Kairatie 2. Do not be put off by the term 'boarding-houses': the Aakenus (Koskikatu 47), Outa (Ukkoherrantie 16B) and Rovaniemi (Koskikatu 27) are not only spotless, but as welcoming as any of the big hotels, if not more so, and the rates at the Outa are 120 FM (single) and 190 (double), as compared with 380 FM for a double at the Ounasvaara. Rovaniemi's Youth Hostel, at Hallituskatu 16, faces Lappia House in the city centre.

Juhani Pallasmaa designed Rovaniemi Art Museum (1986) to occupy part
of the 1930s bus depôt on Lapinkävijäntie 4. The philanthropists Antti and
Jenny Wihuri established their foundation in 1942 to 'promote and support
the cultivation of the Finnish people spiritually and financially'; in the early
years grants were made, but acquisitions have played a more significant part
since 1957. The Wihuri Art Collection was donated to the City of Rovaniemi
in 1986 and it is now being shown in conjunction with changing exhibitions.
The collection's main strengths extend over the four decades since 1940.
Opening hours are noon to 6 every day but Wednesday (to 8), Saturday
(10–4) and Monday (closed). There is a permanent exhibition of the
paintings by the naive artist Andreas Alariesto, whose name means 'Below
Riesto'. Born in 1900 in Riesto, the painter now lives in Vuotso, following
the flooding of his village to make the artificial lake called Lokka. Alariesto
portrays Sami folkways in his attractive pictures. In *Vuotso* (1965) he depicts
the northern village as it would have been in 1909, with *kota*s or wigwams not
yet superseded by log dwellings, and no highways to south or north. A winter
kota (shown in a painting of 1972) would be constructed by weaving branches
and saplings between supporting poles, leaving a hole at the top for smoke to
emerge from a fire burning on gravel surrounded by rocks. Birchbark kept
out the damp, and the frame was covered by peat, the floor being kept dry

Vuotso, 1908–9. Painting by Andreas Alariesto.

192

Kemijoki. Logs on the river

and warm by a thick carpet of birch-twigs. I liked best the *Hunting and Storage* narrative painting of 1970, depicting pits dug to entrap deer, which were then slaughtered with knives or spears. Fish was stored on a platform built on a tree-trunk above the reach of land-animals, a face carved on top of the trunk in the hope of scaring away birds. Meat would be stored in the waters of a cold stream, below boulders, and remain fresh up to a week even in summer. A pole or *seita* was carved and set up at the site of a successful hunt in gratitude to the forest spirits who had lured the deer to a kill.

I was lucky enough to spend time in Rovaniemi during the North Calotte Trade Fair, in the first week of August. Lapin Systema were showing the new Canon Fax 220, Lapin Auto the Peugeot 309: all the technological expertise of the modern world has arrived in Lapland.

Next I took a river cruise along Kemijoki from the boat harbour. The ninety-minute jaunt starts at 10, 12.30, 3, 6 and even ten o'clock(!) in June and July, slackening off to noon, 2.30, 5 and 7.30 in August and September. M/s *Lapinneito* is an endearingly sluggish old craft of 1935, aptly slow in a monotonous riverscape where things to see, 'Sehenswürdigkeiten' if on the Rhine or Mosel, become few and far between once you have passed below the Valtatie Bridge and the narrows in view of Pöykkölä. Captain Juntunen reminisced about his times in Buenos Aires, and about his years at Hanko up to 1972, when *Lapinneito* made what will be its last long journey, up the Bothnian coast to the north.

The regular city tour begins on Sundays at 3 and Tuesdays at 5 from the City Tourist Office at Aallonkatu 2 C between 15 June and 17 August, visiting the Provincial Museum, Ounasvaara Hill, and the Arctic Circle complex.

Scheduled buses to the Arctic Circle (8 km northward, on Highway 4) leave the bus station from bays 3 and 4 at 7.35, 8.10, 11.30, noon, 3.15, 4.15, 5.15, 5.20, 6.20, 8.50 and 9.10, but the sixth, seventh, ninth and eleventh do not operate on Saturdays. The Santa Claus village on the Arctic Circle replies annually to millions of letters sent by children to Father Christmas, and entertains large numbers of tourists with Finland's nearest approach to

'Santa Claus Village' near Rovaniemi. Reindeer compound

Disneyland. The nearest zoo is at Ranua, but you can see munching reindeer in enclosures here, and children will adore the play area, souvenirs, certificate for crossing the Arctic Circle, and Santa Claus's post-office, with its special postmark. Wooden clocks on sale reminded me of a sober Swiss valley (without the cuckoos), and women and children pounced eagerly on splendid clothes for all ages, inventive toys, and leatherwork. My own eye was caught by Pentik ceramics of high style, knives by the Rovaniemi knifesmith Marttini, and spectacular furs by A. & K. Turkis (a good model retailing here at 4000 DM, confided a German woman, would cost her 8000 DM back home). She would also recover 11% of the purchase price at the border, as a tax-free shopper. Reindeer skins cost 170 FM each (@ 4.5 FM to the US$), but equally characteristic are juniper table-mats and breadboards, little bottles made from antlers, and Lappish spoons.

The Arctic Circle complex is visited by Arctic Safaris (Valtakatu 26), who arrange trips by snowmobile and four-wheel-drive Land Cruiser from the city or airport, or a night safari with a meal of sautéed reindeer at a traditional Lapp conical tent lit by 'lumberjack candles', three-foot high torches made of 200-year-old pine, with a sauna, and a chance to earn a reindeer-driving licence. Canoe safaris can be arranged on Raudanjoki, Sinettäjoki and Vikajoki, the price including canoe-hire, lifejackets, paddles, two guides, transportation to the starting-point, coffee and food.

Virtually any type of car or caravan may be hired in Rovaniemi. Canoes may be rented from Otemuovi at Pallarintie 14, and bicycles from Urheilupyörä at Valtakatu 17.

North Again

Finnair arranges one-night excursions from Helsinki to Rovaniemi (no accommodation) during the long summer nights from 1 June to mid-July, from Helsinki to Ivalo (accommodation in a log cabin) from 1 June to 30 September, and a three-day North Cape Safari, with self-drive Suzuki jeeps from Ivalo to Inari (night in a cabin at Muotkan Rouktu), North Cape (night at the inn in Karasjok) and back to Ivalo via a Lapp reindeer farm at Kaamanen, on Lake Aksu.

The public bus is the cheapest way to see the North Cape, and has the advantage that you can meet other Finns (and very few tourists) on the way. As a rough guideline, throughout the year, you leave Rovaniemi bus station (near the rail station) at noon, with stops in Sodankylä (20 minutes at 2.15) and Ivalo (half an hour at 5.30), arriving for the night at Karasjok at 7.45. You leave Karasjok at 7 next morning, changing at Russenes at 9.45 to a bus arriving at Kåfjord at 11.30, changing again for buses at 11.30 or 8.30 p.m.

for the hour's ride to Honningsvåg. It takes 50 minutes to drive thence to the North Cape, with daily departures at 12.20 and additional summer departures at 4, 7.30 and 9.45 p.m., returning at 2.10, 5.50, 9 p.m. and half-past midnight.

Car/sleeper trains provide daily service from Helsinki, Turku and Tampere. Lapland Travel Ltd, Koskikatu 1, Rovaniemi 20, provide a comprehensive brochure offering a wide range of summer cottages, hunting safaris, sailing safaris, fell-skiing and ski-doo safaris, and hiking or caneoing holidays. Cross-country skiing has become a leading pastime in Lapland, even more than in the rest of the country, and you will see athletes whirring along on summer skis even on warm days when the first snowfall seems a generation off.

One joyous morning in August I entered a bus marked Sodankylä – Ivalo. Families on holiday, soldiers returning from leave, solitary individuals of all ages including the mandatory complement of dazzlingly beautiful blondes: it was an average Finnish busload, though possibly a trace quieter even than usual. Roads and railtracks are made negotiable twelve months of the year, despite temperatures well below freezing over a period of several consecutive months. The standard of roadbuilding and road maintenance is first-rate throughout Finland, and Lapland is no exception. I chatted with a young man on his way to Ivalo, to spend time with his family. His English was slow, measured and careful: it was obvious that he was being polite to an inquisitive intruder, rather than sociably making pleasurable conversation. He would draw in his breath, murmuring 'jo' (pronounced *yaw*) then anglicizing it to 'yes' for my benefit. This Swedish colloqualism replaces the classical Finnish 'kyllä' in familiar speech. The conductor collected my 72 FM (less than US$15) for the 260 km round-trip to Sodankylä as the forest began to close in on both sides of the two-lane Highway 4 before Ylinampa, then we stopped, virtually in the middle of a Lapp forest, at Vikajärvi crossroads. Keidas Baari bore the sign 'Foods/Matvaror/Livsmedel/ Lebensmittel' in the order English, Finnish, Swedish and German, and I drank black coffee and ate a bun (the ubiquitous *pulla*) in the company of Jaakko, respecting his silence. The sun began to pierce through the birchwoods as we boarded the bus, which had little posters exhorting us to 'Pidä Lappi Siistinä', 'Keep Lapland Clean', an amusing request in thousands of square miles of woods where only birds and wild animals roam.

Then on, relentlessly on through forest, forest, glinting lakeshores, forest, forest. Beware of the Lappish madness, which will forever change your life, swivelling your viewpoint from its former position, like any long sojourn in the Sahara desert or Amazon jungle. The great lakes of the south induced in me a quiet rapture that rose to a crescendo in the north. Who could fail to respond with reverence to the great forests, and the oncoming fells? If the wilderness does not drive you crazy, it will lure you inevitably back. Many Finns have settled in Canada (though 95% of them in the cities), and the geographical analogies press home on you from all sides: vastness, great blue skies, a long hard winter, solitude and a toughness of body and spirit defined in Finnish as *sisu*, in geology as granite, on which the country was born, on which you walk, in which you sculpt, an immanent presence vibrating in and through every landscape.

At ten a.m. we drew into the Linja-Autoasema (Bus Station) at Sodankylä, a town built between the rivers Kitinen and Jeesiö, with an open-air museum 2.5 km south of the centre open from 1 June to 30 August between 10–4 every day but Sundays (12–6). The Old Church (1689) and New Church (1859) remain open from 10–6 every day from early June to mid-August.

Tankavaara. My 'summer cottage'

Our bus returned from its Post Office delivery and pick-up half an hour later, and we sped along Highway 4 through the village of Sattanen, with sturdy one-family wooden homes on all sides, travelling along rivers and lakes between Petkula and Peurasuvanto. A gloriously sunny day made the half-hour drive to the village of Vuotso memorable for scintillas of gold radiating like burnished arrows through the endless forests.

I arrived at the village of Tankavaara at 12.15, just in time for a welcome lunch with Inkeri Syrjäinen. She has lived in Lapland for fifteen years, ten of them at Tankavaara, a gold-panning village. Most of her guests are Finns, Swedes and Germans, high season being June-September, 20 December-6 January for the cross-country slalom, and mid-February to mid-May for skiing, and the husky-drawn sleigh ride between Tankavaara and Pikku Tankavaara, taking an hour for the round trip. Over meat and potato soup, exquisite salmon, and Arctic cloudberry waffles, Inkeri told me about a friend of hers in Helsinki who refused to travel to the Hansa town of Lübeck because it was too far, but travelled every summer to Ivalo, which is a great deal farther. Mosquitoes are not so bothersome in August, the worst time being June and July. Outside, raindrops still glittered on leaves and branches from last night's shower: blueberries and cranberries tantalisingly tiny, though surprisingly numerous. My hotel suite, comprising a quarter of a house, consisted of a combined bedroom, log fireplace and sitting-room with dining-table, and a little attic area reached by a ladder with two children's bunks. Ten family cottages nearby accommodate three or four persons each, all furnished in plain, sturdy pine.

Gold-panning is a way of life over many decades in this part of the country, and the world championships were held at Tankavaara from 9 to 16 August 1987. I tried my fortune, exchanging hiking boots for wellingtons, and paddling to a log where where expert tuition was provided by Sari from Oulu. I scooped up brown mud in a very fine sieve, shaking it rapidly from side to side to lodge stones and pebbles on one side, then brushing these out into the waters and panning again. After ten minutes of careful sieving my results were: nothing at all, but a tiny speck of local local gold was nevertheless attached to a souvenir card for me, to reward my enthusiasm. In the end, I found the Gold Museum more rewarding than I found the panning, even if the total amount of gold ever found in Lapland would hardly have excited Klondike prospectors. Agricola recorded gold-prospecting in Lapland in *De veteribus novis metallis* (1546) but private prospecting was not officially licensed until 1837. Three sailors panned more than 2 kg of gold from Ivalojoki in the space of five weeks in 1869, causing the Tsar to set up in 1870 a state body to control prospecting: Kultala Kruunu, under whose auspices 335 visitors panned in that season, the largest find being about 19 kg, while a total of 57 kg was panned by 500 prospectors in the 1871 season,

Tankavaara. Panning for gold

dropping thereafter. In the 1920s the Ivalojoki Company began mechanical prospecting of gold veins at Laurila and Ivalojoki, but within a few years the seams proved uncommercial. Another company, Lapin Kulta Oy, invested heavily at the same time but gave up. In 1935 the biggest gold nugget found so far in Finland, at Luttojoki, weighed 395 grams. To put Lapp gold into perspective, it is estimated that the total found so far weighs 600 kg, the same amount that Outukumpu copper, gold and silver mines (between Joensuu and Kuopio) produce in a average year. Finland's annual average of 1,000 kg compares with figures of 852,300 kg in South Africa, 280,000 in the U.S.S.R., and 60,000 in Canada. A separate mineralogy museum displays all the types of local stone, semi-precious and precious alike. Reindeer in a nearby enclosure watched me warily as I wandered past them,

199

anywhere, then farther into the woods. Every birch is unique, an individual, with its own bark, its own history of insects and weather; yet if you look at each of them individually you would go mad; because there are too many of them. I began to suffer the amazement of the cosmologist, trying to fix himself as a meaningful human being in countless aeons amid numberless galaxies. On Highway 4, tiny cars hummed like beetles, escaping agoraphobia at eighty miles an hour. Around me on every side, the fells swayed and curved like *Kalevala* heroes asleep, breathing gently on their side. In a few weeks, the time called *ruska* would – virtually overnight – enchant green colours into browns, reds, yellows, lilacs. *Ruska aika* does not endure: from the long summer transition is brief to the much longer winter. Nerves fray as the Finn desperately seeks to prolong the glorious days of summer (longest in Ahvenanmaa and the Turku archipelago) by staying up all night, or taking weekend breaks in the wilderness to prolong the illusion that cities are a mirage. Plotinus graded knowledge into three stages: opinion, based on sense; science, based on reason; and illumination, based on ecstasy, or apprehension of reality beyond the gift of words. The nearer one comes to nature, then, the higher the risks of ecstasy, and what I experience in the deserts of Arabia or the Pacific seas comes as close to illumination as did 'the dark night of the soul' of San Juan de la Cruz.

As a redwing sprang its invisible cord of flight from one birch to another, I entered that wordless movement, instinct with dread of capture and the exhilaration of eluding it.

The Prey

> pace lost, aim tracked,
> falcon clouded, vixen tensing,
>   flutter shrill
>   between howl echoes,
>   curled talons
> I am the gaudy prize
>   before today's full moon
>   after yesterday's eclipse

a solitary wolverine sniffing up

Lapland is an excellent region to study the northern lights, or aurora borealis. Sodankylä has a northern lights observatory, which might offer to show you something of the phenomenon, but there is no resident tourist guide, so you would be better advised to visit the northern lights planetarium at the Tankavaara guide centre. The aurora borealis, first so called in a

French book of 1733, is linked to the occurrence of sunspots, the shape being a rainbow arc, seen in clear weather on dark nights in northern Lapland, especially around April and October. Occasionally, lights flare up late into the night, cloudy patterns shimmering, glowing and fading in brilliant greens, whites, oranges.

I breakfasted next day with a group of Swedes who had just returned, breathless from jogging on the forest tracks, where they had been caught by a heavy shower. Refreshed by porridge and strawberry jam, apple juice, bread and butter with cheese and ham, and coffee, I headed for the adjacent Urho Kekkonen National Park, extending from Highway 4 to the Soviet border, which was established in 1983 to preserve the forest, wet lands and fells of 2,550 sq km of southeastern Lapland. Hikers and campers are encouraged to wander everywhere except close to the border zone, but hunting is limited to local residents and a prior fishing permit must be obtained by anglers from the National Forestry Board.

Accommodation is provided at six peat-covered Lappish wigwams, twelve locked huts (to which keys may be obtained at Kiilopää in advance) and many unlocked huts. Hotels are dotted about Saariselkä's fells, from the luxurious old-established Laanihovi at Laanila to the modest Muotka Maja (only 60 FM ($12) a night including breakfast and sauna). Tankavaara, Saariselkä and Kiilopää have nature trails, along which the visitor is introduced to aspects of the park's natural history. Ski tracks are marked out (and illuminated for 16 km) all over the region.

The acidic rocks support sparse vegetation, with some deciduous trees in sheltered gullies, but the first trees to preponderate after the melting of the glaciers beginning ten thousand years ago were birch; then with the gradual warming of the environment pine forests began to spread, and three thousand years ago the spruce dug in its roots, since when climate and vegetation have remained much the same. Lakes in the zone are few and insignificant, the largest being Luirojärvi, below Saariselkä fells. Continuing south-east, hikers will come to the surprise of Jaurujoki, a wilderness river meandering amid pine-heaths and spruce-gullies. Virtually unpopulated wilds bring you to Kemijoki, which will wind its way down to Kemijärvi, Rovaniemi and finally to the Gulf of Bothnia at the port to which it gave its name. Quite a different environment is the bogland of Sompio, with treacherous areas, parts of which are closed off completely to visitors as a strict reserve.

The park's ecosystem remains fragile, and one should avoid approaching timid reindeer, especially during the spring, when females are liable to miscarry. Reindeer lichen (*Cladonia*) is to be found on dry pine heaths, like those in the vicinity of Saariselkä. Kiilopää bears a covering of low fell birch scrub; the upper fells have low dwarf birch (*Betula nana*), crowberry

(*Empetrum nigrum*)and meadows of wild azalea (*Loiseleuria procumbens*).

Brown bears still roam the park, as do wolves and wolverines, outnumbered by the twenty-five thousand reindeer belonging to three different associations.

The wetlands harbour a wide variety of birds: spotted redshank, greenshank, jack-snipe, broad-billed sandpiper, meadow-pipit, wood sandpiper, ruff and yellow wagtail. Coniferous forests yield common sightings of brambling, redwing and willow warbler; fell birch groves form the habitat of ptarmigan, redpoll, bluethroat, wheatear and golden plover.

In the National Park Centre, Raili Outakoski took me upstairs to see six newly-born lemmings, sightless and helpless, less than one day old. The adult lemmings, crazily trying to tear and bite their way out of their narrow cages, were given milk powder and tiny pieces of apple. The veteran, one year old, slower and more methodical in his escape attempts, watched me, another potential enemy, out of the corners of his busy eyes. Outside, I followed a nature trail on duckboards raised above the bracken, with markings for berries, a tall spruce, a three-hundred-year old pine, then the duckboards ended and at a bifurcation I chose the 6-km *Kuukkelilenkki* ('Long Trail') in preference to the 1-km *Urpiaislenkki*. Stops included the track to Saariselkä, a 'raita' tree, birches killed by fungi, a pumping station, a pine gnawed from the top, a glacier line, and a feature on the fells.

Invigorated by the warm sun, gentle breezes, and air tangy with scented pines, I began to hike north along Highway 4. Roller-skiers in groups of four to six whooshed up to me and past, heads purposefully down, in training for the first snows. Reindeer loafed by the roadside, occasionally crossing in the hope of better grazing on the other side. I tried to name whatever I saw in Finnish: *poro*, for reindeer; *koivu*, for birch; *tunturi*, for fell.

I defy anyone sceptical of the magical connections between language and nature to remain indifferent to the resonant beauty of Finnish words in the forests and lakes: *aurinko* (sun), *hiljaisuus* (stillness, silence), *huurteinen* (rimed with hoarfrost), *kanerva* (heather), *raskasmielinen* (melancholic), *kaukainen* (distant), *vadelma* (raspberry), *karhunvatukka* (blackberry), the stress always on the first syllable like a delicate xylophone hammer.

Off right I saw a turn to Kiilopää, a wilderness centre from which campers can set out to discover Rautulampi on a recognised hiking and skiing route, then another road meandered off left towards the isolation of Kuttura: a road I longed to take. I chatted to a Lapp selling knives, bone carvings, whole antlers, and reindeer skins in a covered stall by the side of the road, exchanging simple German. He was roasting meat over an open log fire, flames flickering up to the dripping carcase. As I wended north again towards Laanila, cars headed off towards Saariselkä tourist centre. Reindeer munched on grass by the side of the road: two together, then four, then

Kaunispää. Forest View.

three, wary of my approach. They are branded with ownership marks from the end of June to the beginning of July, and some clearly feared that I could be yet another brander, tormentor, rounder-up. As I rounded another bend, climbing ever upwards into fell-country, I imagined these contours in *kaamos*, that deep-blue wintry sleep from the early snows to late February, when day emerges for only a few uneasy hours between twilight and twilight.

This year I should never reach Ivalo, much less Inari. I trudged, a solitary labouring ant on a great path, along a way marked 'Kaunispää', meaning 'belvedere', recalling the tolerant amusement of a Finn from Haapajärvi on learning where I was destined that afternoon. 'Kaunispää? In Lapland, *everywhere* is a kaunispää'.

Yes, as I rested at the top, I admitted to myself that I might have saved myself the exhilarating climb to this vantage point. At the foot of Kaunispää, the view had been almost as magnificent: miles of conifers, hundreds of thousands of single trees, each with their own lives and destinies. I turned full circle, and the clear skies hovered like all-encompassing angels enfolding the majesty of the pagan forests. Dizzily, I closed my eyes against the Lappish madness, and slowly paced again downhill. To Tankavaara in an evening that never fell, tomorrow to Rovaniemi, to Kemi, to Helsinki, and away back home . . . I write the last words down, and the shock of Finland returns with a vigour that never diminishes with passing time. I thought I had returned unscathed, but the Lappish madness, more insidious than summer gnats or blackfly, still has me in its jealous grip.

USEFUL INFORMATION

When to Come

Sportsmen will know when to come to Finland for their own favourite activity, such as cross-country skiing in the winter or hiking in the summer or autumn. But for those wanting to explore Finland at its best, the time to travel is from late June to mid-August, when days are long, museums and galleries are open, and summer theatres prolong the day from six in the morning to after eleven at night. Spring may last only a couple of weeks, when the last snows begin to give way with miraculous suddenness to warm summer with scarcely time for you to draw breath between; but autumn – a couple of weeks in September – rightly attracts many fans year after year for the sublime colours, swiftly changing like mannequins at nature's fashion show. October has little to recommend it, but the first northern snows in November or December will quicken the pulse of winter sports enthusiasts. December and January have very short days, as though night has taken up its option on a mortgage of the land. February temperatures may drop to –40°C in Lapland, and March is often the best month for skiing in the south. April and May promise springtime, so long in the expectation, and days lengthen with coats of lilac in the cities.

You may be surprised by summer heat, due to the Gulf Stream from the west, and dry continental conditions from the east. Take summer clothes, with a sweater for the evenings or steamer-trips, if travelling from June to August, with a raincoat or umbrella. Extra pullovers will be needed in spring and autumn, and in winter there is really no limit to the clothing that you should take, including woollen underwear, heavy anoraks (and furs if your conscience will allow), gloves and headgear.

These are the average temperatures in Helsinki at midday throughout the year, in degrees Centigrade:

January	-4.7	July	19.5
February	-4.1	August	18.3
March	0.1	September	13.6
April	5.1	October	8.0
May	11.5	November	2.0
June	17.6	December	-2.0

How to Come

Finnair operates non-stop services between London (Heathrow) and Helsinki twice daily (except Saturdays) between April and October, and twice daily (except Tuesdays and Saturdays) between November and March. From New York, services are five times a week and from Montreal twice a week. Consult Finnair or your travel agent for the arrangement best suited to your requirements. In London, Finnair is at 14 Clifford St., W1X 1RD, tel. (01) 408-1222; in New York, 565 Fifth Avenue, tel. (212) 689-9300; in Montreal, 625 President Kennedy Avenue, tel. (514) 282-1173.

A four-tier tariff operates over the route London-Helsinki. The most economical is the APEX fare with a 14-day advance purchase rule and a minimum stay of 14 days. The next level is the instant purchase fare (PEX), with a requirement of one Saturday overnight following the day of travel to Finland. This is followed by the Eurobudget fare, which has an open return option, while the Executive class fare has no restrictions and a ticket validity of one year, allowing total flexibility. APEX, PEX and Eurobudget fares allow travel every day on direct services between the United Kingdom and Finland.

Abroad, or once in Finland, non-Scandinavians may obtain a special Finnair Holiday Ticket, allowing unlimited travel over 15 days for a fixed sum during June, July and August, as well as on Karair's domestic routes (but not on Finnaviation). Finnair offices can be found in Manchester and in the following North American cities: Atlanta, Boston, Chicago, Dallas, Los Angeles, San Francisco, Seattle, Vancouver and Washington.

Helsinki offices of Finnair are at Töölönkatu 21, Aleksanterinkatu 17, Eteläesplanadi 20, Elimäenkatu 14-16, Mannerheimintie 46-48 and 102, and at Vantaa Airport. In Turku the address is Aninkaistenkatu 3; in Tampere at Hotel Cumulus, Kyttälänkatu 2, and in Rovaniemi at Hotel Pohjanhovi, Koskikatu 1.

Domestic airports served by Finnair, other than the cities just mentioned, are Maarianhamina, Pori, Vaasa, Kokkola, Oulu, Kemi, Kittilä, Ivalo, Kuusamo, Kajaani, Joensuu, Kuopio, Varkaus, Savonlinna, Lappeenranta, Mikkeli, and Jyväskylä. Fares seem low by European standards; schedules are precise; and the views magnificent everywhere, from the Turku archipelago to the lakes of Tampere and the east, to Lapland's remote wilderness.

Rail Travel is efficient, luxurious, and even cheaper, naturally covering many more destinations than aircraft, and allowing a closer view. Try the circular tour from Pori (west coast) to Virrat, Jyväskylä, Pieksämäki, Hämeenlinna, Toijala, Loimaa, and Turku.

If you want to travel out to Finland by train, the connections are Ostend, Cologne, Hamburg, Stockholm; or Hoek van Holland, Bremen, Hamburg, Stockholm.

The Nordic Tourist Rail Ticket is a bargain, permitting unlimited rail travel in the four Nordic lands; Finnrail also offers a cheap pass for periods of 8, 15, 22 and 30 days.

Sea Travel may appeal to certain visitors, and in that case you can drive to Travemünde (BRD) and take the 22-hour Finnjet car ferry to Helsinki, operating throughout the year. Taking your car across Sweden, you can depart from either Newcastle or Felixstowe in summer (24 hours) to Gothenburg, then drive to Stockholm, and ferry from Stockholm to Turku or Helsinki. Some services stop at Maarianhamina (Åland).

Cars and Car-Hire. I was reminded of Ireland by the traffic-free roads in Finland. Once outside Helsinki, there is no stress at all, as long as you remember *never* to drink alcohol before driving, *never* to use the horn except in dire emergency, *always* to drive on the right, overtake on the left, and keep your lights on at all times. Exercise great care if there is the chance of reindeer roaming (in the north) and elk (elsewhere) particularly at twilight. If a speed limit is not shown, it will be 80 kph, or 50 mph. Report any animal casualty, or any accident to the local police.

You must have a driving licence valid in your own country, and a national sticker on the back of your car; don't lend, transfer or sell your car in Finland unless you pay duty, on penalty of confiscation. The green card is not mandatory, but highly desirable in case of accident. Report any accident to the Motor Insurance Bureau in Helsinki at Bulevardi 28 (tel, (90) 19251). A warning triangle must be carried, and used in emergencies.

Distances from Helsinki are: Rovaniemi 835 km, Tampere 175 km, and Turku 165 km. Service stations are numerous only on major roads, and open from about 7 a.m. to 8 p.m. If you can't see a petrol pump, ask at the village shop. A breakdown service is operated in Helsinki by the Automobile and Touring Club, Kansakoulukatu 10 (tel. (90) 069 0496). Here are some of the most important road signs, in addition to the usual pictograms.

Aja Hitaasti	Drive slowly
Heikko Tienreuna	Soft shoulders
Hirvivaara	Beware Elk!
Kapea Silta	Narrow Bridge
Kelirikko	'Broken Going' (bluntly, you may not be able to get through!)
Liukas Tie	Slippery Road
Lossi	Ferry
Porovaara	Beware Reindeer!
Tietyö	Roadworks

Car-hire is available from major companies in all important towns and cities. Some companies require the driver to be at least 25; others over 21. All stipulate a current national driving licence and *either* ownership of a major credit card or a cash deposit representing a proportion of the likely charge. Rates include third-party insurance.

Campers will recognise the traditional blue and white sign on campsites, with a picture of a tent inside a 'C'. The camping season runs from late May to September in the south, but mid-June to mid-August in the north. The Finnish Tourist Board will give you a brochure with current lists of over three hundred campsites. Never camp outside these marked sites without obtaining permission beforehand and *never* light a fire in the open nor dump litter anywhere except in the receptacles provided.

Bus routes are widespread, efficient, and frequent, serving even the most isolated districts once a day, whether by private bus companies or post-buses. Here is your chance to see most of the countryside that you would see by private car, but with the added opportunity to meet the average Finn, who is much more friendly than foreigners' folklore would have us to believe. In cities, buses prove the best way of getting around from one central bus station to the outskirts in Helsinki, Turku and Tampere. But Naantali, Porvoo, Ruovesi and Hämeenlinna are too small for buses to be useful; walking becomes an adventure because many details strike the wayfarer who allows plenty of time: the Jugendstil details in architectural decoration in the three cities; the prevalence of granite in Helsinki; shopsigns and imaginative shop-window displays; flowerbeds; the sheer beauty and elegance of women passing by.

In Helsinki, pay bus-conductors sitting at the back of the vehicle or, on buses and trams marked 'E' black on yellow, pay the driver. A tourist ticket valid for 24 hours on all public transport can be bought at city transport offices; or you might prefer books of ten tickets that can be bought in advance. Tickets for buses and trams are also valid on the metro line from Railway Square to Itäkeskus.

Taxis are black, with a yellow light illuminated when free. Try to obtain a 'taksi' from a rank or in the street, because if you telephone, the metred charge starts from the car's departure point, not when it picks you up. Surcharges apply not only at night, but also at weekends

Boats must be recommended as a quintessential part of Finnish life, and I describe trips in Helsinki harbour, to Porvoo; around Turku archipelago and to Naantali; from Tampere north to Virrat and south to Visavuori and Hämeenlinna; and along Kemijoki near Rovaniemi. If you have time, I suggest you add to your itinerary a boat trip on the lake system of Saimaa, lasting between several hours or up to a week, calling at Lappeenranta, Savonlinna, Mikkeli, Kuopio, Varkaus and Joensuu.

Accommodation

Finnish hotels tend to be expensive, because capital building costs are high and facilities superb. Your local Finnish Tourist Board office will supply lists of hotels with current rates, and there is a booking service on the lower level of Helsinki Rail Station. All local tourist offices in Finland will provide you with up-to-date lists of hotels at all price levels; you might care to consider a combination of the following ideas. Holiday villages, like Aulanko near Hämeenlinna or Maisansalo near Tampere, have flats or bungalows in rural settings. Summer cottages are a national institution which form part of the Finnish mystique, and you can hire majestic villas or rustic cabins in most parts of the country. Farmhouses take paying guests and in some cases the family will even arrange summer work on the farm by prior arrangement. Summer hotels, such as Domus Aboensis in Turku or Dipoli in Espoo, consist of very comfortable student quarters open to the public while the undergraduates are away. Youth hostels, with no age restrictions, are found in most towns. Private boarding-houses offer splendid value: ask for a 'matkustajakoti' if tourist offices are not quite sure what you mean. Some accommodation in private homes is offered, but standards are so strict that charges will inevitably seem much higher than you would expect outside Scandinavia. Motels are a new growth industry, and can be utilised if you find yourself benighted and do not want to find lodgings in a town centre. Finally, one must not omit the famous 'wilderness hut', or *autiotupa*. Hikers use this in Lapland, and to a lesser extent in the forested south; ideal for backpackers, they are really just a log-cabin with open fireplace in which to doss down for the night. Even if they seem by a sign to be semi-private, they are mostly open to everyone, as long as you remove all litter and replace firewood you have used by cutting locally.

Restaurants

Cuisine seems not to have made Finland famous, a curiosity attributable to the fact that the country is still considered by the less well-informed as 'cold, distant, and expensive' or 'kylmä, kaukana, ja kallis'. It may be all three, but in fact there is as wide a range of restaurants as in the U.S.A. or West Germany. Yes, *à la carte* meals will be relatively expensive, but *table d'hôte* menus are invariably excellent and usually good value. So too is the *voileipäpöytä* (literally 'bread and butter table') or *seisovapöytä*, the Finnish *smörgåsbord* of appetising hot and cold dishes usually provided at breakfast, lunch and dinner. At lunchtime you will see the Finns starting with herring dishes, then fish and seafood, then meats and salad, followed by fruit, finishing with coffee. There is no need to copy that order, but 'when in Rome' . . . Splendid breads and cheeses should be sampled, as should mushrooms during their short but dramatic season, when the conversation turns on little else. Don't tip more than you have to: a service charge (higher at weekends) is automatically added to your account. Waiters and waitresses do not expect tips, which will be a relief to those who only tip for swift service. Service in the best restaurants can be lackadaisical.

Hot and cold food is available on trains, at major bus stations, and in many museums and art galleries.

Passports and Visas

You need a valid passport to enter Finland, but nationals in Europe and North America do not require a visa for holiday visits or study up to three months long.

Diplomatic Representation and Tourist Information

The Australian Embassy at Sergels Torg 12, 10342 Stockholm has responsibility for Finland. The Canadian Embassy is at Pohjoisesplanadi 25B, 00100 Helsinki 10; the British Embassy and Consulate at Uudenmaan-katu 16–20, 00120 Helsinki 12; and the U.S.A. Embassy at Itäinen Puistotie 14, 00140 Helsinki 14.

Finnish embassies are to be found in the U.S.A. at 3216 New Mexico Avenue, N.W., Washington, D.C. 20016; in Britain at 38 Chelsea Place, London, SW1X 8HW.

In North America the Finnish Tourist Board can be found at 655 Third Avenue, New York, N.Y. 10017, tel. (212) 949–2333. In the U.K. write to 66/68 Haymarket, London SW1Y 4RF. If you are in transit through Scandinavia towards Finland, you can obtain information from the Finnish

Tourist Board offices at Vester Farimagsgade 3, 1606 Copenhagen V, Denmark; Lille Grensen 7, 0159 Oslo 1, Norway; and Kungsgatan 4A, 11143 Stockholm, Sweden.

Helsinki City Tourist Office is located at Pohjoisesplanadi 19, 00100 Helsinki; Tampere's at Verkatehtaankatu 2; Turku's at Käsityöläiskatu 3, and Rovaniemi's at Aallonkatu 2C.

You must be guided by your conscience (and your budget!) when it comes to furs, but furlovers will find Helsinki incredibly rich in quantity, style, and workmanship. For Finnish music, try Stockmann Melodia (5th floor of Stockmann's, Aleksanterinkatu 52) and Fuga, Unioninkatu 28. Hats and caps are the speciality of E.R. Wahlman, Pohjoisesplanadi 35. Confectionery is supplied by Oona and Oliver in Senaatti Center and Karkkipussi, Keskuskatu 6.

In Helsinki Summer Finns are smiling, outgoing, extravert enthusiasts who eat ice-cream, swim, sail, shop on the Kauppatori open-air market, and visit summer theatres and Linnanmäki Amusement Park (daily except Mondays from 10 May to 1 September). Winter Finns are an entirely different race: dour, unsmiling, wrapped in heavy clothing, introvert people who emerge with the first Siberian blasts, vanish again for a few months only when the ice melts and watery sunshine splashes pale golden light on roofs and unsuspecting windowpanes. Winter Finns go to opera, and ballet at the National Opera, Bulevardi 23–7 (seats from 25 up to 95 FM), theatre at the Finnish and Swedish theatres, and films starting at 7 and 9.

Summer theatre performances in Helsinki (tickets from Lippupalvelu, Aleksanterinkatu 23, tel. 643 043) take place at the Summer Theatre (end of Lääkärinkatu), Töölönranta Summer Theatre, Suomenlinna (Good Conscience Bastion), Student Theatre at Mustikkamaa, Operetta Theatre at the Rowing Stadium, and the Vanha Mylly (Old Mill), Herttoniemi Manor.

Classical music concerts are held at the House of Nobility (1863, on Aleksanterinkatu) and the Rock Church. Sacred music can be heard at the Espoo Church and S. John's as well as at the Cathedral.

The open-air market at Kauppatori stays open until 8, and at 7 p.m. folk-dance concerts take place at Seurasaari. Obtain current information on all local events from Helsinki City Tourist Office, Pohjoisesplanadi 19, tel 169 3757 and 174 088, open from 16 May to 15 September between 8.30 and 6 on weekdays, and 8.30–1 on Saturdays, and in winter between 8.30 and 4.30 on Mondays, and 8.30–4 Tuesdays through Fridays. There (and at the Rail Station) you can buy the special Helsinki Card valid for 1,2 or 3 days. Quite apart from its financial savings, the card will save you time and trouble because you can use it without charge on the Metro, trams, and the blue city buses (though not those which go outside the city), as well as the sightseeing bus and the ferry to Suomenlinna (and a free guided tour) and

Pihlajasaari, a free leather shoe-shine by Leonti Ivanov at the Rail Station, free entry to Vermo trotting track (Wednesdays at 6 and weekends at 1 throughout the year), a free ticket at 45 cinemas, free programmes at Helsinki Festival events and most theatres, admission and guided tour and folkdancing at Seurasaari, the zoo on Korkeasaari and the botanical garden at Unioninkatu 44, as well as the Winter Garden at Hammarskjöldintie 1 and Linnanmäki, Tivolikuja. The Helsinki Card allows free guided tours in English through the Finnish Parliament building, Mannerheimintie 30, and through Aalto's 1970s Finlandia Hall, Karamzininkatu 4. Most museums and galleries offer free entry to cardholders, including the Lauri and Lasse Reitz Foundation, Apollonkatu 23 B 64 (6th floor) on Wednesdays and Sunday afternoons from 3 to 5 and Helsinki Art Exhibition Hall, Nervanderinkatu 3 (behind Parliament House).

Tram 3T offers free travel on its figure-of-eight hourlong cruise through central Helsinki; a ninety-minute bus ride is free to cardholders from Asema-aukio (between the Rail Station and the Post Office) at 1 every Saturday throughout the year, and every day between 1 June and 31 August.

The Helsinki Card entitles you to a return ticket to Luoma (2 km walk to Hvitträsk) on trains E, L or Y which depart about every half-hour.

Those interested in the Finnish Design Center and the specialised Friends of Finnish Handicrafts will head smartly for the Museum of Applied Arts (1873) (Finland's answer to the Victoria and Albert Museum of 1851) on Korkeavuorenkatu 23, open from Tuesdays to Fridays between 11 and 5, and at weekends from 11 to 4. It is the third most popular museum in Finland, and nobody should leave Helsinki without exploring at least its permanent exhibition, even if you have no time for its temporary shows.

Customs and Currency

The easy-going Finns make immigration, customs and currency checks trouble-free. Just remember that you must have Bank of Finland permission to import and export 500 FM notes, you can bring in goods worth up to 500 FM duty-free, and in addition you can bring in (from Europe) 200 cigarettes, a litre of spirits and a litre of wine (400 cigarettes if coming from outside Europe). Returning to the U.S.A. or Canada you can import from Finland 200 cigarettes and either a litre of spirits or a litre of wine. Returning to the U.K. you can import from Finland 200 cigarettes, a litre of spirits and 2 litres of wine. There are no restrictions on the import of currency to Finland, and you may export currency up to the value you brought in.

Banknotes are issued in denominations of 500, 100, 50, 10 and 5 FM, and coins in 5 and 1 FM, 50, 20, 10 and 5 *penniä* (sg. *penni*). You can change money at international airports, ports, and Helsinki rail station. Your passport is needed to exchange travellers' cheques, which are quickly and easily exchanged not only at banks, hotels (adverse exchange rate!) and restaurants, but also in many big shops and department stores.

Health

Medical services are as fine as anywhere on earth in welfare-conscious Finland. By all means take out health insurance before you set out, as you would anywhere else, but repose perfect confidence in doctors, dentists and pharmacies. A pharmacy is signed *Apteekki* and does not sell the range of goods you expect in an American drug-store or British chemist's. Every hospital has a doctor on call day and night, and most speak English. I know: I was treated by one with speed, courtesy and efficiency. You can drink tap water with impunity in both cities and rural areas.

Speaking the Languages

In the U.K. you can learn Finnish at the School of Slavonic and East European Studies, Senate House, Malet St., London WC1E 7HU; at the Dept. of Scandinavian Studies, Newcastle-upon-Tyne, Newcastle NE1 7RU; and at the School of Modern Languages and European History, University of East Anglia, Norwich NR4 7TJ. In the U.S.A. there are courses at UCLA; Indiana University; University of Massachusetts; Suomi College, Hancock, Michigan 49930; University of Minnesota; Columbia University, New York; Brigham Young University, Provo, Utah; the University of Texas at Austin; Foreign Service Institute, Dept. of State, 1400 Key Blvd., Arlington, Va. 22209; and the University of Wisconsin.

Beginners can study while living in Finland (clearly the ideal solution), with a choice of Tampere, Helsinki and Espoo, Jyväskylä and Rauma. You can write for the latest details to the Council for Instruction of Finnish for Foreigners, Ministry of Education, Vuorikatu 5 B 18, SF-00100 Helsinki. The courses especially recommendable for those with English as a first language are: Summer University of Helsinki, Fredrikinkatu 39, SF-00120 Helsinki (40 hours in June, July or August); Summer University of Tampere, Vuolteenkatu 11, SF-33100 Tampere (Elementary, 18 days in June, followed by Continuation course, another 14 days ending about 4 July); and the Summer University of Jyväskylä (Elementary and Continuation courses, July and August).

Records and tapes and textbooks should be obtained in advance, and a dictionary, such as one of those by Aino Wuolle, published by Söderström. Books are very expensive in Finland, and few second-hand bookshops can be found, so if you can buy books about Finland before travelling, you will save a great deal.

Many anglophone visitors are surprised to learn that Finland has a second official language: Swedish, spoken as a first language by about seven per cent of the population, but understood or spoken as a second language by a great many more. It is hardly a compliment to call many Finns bilingual, for any educated Finn is likely to be at home in four languages, including English and German, and many understand French, Italian, Russian and can make a point in Estonian, a kindred language of the Soviet Republic across the water.

Words and Phrases

Stress the first syllable, lengthen double vowels, treat ä, ö, and y as German ä, ö, and ü, and give every letter uniform clarity (*tie*, 'road', is thus 'tee-eh'). It really does make a difference if you can learn at least the courtesies. No more is expected.

Do you speak English?	Puhutteko englantia?
I do not speak Finnish	En puho suomea
Yes	Jo; kyllä
No	Ei
Good morning!	Hyvää huomenta!
Good afternoon!	Hyvää päivää!
Good evening!	Hyvää iltaa!
Good night!	Hyvää yötä!
(If you get this correct, consider yourself an honorary Finn)	
Hello!	Hei, hei!
Goodbye!	Näkemiin
I should like. . .	Haluaisin. . .
. . . a city map	. . . kaupungin kartta
. . . a round-trip ticket	. . . lipun meno-paluu
Bus stop	Pysäkki
Excuse me	Anteeksi
No Smoking	Tupakointi kielletty
Where is the tourist office?	Missä on matkailutoimisto?
Entrance, Exit	Sisään, Ulos
Please help me	Auttakaa minua
I don't understand	En ymmärrä
How much is it?	Paljonko se maksaa?
Admission Free	Vapaa pääsy
Please	Olkaa hyvä
Thank you (very much)	Kiitos (paljon)

Waiter, waitress	Tarjoilija, neiti
Just a moment	Hetkinen
You're welcome	Ei kestä
Open, Closed	Avoinna, suljettu
Drinking Water	Juomavettä
Polluted Water	Juotavaksi Kelpaamatonta Vettä
Large, small	Iso, pieni
Here, there	Täällä, siellä
Free, occupied (reserved)	Vapaa, varattu
Cheap, expensive	Halpa, kallis
New, old	Uusi, vanha
Left, right	Vasen, oikea
Hot, cold	Kuuma, kylmä
Difficult, easy	Vaikea, helppo
Up, down	Ylös, alas
Forbidden	Kielletty
Finnish	Suomalainen
Finland	Suomi
American	Amerikalainen
U.S.A.	Yhdysvallat
English	Englantilainen
G.B.	Iso-Britannia
England, Scotland	Englanti, Skotlanti
Ireland, Wales	Irlanti, Wales (Vahless)
Where are the toilets?	Missä on wc? (Vaysay)
Men's Toilet	M, Miehille
Women's Toilet	N, Naisille
What time is it?	Paljonko kello on?
Restaurant; small restaurant	Ravintola, grilli
Snack-bar, coffee-bar	Baari, Kahvila (Kahvio)
Breakfast, lunch	Aamiainen, lounas
Dinner, supper	Päivällinen, illallinen
Tea, Coffee	Teetä, kahvia
Street, Lake	-katu, -järvi
Road, Hill	-tie, mäki
Bus stop	Pysäkki
River, Park	-joki, -puisto
Hall, Church	-talo, -kirkko
Castle, Square	-linna, -tori
Island, Archipelago	-saari, -saaristo
Telephone	Puhelin

Numbers and Days of the Week

1 yksi 2 kaksi 3 kolme 4 neljä 5 viisi 6 kuusi 7 seitsemän 8 kahdeksan 9 yhdeksan
10 kymmenen 11 yksitoista 20 kaksikymmentä 23 kaksikymmentä kolme 100 sata
145 sata neljäkymmentä viisi 200 kaksi sataa 1,000 tuhat 2,000 kaksi tuhatta

Sunday	Sunnuntai
Monday	Maanantai
Tuesday	Tiistai
Wednesday	Keskiviikko (*lit.* 'midweek', *Ger.* Mittwoch)
Thursday	Torstai
Friday	Perjantai
Saturday	Lauantai
Weekdays	Arkisin

Months and Seasons

January	Tammikuu	Winter	Talvi
February	Helmikuu		
March	Maaliskuu		
April	Huhtikuu	Spring	Kevät
May	Toukokuu		
June	Kesäkuu	Summer	Kesä
July	Heinäkuu		
August	Elokuu		
September	Syyskuu	Autumn	Syksy
October	Lokakuu		
November	Marraskuu		
December	Joulukuu	Christmas	Joulu

Holidays and Festivals

Museums and galleries are normally closed on Mondays. Set holidays falling annually are New Year's Day, Labour Day (Vappu, 1 May), National Day (6 December), and 24–26 December. Moveable holidays include: Epiphany (the Saturday between 6–12 January), Good Friday, Easter Monday, Ascension Day (the fifth Saturday after Easter), the day before Whitsun Day, Midsummer Day (Juhannus, the Saturday between 20–26 June) and All Saints' Day (the Saturday between 31 October and 6 November).

Local festivals are too numerous to list, but here is an indication of some of the most outstanding.

5 February	Runeberg Day, celebrated in Helsinki and elsewhere in honour of the national poet
Last Sunday in March	Lapp church festivals, often coinciding with weddings (also in early September)
Mid-July to early August	Savonlinna Opera and Music Festivals
Second week of August	Turku Music Festival and Ruissalo Rock Festival
Mid-August	Tampere Theatre Festival
Late August to early September	Helsinki Arts Festival

Index

224

THE OLEANDER PRESS

COASTAL FEATURES OF
ENGLAND AND WALES
J.A. Steers

A DICTIONARY OF COMMON FALLACIES
Philip Ward

THE GERMAN LEFT SINCE 1945
W.D. Graf

INDONESIA: A BIBLIOGRAPHY OF
BIBLIOGRAPHIES
J.N.B. Tairas

JAN VAN RYMSDYK: MEDICAL BOOK
ILLUSTRATOR
J.L. Thornton

THE LIFE AND MURDER OF
HENRY MORSHEAD
Ian Morshead

MEDICAL BOOK ILLUSTRATION:
A SHORT HISTORY
J.L. Thornton & C. Reeves

THE SMALL PUBLISHER
Audrey & Philip Ward

OLEANDER LANGUAGE AND LITERATURE

THE ART & POETRY OF C.-F. RAMUZ
David Bevan

BIOGRAPHICAL MEMOIRS OF
EXTRAORDINARY PAINTERS
William Beckford

CELTIC: A COMPARATIVE STUDY
D.B. Gregor

FRENCH KEY WORDS
Xavier-Yves Escande

FRIULAN: LANGUAGE & LITERATURE
D.B. Gregor

GREGUERÍAS: Wit and Wisdom of
R. Gómez de la Serna

INDONESIAN TRADITIONAL POETRY
Philip Ward

A LIFETIME'S READING
Philip Ward

MARVELL'S ALLEGORICAL POETRY
Bruce King

ROMAGNOL: LANGUAGE & LITERATURE
D.B. Gregor

ROMONTSCH: LANGUAGE & LITERATURE
D.B. Gregor

OLEANDER GAMES AND PASTIMES

**CHRISTMAS GAMES FOR ADULTS
AND CHILDREN**
Crispin DeFoyer

DARTS: 50 WAYS TO PLAY THE GAME
Jabez Gotobed

DICE GAMES NEW AND OLD
W.E. Tredd

**ENLIGHTENMENT THROUGH THE ART
OF BASKETBALL**
Hirohide Ogawa

ENNEAGRAMS: NINE-LETTER WORD GAME
Ian D. Graves

PUB GAMES OF ENGLAND
Timothy Finn

**SUMMER GAMES FOR ADULTS
AND CHILDREN**
Hereward Zigo

OLEANDER MODERN POETS

CONTEMPORARY GERMAN POETRY
comp. Ewald Osers

THE HIDDEN MUSIC
Östen Sjöstrand

A HOUSE ON FIRE
Philip Ward

IMPOSTORS & THEIR IMITATORS
Philip Ward

LOST SONGS
Philip Ward

ONCE OFF (Lenier poems)
Royal College of Art

RAIN FOLLOWING
Sue Lenier

THE SCANDALOUS LIFE OF CÉSAR MORO
César Moro

SWANSONGS
Sue Lenier

UNDERSEAS POSSESSIONS
Hans-Juergen Heise

LIBYA PAST AND PRESENT

APULEIUS ON TRIAL AT SABRATHA
Philip Ward

THE LIBYAN CIVIL CODE
I.M. Arif & M.O. Ansell

LIBYAN MAMMALS
Ernst Hufnagl

THE LIBYAN REVOLUTION
I.M. Arif & M.O. Ansell

MOTORING TO NALUT
Philip Ward

SABRATHA
Philip Ward

TRIPOLI
Philip Ward

ARABIA PAST AND PRESENT

OLEANDER TRAVEL BOOKS

THE AEOLIAN ISLANDS
Philip Ward

ALBANIA: A TRAVEL GUIDE
Philip Ward

BANGKOK: PORTRAIT OF A CITY
Philip Ward

COME WITH ME TO IRELAND
Philip Ward

JAPANESE CAPITALS: NARA, KYOTO, TOKYO
Philip Ward

ROSSYA: THE TRANS-SIBERIAN EXPRESS
Michael Pennington

TOURING CYPRUS
Philip Ward